A Source-book of Scottish Witchcraft

A Source-book of Scottish Witchcraft

Compiled by
Christina Larner
Christopher Hyde Lee
and
Hugh V. McLachlan

The Grimsay Press
2005

The Grimsay Press
an imprint of
Zeticula
57 St Vincent Crescent
Glasgow
G3 8NQ

http://www.thegrimsaypress.co.uk
admin@thegrimsaypress.co.uk

Transferred to digital printing in 2005

First published in Great Britain in 1977 by
Department of Sociology, The University, Glasgow, G12 8RT,
ISBN 0 85261 145 5

ISBN 1 84530 028 9

Preface to the 2005 reprint

A Source-book of Scottish Witchcraft, by Larner, Lee and McLachlan, first published in 1977, is here reprinted in its original form.

For almost thirty years, *A Source-book of Scottish Witchcraft* has been the most authoritative reference book on Scottish Witchcraft. It has been invaluable to the specialist scholar and of interest to the general reader. It provides, but provides much more than, a series of lists of the 'names and addresses' of long-dead witches. However, although it is widely quoted and held in high esteem, few copies were ever printed and most are owned by libraries or similar institutions. Until now, it has been difficult to obtain and even more difficult to buy.

In 1938, George F. Black, a Scotsman who was in charge of New York Public library, published *A Calendar of Cases of Witchcraft in Scotland 1510-1727*. This was a fairly comprehensive compilation of brief accounts of references, in printed sources, to Scottish witchcraft cases. The *Source-book* built upon this study but went beyond it by including, through an examination of actual ancient manuscripts, information on previously unpublished cases. It also presented the material in a more systematic way in relation, where known, to the names of the accused witches, their sex, their fate, the place of the case, its date and the type of court that dealt with it. Some such information is presented in the form of tables. Transcriptions of documents pertaining to witchcraft trials - such as examples of the evidence of supposed witnesses - and other salient legal documents - including, for instance, an ancient account of when and why the testimony of female witnesses might be legally acceptable in Scottish courts - are also presented.

Recently, Stuart Macdonald of Knox College, University of Toronto has produced a CDROM based on the material of the Source-book. More recently still, the team of the "Survey of Scottish Witchcraft 1563-1736" at Edinburgh University - Julian Goodare, Louise Yeoman, Joyce Miller and Lauren Martin - have used the *Source-book* as the basis of a study, the results of which are now available on-line. (See: www.arts.ed.ac.uk/witches) Marvellous additions to knowledge in this fertile field as these studies make, their output and its electronic formulation is complementary to the Source-book. It does not replace or supersede it. *A Source-book of Scottish Witchcraft* remains the most authoritative printed reference book for and catalogue of Scottish witchcraft cases.

Biographical Notes

The late Professor Christina Larner is the author of *Enemies of God*, (Chatto and Windus, 1981; John Donald, 2000) and acknowledged as one of the brightest leading lights of witchcraft scholarship. Dr Christopher Lee returned to America after working on the book and her current position and location are not known. Dr Hugh V McLachlan is the author of *Social Justice, Human Rights and Public Policy*, (Humming Earth, 2005) and is a Reader in the School of Law and Social Sciences, Glasgow Caledonian University.

Hugh V. McLachlan, Glasgow, 2005.

CONTENTS

The compilers would like to thank J.K. Swales for help with the computer programme, Wilma Purser for work on the coding, Patrick and Gavin Larner for compiling the index, and Ruby Love who typed it all.

Introduction

In 1938 the New York Public Library published A Calendar of Cases of Witchcraft in Scotland 1510-1727 by G.F. Black, which was reprinted without amendment in 1971. It consisted of a list of extracts from printed sources arranged in rough chronological order. Up till now it has been the only piece of systematic research on Scottish witchcraft available.

The present compilation was made possible by the award of a grant by the Social Science Research Council [1] for a three-year period of research into "Witchcraft Accusations and Prosecutions in Scotland". It is intended to replace Black as a work of reference, for what Black's Calendar, valuable as it was, did not do, was to systematise the material other than by year, or indicate to what extent it was comprehensive; to what extent defective.

Prosecutions for Witchcraft in Scotland

In Scotland witchcraft was a criminal offence from 1563, when it was included in statute law,[2] until 1736, when it was repealed together with the English Witchcraft Act of 1604.[3] After 1736 it was possible only to prosecute for 'pretended witchcraft' and to impose a maximum penalty of a year's imprisonment. There were known executions for witchcraft in Scotland before 1563, but the process was obscure and these cases are not included in the present Source Book.

The great majority of prosecutions and executions for witchcraft took place between 1590 and 1680. Before 1590, when James VI personally conducted a large scale sorcery trial, and after 1680, cases were rare and isolated, apart from the Paisley outbreak of

---

1. SSRC Grant HR 2317/1. Final Report available on application to Dr. C.J. Larner, Department of Sociology, University of Glasgow.
2. Acts of the Parliament of Scotland, Vol. II, p.539. See below p.283.
3. The Statutes at Large, Vol. VI, pp. 206-7. See below pp.283-5.

1697. Within the period 1590 to 1680 there were four intensive outbreaks of prosecutions. The first was from 1590 to 1597. Very little is known about this outbreak because the prosecutions took place locally, but we know from casual references [1] and from the edict of the Privy Council which finally supressed it [2] that it was very extensive. The other three were 1628 to 1630, 1649, and 1661-62. Apart from these peaks, the whole period 1640-1662 saw a large number of prosecutions.[3]

The prosecutions were most frequent in particular areas: the east coast and environs from Aberdeen to the Borders; inland areas around Edinburgh, Stirling, and Lanark; the Orkneys, and towards the end of the period, Ayrshire and Galloway. This correlates partly, but not completely, with those areas of Scotland which were fully administered by a system of kirk sessions, presbyteries, secular courts, and access to central authorities in Edinburgh.

There were a variety of ways in which a witch could be prosecuted, and this is one of the factors which makes the researcher's task a difficult one. The treason trials of 1590 to 1591 were conducted in special courts of justiciary frequently presided over by the king. The trials which took place, mainly in Aberdeenshire, Fife, and the Lothians, from 1590-1597, and whose records are mainly lost or contained in family papers, were conducted in local courts under the general commission for trying witches issued by the Privy Council in 1591.[4] When this was withdrawn in 1597 the Privy Council reserved for itself the right to consider each application for a commission to try a witch. Penalties were to be imposed on those who prosecuted witches without their authority. In the confused and flexible system of criminal justice which operated in the sixteenth and seventeenth centuries this does not mean that the control of the Privy Council over witchcraft trials was total; it does mean that Privy Council commissions to local landowners and

---

1. See Christina Larner, The Enemies of God, Chatto for Sussex University Press, forthcoming.
2. Register of the Privy Council, V.5., p.409.
3. See below pp.238-9, tables 4 and 5.
4. Register of the Privy Council, V.4., p.680.

officials became the commonest single way of trying a witch. The second commonest way was through the Court of Justiciary and its circuit courts, and the least common was through commissions of Parliament. During the second half of 1649 however, the Committee of Estates issued commissions for one hundred and fifty seven trials. All these ways were more or less legal: legality itself was an elusive concept closely related to power struggles between various courts and organs of government. There are, however, quite apart from the period 1590 to 1597, enough references to executions of witches whose cases never reached the central authorities to raise queries about the proportion of dubiously legal to official executions, and about the validity of any figures and projections for the total numbers of witches tried and executed.

The Source Material

The compilers have concentrated on the central sources partly because they have never been used systematically before, partly because in the early days of the research project we assumed, wrongly, that in this way we could collect all the executions.

There are three main groups of sources for the central government prosecutions for witchcraft. The first is that for the Court of Justiciary; primarily the Books of Adjournal, which are the manuscript minutes of trials in that court. These are held in the Scottish Record Office in Edinburgh. They have a manuscript index for much of the period. There are gaps, some appeared after and some before the index was made; from July 1650 to October 1652 and from July 1655 to June 1661. The National Library of Scotland has abridged Books of Adjournal which cover some of these gaps. In addition there are, in the Record Office, unindexed boxes of pre-trial material. Some, but not all, of these boxes have a dittay roll within them with a list of crimes, but these refer to crimes which the official concerned wanted tried, and do not always relate to material in the box. Sample examination has produced papers which refer to witchcraft cases which never came to trial. There may well be more in these boxes. There are also the Circuit Court minutes; the records of the travelling justiciary. These are sometimes bound up with the Books of Adjournal, but it is not clear to what extent these records are complete, and some witchcraft trials of the circuit courts may have been lost to us. Some of this High Court material is available in print; notably in Robert Pitcairn, <u>Criminal Trials in Scotland</u>; G.F. Black, <u>Some Unpublished Witchcraft Trials</u>, and W.G. Scott-Moncrieff's edition of an abstract of the Books of Adjournal.[1]

The second main source, containing the largest number of cases, is the Privy Council. The Privy Council minutes are available in print up to 1691. They are complete in so far as they include all the cases discussed. Some of the accounts may be truncated, but a sample examination of witchcraft cases in manuscript suggests that these are usually printed entire. But as in the case of the Justiciary Records there is unindexed material. This has been left unexplored by this research team. They cannot be used cost-effectively for individual cases until they have been surveyed by the archivists. They are more extensive than those for the High Court.

The third main group of central sources is the Parliamentary records and those associated with them. In fact only a few witchcraft cases were processed through Parliamentary commissions, and these can be found in the printed <u>Acts of the Parliament of Scotland</u>. The manuscript records of the Committee of Estates, whose witch-processing activities in 1649 have been referred to, are also available in the Scottish Record Office.

The defects of the material lie partly in what is actually missing. There are hardly any records for the extensive witch-hunt of 1590-1597. There are the gaps in the Justiciary records which have been mentioned, and clearly many of the background process papers have been lost. One of the biggest gaps is that there is no feedback on the fate of the witches for whose trial Privy Council commissions were granted, except in the rare cases of appeal procedures. It is an understatement to say that Scotland was not

---

1. See below, Section IV, p.306.

a fully bureaucratised society in this period, and the horseman from the Burgh of Ayr, having extracted his commission for a local trial, had no motive to ride back again and report the results. Such records as survive for these trials by local landowners (which were by far the commonest type of trial), are likely to be found in private family papers and sheriff court records, which until 1745 were likewise the private property of hereditary sheriffs.

The material which does survive is also defective in terms of the type of information presented. The fate of the witch is often unreported, and likewise his or her marital and social status. Never, even in the processes, do we get an account of the type of questions asked, and the way in which confessions are extracted has to be inferred. In these respects the Scottish records are very often much less complete and informative than continental or English records. Record-keeping itself, even at central governmental level, seems to have been an under-systematised and undervalued activity compared with contemporary standards elsewhere.

In theory, however, these central records, even if they do not tell us much about them, should yield all the witches who were put on trial. The local records should contain only the early procedures against these witches, plus the witches who were dealt with by the kirk sessions through minor punishments or not proceeded against at all. In fact it is clear that an unknown number of witches were executed without going through the 'legitimate' channels. Black's Calendar refers to some of these, and other researchers in Dundee [1] and Galloway [2] have uncovered more cases of this nature. In addition there is the case of Orkney which had devolved administrative powers and operated rather like a separate kingdom during this period.

The local records are essential for an understanding of the origins of witch labelling and witch accusation. There is a good

---

1. Maureen Anderson, undergraduate dissertation, University of St. Andrews, 1976.
2. A.E. Truckell, Archivist at Dumfries Burgh Museum, unpublished list of witchcraft cases in Galloway and Dumfriesshire.

deal of local material contained within the pre-trial processes which relates to the content of neighbours' original accusations against the witch, but these need to be supplemented by information about the type of case which never got as far as being taken to court. Scottish local records are far more defective than the central ones in the sense that their survival has been haphazard, and there are few complete records, but where they exist they are extremely rich in social information.

The main types of local source material are kirk sessions, and presbytery records, sheriff courts, baron courts, burgh councils, and family papers. Some of these are available in the Scottish Record Office. Others are kept locally.

Coverage of the Material

The members of the research project have covered all the central sources described. It would probably be possible for further researchers to uncover further names of accused witches in the pre-trial material, and material relating to the Privy Council cases, but in the opinion of the compilers of this volume it would not be cost-effective until archivists have done some classification and indexing. That does not mean that there is no work to be done on the central records. As has been suggested, the central records also provide valuable information on local witchcraft, and for some of the cases, particularly during the major outbreaks, there is enough material to make a detailed analysis possible. So far as the local material goes we have covered only samples. Our view is that while it would probably be possible to add considerably to the list of witches by intensive work on small areas, it would again probably not be cost-effective, unless the researcher were to concentrate on the major years of persecution. There is a substantial piece of work still to be done collating local and central records for the years 1649 and 1661-62 for example. So far as other years go, however, it would be possible to read a manuscript kirk session register extending over a considerable period and find less than half a dozen cases which had any connection with witchcraft or charming.

In the absence of any previous systematic examination of this type of record, it seems that the most interesting and productive way forward at the present time would be to analyse individual records in their entirety. In this way it would be possible to lay out the apparatus of social control in general, and put witchcraft into its perspective among the other crimes and misdemeanours: at local level: fornication, adultery, foul speaking, sabbathbreaking, and drunkenness. An SSRC supported survey of criminal sources for early modern Scotland is being undertaken (academic session 1976-77) by B. Lenman and G. Parker, Department of History, University of St. Andrews.

Plan of the Book

A Source-Book of Scottish Witchcraft is divided up in the following way. In Section I all cases of witchcraft known to the compilers are divided into groups. Five of these groups represent the type of court in which the case was either tried or the individual mentioned.[1] These are (1) Court of Justiciary, (2) Circuit Courts, (3) Parliamentary Commissions, (4) Committee of Estates, (5) Privy Council Commissions. The sixth group consists of other known cases. Within each group the cases are listed in chronological order, in so far as this is possible given that certain cases were dealt with over a considerable period of time. Each case is numbered and in the other sections of the Source Book the case is referred to by this number in order that the reader can trace it back to the original source material. In these grouped lists the following information is given: name, place (usually the witch's area of residence, sometimes the place of trial), date (usually of the court case, i.e. date of trial in the Court of Justiciary; date of granting of commission in the case of the Privy Council), sex, marital status where known, outcome of trial where known, primary source, and whether the case was already known to Black or has been discovered since then. This is partly to make it easy for readers to refer

1. Many of the witches in our list have merely had their names mentioned by neighbours or other witches, and there is no record of their having been further proceeded against.

back to Black where appropriate for his brief quotations from the sources, which are lacking in our lists, and for his comments; partly to indicate the amount of new material contained in the present volume. What the lists do not include is the social and economic status of the accused, because this information is available only for a small proportion of the cases. The cases for which this is known are analysed separately in the collection of tables.

The cases in the last group which are also listed chronologically, consist of those which are recorded but are not known to the central records or on which there is further material elsewhere. In this group there are three main types of case: (1) those that one would not have expected to reach the central records because they were accounted for locally and given minor punishment or let off, (2) those who were executed and who therefore ought properly to have appeared in central records, (3) those whose fate is unknown and the question therefore of whether they ought to have been in central records unanswerable. In addition there are cases already mentioned in the other lists to which there are further references, and some duplications which only became apparent with the completion of the index.

It should be noted that the numbers in Section I represent cases and not individual witches. Some witches were charged more than once or in more than one court. In the index of named witches at the end of the Source Book, where there is more than one reference to what is without doubt the same person these references are collated. Where there is any doubt about the identification, the name is replicated as appropriate. It should also be noted that there was no orthodox orthography in this period. Some scribes spelt the same name in different ways on the same page. The spelling of place and personal names in the lists is intended to be as it was in the source from which it was taken.

Section II of the Source Book contains analyses of the cases in terms of sex, marital status, social status, the proportion executed, acquitted, and unknown over the period, presented in table form. Section III consists of sample transcripts of previously unpublished material. Section IV is a list, with commentary, of primary and secondary source material.

Christina Larner
Christopher Hyde Lee
Hugh V. McLachlan

Department of Sociology
University of Glasgow.
March 1977.

SECTION I.

CASES OF WITCHCRAFT

Abbreviations and Explanatory Notes.

No.		Project number of the case. Some individuals appear more than once.
Date		The date is, where appropriate, that of the trial, the commission, or the last mention in the processes.
Sex	F	Female
	M	Male
Mar. Stat		Marital Status
	U	Unknown
	M	Married
	S	Single
	W	Widowed
Trial Stat		Trial Status
		The level to which the case was taken.
	T	Taken to trial
	Proc.	Preliminary proceedings taken in pre-trial processes.
	Men.	Mentioned as a witch by an accused person.
	Com.	Privy Council or Parliamentary Commission to named individuals for a local trial.
Fate	Ex.	Executed
	NK.	Not known
	NCP	Non-capital punishment
	Misc	Some other outcome (escaped, died in prison)
	Acqu	Acquitted
Source		
New Case		An asterisk indicates that the case is not in G.F. Black's Cases of Witchcraft in Scotland, New York, 1938.

ABBREVIATIONS FOR PRINCIPAL SOURCES

APS	*Acts of the Parliament of Scotland*, London 1814
D	Circuit Minute Books, Scottish Record Office
JC	Justiciary Court MSS., Scottish Record Office
Pit	R. Pitcairn, *Criminal Trials in Scotland*, Edin. 1833
Proc.SRO List	Scottish Record Office hand list of processes
R.P.C.	*Register of the Privy Council*, Edin. 1880 -
RCE	MS. Records of the Committee of Estates, Scottish Record Office
SJC	*Selected Justiciary Cases*, Stair Society
SRO Adj List	Index to Books of Adjournal, Scottish Record Office

HIGH COURT OF JUSTICIARY									
No.	Name	Date	Place	Sex	Mar. Stat	Trial Stat	Fate	Source	New Case
1	Nik Neving	- - 1563	Monaie	F	U	Men.	Ex.	SJC.V3 p.598	*
2		- - 1563		F	U	T	NK.	Pit.V1 p.510	*
3		- - 1563		F	U	T	NK.	Pit.V1 p.510	*
4		- - 1563		F	U	T	NK.	Pit.V1 p.510	*
5		- - 1563		F	U	T	NK.	Pit.V1 p.510	*
6	Agnes Mullikine	- - 1563	Dunferm- line	F	U	T	NCP	Pit.V1 p.432	
7	Janet Boyman	- - 1572	Edinburgh Cowgait	F	M	T	Ex.	JC26/1	
8	Bessie Dunlop	-.11. 1576	Ayrshire Lyne	F	U	T	Ex.	Pit.V1 pp.49 -58	
9	Eduart Kyninmonth	- - 1577	Angus ?	M	U	T	NK.	Pit.V1 p.70	
10	Violet Mar	- - 1577	Perthshire Kildeis	F	U	T	NK.	JC2/1	
11	William Gilmour	- - 1582	Ayrshire Bonetoune	M	U	T	Misc	Pit.V1 p.144	
12	Tibbie Smart	- - 1586		F	U	Proc.	NK.	PROC. S.R.O. List	*
13	Alesoun Piersoun	28. 5. 1588	Byrehill	F	U	T	Ex.	JC2/2	
14	Marjory Blaik	26. 7. 1588	Perthshire Cairny	F	U	T	Misc	Pit.V1 p.167	
15	John Myllar	26. 7. 1588	Perthshire Cairny	M	U	T	Misc	Pit.V1 p.167	
16	Lady Fowlis	28.10 1589	Ross-shire	F	M	T	Acqu	JC2/2	
17	Familiars of Lady Fowlis	22. 7. 1590		U	U	Men.	NK.	Pit.V1 Part 2 p.191	*

HIGH COURT OF JUSTICIARY									
No.	Name	Date	Place	Sex	Mar. Stat	Trial Stat	Fate	Source	New Case
18	Lady Fowlis	22. 7. 1590	Ross-shire	F	M	T	Acqu	Pit.V1 pp.191 -201	
19	Hector Munro	22. 7. 1590	Ross-shire	M	U	T	Acqu	Pit.V1 pp.201 -204	
20	Marioune McIngaruch	22. 7. 1590	Ross-shire	F	U	Men.	NK.	Pit.V1 pp.201 -204	*
21	John Bane's Wife	22. 7. 1590	Ross-shire	F	M	Men.	NK.	Pit.V1 pp.201 -204	*
22	John McConeill-Gar's Wife	22. 7. 1590	Ross-shire	F	M	Men.	NK.	Pit.V1 pp.201 -204	*
23	John McConeill--Gar	22. 7. 1590	Ross-shire	M	M	Men.	NK.	Pit.V1 pp.201 -204	*
24	Cristiane Roiss	22. 7. 1590	Ross-shire	F	U	Men.	Ex.	Pit.V1 p.193	
25	Marion Neyne McAlester	22. 7. 1590	Ross-shire Taine	F	U	Men.	NK.	Pit.V1 pp.195 -196	
26	William McGilliewareycht-Dame	22. 7. 1590	Ross-shire Taine	M	U	Men.	Ex.	Pit.V1 pp.195 -196	
27	Thomas Caffindonisch	22. 7. 1590	Ross-shire Taine	M	U	Men.	NK.	Pit.V1 pp.191 -201	*
28	Agnes Roy	22. 7. 1590	Ross-shire Taine	F	U	Men.	Ex.	Pit.V1 pp.191 -201	*
29	Thomas McKane More McAllane McEuoch	22. 7. 1590	Ross-shire	M	U	Men.	Ex.	Pit.V1 pp.191 -201	*
30	Cristian Smyth	-. 7. 1590	Ross-shire Taine	F	U	Men.	NK.	Pit.V1 pp.195 -196	

HIGH COURT OF JUSTICIARY									
No.	Name	Date	Place	Sex	Mar. Stat	Trial Stat	Fate	Source	New Case
31	Violat Auchinlek	9. 8. 1590	Aberdeen-shire	F	M	T	Misc	JC2/2	
32	Janet ~~Clark~~ Grant	17. 8. 1590	Aberdeen-shire	F	U	T	Ex.	JC2/2	
33	Bessie Roy	18. 8. 1590	Aberdeen-shire	F	U	T	Acqu	JC2/2	
34	Marion Bruce	18. 8. 1590	Aberdeen-shire	F	U	Men.	NK.	Pit.V1 p.208	
35	Jonet ~~Grant~~ Clark	19. 9. 1590	Aberdeen-shire	F	U	T	Ex.	JC2/2	
36	Meg Dow	28. 4. 1590	Gilmerton	F	U	T	Ex.	JC2/2	
37	Bessie Paul	18. 8. 1590	Aberdeen-shire	F	U	Men.	NK.	Pit.V1 p.208	
38	John Fean	-.11. 1590	Preston-pans	M	S	T	Ex.	Pit.V1 pp.209 -223	
39	William Leslie	- - 1590	Aberdeen-shire	M	M	T	Misc	JC2/2	
40	Janet Pook	- - 1590	Falkirk	F	U	Proc.	NK.	JC26/2	
41	Johne McGillis	- - 1590	Preston-pans	M	U	Men.	Ex.	JC26/2	
42	Agnes Sampsoune	- - 1590	Nether Keith	F	M	T	Ex.	JC26/2	
43	Wife of Nicoll Murray	- - 1590	Preston-pans	F	M	Men.	NK.	JC26/2	
44	Jonet Gall	- - 1590	Preston-pans	F	U	Men.	NK	JC26/2	
45	Anny Rychesoun	- - 1590	Preston-pans	F	U	Men.	NK.	JC26/2	
46	Wife of John Ramsay	- - 1590	Preston-pans	F	M	Men.	NK.	JC26/2	
47	Issobell Gylloun	- - 1590	Preston-pans	F	U	Men.	NK.	JC26/2	

HIGH COURT OF JUSTICIARY									
No.	Name	Date	Place	Sex	Mar. Stat	Trial Stat	Fate	Source	New Case
48	Bessie Wright	- - 1590	Preston-pans	F	U	Men.	NK.	JC26/2	
49	Catherine Duncane	- - 1590	Preston-pans	F	U	Men.	NK.	JC26/2	
50	Wife of the Portaris of Seytoune	- - 1590	Preston-pans	F	M	Men.	NK.	JC26/2	
51	Johhne Gordoun	- - 1590	Preston-pans	M	U	Men.	Ex.	JC26/2	
52	Jonett Logane	- - 1590	Preston-pans	F	U	Men.	NK.	JC26/2	
53	Janet Campbell	- - 1590	Preston-pans	F	U	Men.	NK.	JC26/2	
54	Meg Bogtoun	- - 1590	Preston-pans	F	U	Men.	NK.	JC26/2	
55	Katherene Wallace	- - 1590	Preston-pans	F	U	Men.	NK.	JC26/2	
56	Margarett Aichesoun	- - 1590	Preston-pans	F	U	Men.	NK.	JC26/2	
57	Katherine Gray	- - 1590	Preston-pans	F	U	Men.	Ex.	JC26/2	
58	Wife of George Moitis	- - 1590	Preston-pans	F	M	Men.	NK.	JC26/2	
59	Margaret Thomson	- - 1590	Preston-pans	F	U	Men.	NK.	JC26/2	
60	Barbara Keand	- - 1590	Aberdeen	F	U	Men.	Ex.	SP.Misc. V2 p.65	
61	Gilbert McGill	- - 1590	Preston-pans	M	U	Men.	Ex.	JC26/2	
62	Wife of Thomas Brounhill	- - 1590	Preston-pans	F	M	Men.	NK.	JC26/2	
63	Thomas Brounhill	- - 1590	Preston-pans	M	M	Men.	NK.	JC26/2	
64	Bessie Broune	- - 1590	Preston-pans	F	M	Men.	NK.	JC26/2	

HIGH COURT OF JUSTICIARY									
No.	Name	Date	Place	Sex	Mar. Stat	Trial Stat	Fate	Source	New Case
65	Bessie Cowane	- - 1590	Preston-pans	F	U	Men.	NK.	JC26/2	
66	Marioun Colington	- - 1590	Preston-pans	F	U	Men.	NK.	JC26/2	
67	Duncan Buchquhanne	- - 1590	Preston-pans	M	U	Men.	NK.	JC26/2	
68	Malie Geddie	- - 1590	Preston-pans	F	U	Men.	NK.	JC26/2	
69	Helen Lauder	- - 1590	Preston-pans	F	U	Men.	NK.	JC26/2	
70	Marioune Schaw	- - 1590	Preston-pans	F	U	Men.	NK.	JC26/2	
71	Helen Quhyte	- - 1590	Preston-pans	F	U	Men.	NK.	JC26/2	
72	Issobell Lauder	- - 1590	Preston-pans	F	U	Men.	NK.	JC26/2	
73	Jonet Nicolsoun	- - 1590	Preston-pans	F	U	Men.	NK.	JC26/2	
74	Marioun Bailzie	- - 1590	Preston-pans	F	U	Men.	NK.	JC26/2	
75	Marioune Nicolsoun	- - 1590	Preston-pans	F	U	Men.	NK.	JC26/2	
76	Alexander Quhytlaw	- - 1590	Preston-pans	M	U	Men.	NK.	JC26/2	
77	Marie Patersone	- - 1590	Preston-pans	F	U	Men.	NK.	JC26/2	
78	Masie Aichesoune	- - 1590	Preston-pans	F	U	Men.	NK.	JC26/2	
79	Cristian Kerington	- - 1590	Preston-pans	F	U	Men.	NK.	JC26/2	
80	Meg Dun	- - 1590	Preston-pans	F	U	Men.	Ex.	JC26/2	
81	Catherene McGillis	- - 1590	Preston-pans	F	U	Men.	NK.	JC26/2	

HIGH COURT OF JUSTICIARY

No.	Name	Date	Place	Sex	Mar. Stat	Trial Stat	Fate	Source	New Case
82	Barbara Napier	5. 5. 1591	Edinburgh	F	M	T	Acqu	JC2/2	
83	Ewfame Makcalzene	9. 6. 1591	Clifton-hall	F	M	T	Ex.	JC2/2 JC26/2	
84	Junet Strabmy	6. 7. 1591		F	U	Proc.	NK.	JC26/2	*
85	Patrick Herring	19.10. 1591	Stirling ?	M	U	T	Misc	JC2/3	
86	Jonet Straton	– – 1591	Preston-pans ?	F	U	Proc.	NK	JC26/2	
87	Donald Robinson	– – 1591	Preston-pans	M	U	Proc.	NK.	JC26/2	
88	Charles Wat	– – 1591	Preston-pans	M	U	Men.	NK.	JC26/2	*
89	Gelie Duncan	– – 1591	Preston-pans	F	U	Men.	NK.	JC26/2	
90	Thom Cockburn	– – 1591	Preston-pans	M	U	Men.	NK.	JC26/2	*
91	Thome Fean	– – 1591	Preston-pans	M	U	Men.	NK.	JC26/2	*
92	Niniane Chirneyside	– – 1591	Edinburgh	M	U	Men.	Misc	Pit.V1 p.259	
93	Jonat Drummond	– – 1591	Nether Keith ?	F	U	Men.	NK.	JC26/2	*
94	Archie Farquhars	– – 1591	Nether Keith ?	M	U	Men.	NK.	JC26/2	*
95	Jonet Fairlie	– – 1591	Preston-pans ?	F	U	Men.	NK.	JC26/2	*
96	Ane Simson	– – 1591	Preston-pans ?	F	U	Men.	NK.	JC26/2	*
97	Ane Nairn	– – 1591	Preston-pans ?	F	U	Men.	NK.	JC26/2	*
98	Marion Ranking	– – 1591	Preston-pans ?	F	U	Men.	NK.	JC26/2	*

HIGH COURT OF JUSTICIARY									
No.	Name	Date	Place	Sex	Mar. Stat	Trial Stat	Fate	Source	New Case
99	Bessie Thompson	- - 1591	Preston-pans ?	F	S	Men.	NK.	JC26/2	
100	Robert Griersoun	- - 1591	Preston-pans ?	M	U	Men.	NK.	JC26/2	
101	Meg Begtonne	- - 1591	Preston-pans	F	U	Proc.	NK.	JC26/2	
102	Catarine Wallace	- - 1591	Preston-pans	F	U	Proc.	NK.	JC26/2	
103	Jonet Campbell	- - 1591	Preston-pans	F	U	Proc.	NK.	JC26/2	
104	Katherine Muirhead	- - 1593		F	U	Men.	Ex.	Pit.V1 p.259	
105	Earl of Bothwell	- - 1593		M	U	Proc.	NK.	J.PROC. S.R.O. List	*
106	Marioun Dwne	- - 1594	Long-niddry	F	U	Men.	Ex.	Pit.V2 p.543	
107	John Stewart	24. 6. 1596	Orkney	M	U	T	Acqu	JC2/2	
108	Alesoun Balfour	24. 6. 1596	Orkney	F	M	Men.	Ex.	Pit.V1 pp.375 -377	
109	Alesoune Jollie	30. 9. 1596	Mid-lothian Fala	F	M	T	Acqu	Pit.V1 pp.397 -399	
110	C[illegible]	[illegible]11. [illegible]596	Nokwalter	F	U	T	NK.	JC2/3	
111	Jonet Grawie	-.11. 1596		F	U	T	Acqu	Pit.V2 p.1	
112	Jonet Stewart	12.11. 1597	Edinburgh Canongate	F	U	T	Ex.	JC2/3	
113	Christian Lewinstoun	12.11. 1597	Edinburgh Canongate	F	U	T	Ex.	JC2/3	
114	Christian Saidler	12.11. 1597	Edinburgh Blakhous	F	U	T	Ex.	JC2/3	

HIGH COURT OF JUSTICIARY

No.	Name	Date	Place	Sex	Mar. Stat	Trial Stat	Fate	Source	New Case
115	John Damiet	12.11. 1597	Edinburgh Canongate	M	U	Men.	NK.	JC2/3	*
116	Michael Clark	12.11. 1597	Midlothian Lasswade	M	U	Men.	Misc	JC2/3	*
117	Bessie Aiken	12.11. 1597	Leith	F	U	T	Acqu	JC2/3	
118	James Reid	21. 7. 1603	Mussel-burgh	M	U	T	Ex.	JC2/3	
119	Margaret Duncane	23. 7. 1605	Ayrshire	F	U	Men.	NK.	Pit.V2 p.478	*
120	Katherine McTeir	23. 7. 1605	Ayrshire	F	U	Men.	NK.	Pit.V2 p.478	*
121	Patrick Lowrie	- - 1605	Ayrshire Halie	M	U	T	Ex.	JC2/4	
122	Issobel Griersoune	10. 3. 1607	Preston-pans	F	M	T	Ex.	JC2/4	
123	Bartie Petersoun	18.11. 1607	Midlothian Newbattle	M	U	T	Ex.	Pit.V2 pp.523 -526	
124	Barbara Paterson	- - 1607	Drum-langrig	F	U	T	Ex.	Sharpe p.96	*
125	Cristiane Tod	27. 5. 1608	Longniddry	F	U	Men.	Ex.	Pit.V2 pp.542 -544	
126	Johnne Gray-Meill	27. 5. 1608	Longniddry	M	U	Men.	Ex.	Pit.V2 pp.542 -544	
127	Marioun Ersche	27. 5. 1608	Longniddry	F	U	Men.	Ex.	Pit.V2 pp.542 -544	
128	Beigis Tod	- - 1608	Longniddry	F	U	T	Ex.	JC2/4	
129	James Mure	9.11. 1609	Minihagan	M	U	T	Misc	Pit.V3 pp.68 -69	

HIGH COURT OF JUSTICIARY									
No.	Name	Date	Place	Sex	Mar. Stat	Trial Stat	Fate	Source	New Case
130	James Mure	7. 2. 1610	Minihagan	M	U	T	Ex.	Pit.V3 pp.68 -69	
131	Grissell Gairdner	7. 9. 1610	Newburgh	F	W	T	Ex.	JC2/4 p.368F	
132	Marioun Tailyeor	- - 1611	Tarye	F	M	Proc.	NK.	JC27/ 10	
133	Jonet Irving	1.12. 1613	Perth-shire Logy	F	U	Men.	NK.	Pit.V3 pp.260 -264	*
134	Robert Erskine	1.12. 1613	Perth-shire Logy	M	U	T	Ex.	Pit.V3 pp.260 -264	
135	Annas Erskine	22. 6. 1614	Perth-shire Logy	F	U	T	Ex.	Pit.V3 pp.260 -264	
136	Issobell Erskine	22. 6. 1614	Perth-shire Logy	F	U	T	Ex.	Pit.V3 pp.260 -264	
137	Helene Erskine	22. 6. 1614	Perth-shire Logy	F	U	T	NCP	Pit.V3 pp.260 -264	
138	Margaret Wallace	20. 3. 1622	Glasgow Logy	F	M	T	Ex.	JC2/6 pp.71F: 75F:668	
139	Thomas Greave	1. 8. 1623	Fife	M	U	T	Ex.	JC2/6 p.120F	
140	Janet Aitchison	- - 1628	East Lothian	F	U	Men.	Ex.	Spott. Misc.V2 p.45	
141	Margaret Melross	- - 1628	East Lothian	F	U	Men.	Ex.	Spott. Misc.V2 p.45	
142	Isobell Young	4. 2. 1629	Peebles	F	M	T	Ex.	JC2/6 p.264	
143	Alexander Drummond	3. 7. 1629	Auchter-arder	M	U	T	Ex.	Reid pp.67 -75	

HIGH COURT OF JUSTICIARY

No.	Name	Date	Place	Sex	Mar. Stat	Trial Stat	Fate	Source	New Case
144	Katharine Oswald	13.11. 1629	Niddry	F	M	T	Ex.	JC2/6 p.302	
145	Margaret Melvis	– – 1629	Dunbar	F	U	Men.	Ex.	JC2/6 p.169A	*
146	Jonet Achiesone	– – 1629	Dunbar	F	U	Men.	Ex.	JC2/6 p.269A	*
147	Elizabeth Steven	– – 1629	Niddry	F	U	Men.	Ex.	JC2/6	
148	Alexander Hamilton	22. 1. 1630	Haddington	M	M	T	Ex.	SJC.V1 p.143	
149	Michaell Erskine	2. 4. 1630	Newbyres Mylne	M	U	T	Ex.	JC2/6 p.322	*
150	Alesoun Cowine	– – 1630	Dunce	F	U	Proc.	NK.	S.R.O. List	*
151	John Neil	26. 3. 1631	Tweed-mouth	M	U	T	Ex.	JC2/7	
152	Alisone Nisbet	23. 7. 1632	Hilton	F	M	T	Ex.	JC2/7	
153	John Colquhoun	11. 1. 1633	Luss	M	M	T	Misc	S.R.O. 315/03	
154	Thomas Carlips	11. 1. 1633	Luss	M	U	T	Misc	S.R.O. 315/03	
155	Elizabeth Bathgate	9. 1. 1634	Eyemouth	F	M	T	Acqu	S.R.O. 315/03	
156	Elizabeth Bathgate	4. 6. 1634	Eyemouth	F	M	T	Acqu	JC2/7 pp.148 -160	
157	Margaret Kinard	24.11. 1643	Perth-shire	F	U	Men.	NK.	SJC.V3 p.601	*
158	Neane VcClerich	24.11. 1643	Kinross-shire	F	U	Men.	NK.	SJC.V3 p.599	*
159	Nikclerich	24.11. 1643	Kinross-shire	F	U	Men.	NK.	SJC.V3 p.599	*
160	John McIlvorie	24.11. 1643	Kinross-shire	M	U	Men.	NK.	SJC.V3 p.599	*

HIGH COURT OF JUSTICIARY									
No.	Name	Date	Place	Sex	Mar. Stat	Trial Stat	Fate	Source	New Case
161	John Brugh	24.11. 1643	Kinross-shire	M	U	T	Ex.	JC2/8 pp.336 -340	
162	Margaret Lauder	29.12. 1643	Edinburgh	F	U	T	Ex.	JC2/8 p.347F	
163	Janet Barker	29.12. 1643	Edinburgh	F	U	T	Ex.	JC2/8 p.347F	
164	Jeane Craig	- - 1643	Tranent	F	M	T	Ex.	JC2/8 pp.740 -747	*
165	Agnes Finnie	18.12. 1644	Edinburgh	F	U	T	Ex.	JC26/ 10	
166	Helen Clerk	11. 3. 1645	Newhaven	F	M	Proc.	Misc	JC26/ 14 (5)	*
167	Elspethie	- - 1645	Newhaven	F	U	Men.	NK.	JC26/ 13.5	*
168	Elspeth Edie	11. 2. 1649	Carruddne	F	U	Men.	NK.	JC26/ 13	*
169	Christiane Thomsone	1. 7. 1649	Inver-keithing	F	U	Men.	NK.	JC26/ 13	*
170	Rossina Osit	1. 7. 1649	Inver-keithing	F	U	Men.	NK.	JC26/ 13	*
171	Margaret Aytoune	1. 7. 1649	Inver-keithing	F	U	Men.	NK.	JC26/ 13	*
172	Issobell Guthrie	1. 7. 1649	Inver-keithing	F	U	Men.	NK.	JC26/ 13	*
173	Hellen Douglas	10. 7. 1649	Inver-keithing	F	U	Men.	NK.	JC26/ 13	*
174	Margaret Blaikburne	10. 7. 1649	Inver-keithing	F	U	Men.	NK.	JC26/ 13	*
175	Issobel Mitchell	10. 7. 1649	Inver-keithing	F	U	Men.	NK.	JC26/ 13	*
176	Katharine Smyth	10. 7. 1649	Inver-keithing	F	U	Men.	NK.	JC26/ 13	*

HIGH COURT OF JUSTICIARY

No.	Name	Date	Place	Sex	Mar. Stat	Trial Stat	Fate	Source	New Case
177	Barbara Chattow	10. 7. 1649	Inver-keithing	F	U	Men.	NK.	JC26/13	*
178	Hellane Stanhous	10. 7. 1649	Inver-keithing	F	U	Men.	NK	JC26/13	*
179	Emie Angus	10. 7. 1649	Inver-keithing	F	U	Men.	NK.	JC26/13	*
180	Joannet Grege	10. 7. 1649	Inver-keithing	F	U	Men.	NK.	JC26/13	*
181	Mart Grege	10. 7. 1649	Inver-keithing	F	U	Men.	NK.	JC26/13	*
182	Bessie Wilson	10. 7. 1649	Inver-keithing	F	U	Men.	NK.	JC26/13	*
183	Marjorie Fergie	10. 7. 1649	Inver-keithing	F	U	Men.	NK.	JC26/13	*
184	Joannet Smetoune	10. 7. 1649	Inver-keithing	F	U	Men.	NK.	JC26/13	*
185	Margaret Mairtine	11. 7. 1649	Inver-keithing	F	U	Proc.	NK.	JC26/13	*
186	Katharine Grieve	11. 7. 1649	Inver-keithing	F	U	Proc.	NK.	JC26/13	*
187	Issobell Leitch	-. 7. 1649	Inver-keithing	F	U	Proc.	NK.	JC26/13	*
188	Jeane Waster	18. 8. 1649	Carruddne	F	U	Men.	NK.	JC26/13	*
189	Margaret Haskerstoun	- - 1649	Carruddne	F	U	Men.	NK.	JC26/13	*
190	Marione Sprott	-.11. 1650	Dumfries	F	U	T	NK.	JC26/26	*
191	Marion Corsar	-.11. 1650	Dumfries	F	U	T	NK.	JC26/26	*
192	Thomas Paton	-.11. 1650	Dumfries	M	M	T	Ex.	JC26/26	*
193	Elleson Patersone	-.11. 1650	Dumfries	F	U	T	Ex.	JC26/26	*

HIGH COURT OF JUSTICIARY									
No.	Name	Date	Place	Sex	Mar. Stat	Trial Stat	Fate	Source	New Case
194	Bessie Graham	-.11. 1650	Dumfries	F	M	T	Ex.	JC26/ 26	*
195	Janet Diksone	-.11. 1650	Dumfries	F	U	T	NK.	JC26/ 26	*
196	William Knok	- - 1650	Dalkeith	M	U	Proc.	NK.	JC26/ 27	*
197	Janet Diksone	- - 1650	Dumfries	F	U	Proc.	NK.	PROC. S.R.O. List	*
198	Elizabeth Corsan	- - 1650	Dumfries	F	U	Proc.	NK.	PROC. S.R.O. List	*
199	Elizabeth Maxwell	- - 1650	Dumfries	F	U	T	NK.	JC26/ 26	*
200	Marion Chansie	- - 1650	Dalkeith	F	U	Proc.	NK.	JC26/ 27	*
201	Margaret Tasker	- - 1650	Dalkeith	F	U	Proc.	NK.	JC26/ 27	*
202	Florence Sime	- - 1650	Dalkeith	F	U	Proc.	NK.	JC26/ 27	*
203	Christian Black	- - 1650	Dalkeith	F	U	Proc.	NK.	JC26/27	*
204	Helen Hutton	6. 1. 1652		F	U	T	NK.	S.R.O. Index to HC.	*
205	John Wilson	- - 1652	East Lothian	M	U	Proc.	NK.	PROC. S.R.O. List	*
206	Jon Bayne	- - 1654	Nigg	M	U	Proc.	NK.	PROC. S.R.O. List	*
207	Kathrene Smyth	- - 1655	Inver-keithing	F	U	Proc.	NK.	PROC. S.R.O. List	*
208	John McWilliam	5. 2. 1656	Dumbarton	M	U	T	Ex.	Spott. Misc.V2 p.67	

HIGH COURT OF JUSTICIARY									
No.	Name	Date	Place	Sex	Mar. Stat	Trial Stat	Fate	Source	New Case
209	Elspeth Scroggie	- - 1656	Cupar	F	U	Proc.	NK.	PROC. S.R.O. List	*
210	Agnes Pryde	- - 1656	Cupar	F	U	Proc.	NK.	PROC. S.R.O. List	*
211	Issobell Monro	- - 1656	Edinburgh	F	U	Proc.	NK.	PROC. S.R.O. List	*
212	Agnes Nemo	-. 5. 1657	Libberton	F	M	Proc.	NK.	JC26/ 25	*
213	Janet Bruce	- - 1657	Tranent	F	U	Proc.	NK.	PROC. S.R.O. List	*
214	Katherine Kerse	- - 1657	Midlothian	F	U	Proc.	NK.	PROC. S.R.O. List	*
215	Agnes Robert	- - 1657	Linlithgow	F	U	Proc.	NK.	PROC. S.R.O. List	*
216	Bessie Carnochan	- - 1657	Dumfries	F	U	Proc.	NK.	PROC. S.R.O. List	*
217	Janet Bruce	- - 1657		F	U	Proc.	NK.	S.R.O. Index to HC	*
218	Jonet Tulloch	- - 1657	Renfrew	F	U	Proc.	NK.	JC26/ 19B	*
219	Margaret Anderson	2. 2. 1658	Haddington	F	U	T	Ex.	S.R.O. Adj. List	
220	John Corse	2. 2. 1658	Dysert	M	U	T	Ex.	JC26/ 25	
221	Jonnet Gillespie	6. 4. 1658	Ayr	F	U	Proc.	Misc	JC26/25 Port.Roll Ayr 1658	*

HIGH COURT OF JUSTICIARY									
No.	Name	Date	Place	Sex	Mar. Stat	Trial Stat	Fate	Source	New Case
222	Agnes Patersonne	6. 4. 1658	Ayr	F	U	Proc.	Misc	JC26/25 Port Roll Ayr 1658	*
223	Jonnet Mackskinning	6. 4. 1658	Ayr	F	U	Proc.	Misc	JC26/25 Port.Roll Ayr 1658	*
224	Margaret Sunderland	6. 4. 1658	Ayr	F	W	Proc.	Misc	JC26/25 Port.Roll Ayr 1658	*
225	Jonnet Reid	6. 4. 1658	Ayr	F	M	Proc.	Misc	JC26/25 Port.Roll Ayr 1658	*
226	Agnes Mortoune	6. 4. 1658	Ayr	F	M	Proc.	Misc	JC26/25 Port.Roll Ayr 1658	*
227	Marion Leiges	6. 4. 1658	Ayr	F	W	Proc.	Misc	JC26/25 Port.Roll Ayr 1658	*
228	Catheren Mogersland	6. 4. 1658	Ayr	F	U	Proc.	Misc	JC26/25 Port.Roll Ayr 1658	*
229	Jonnet Holmes	6. 4. 1658	Ayr	F	U	Proc.	Misc	JC26/25 Port.Roll Ayr 1658	*
230	Margaret Jamesonne	6. 4. 1658	Ayr	F	U	Proc.	Misc	JC26/25 Port.Roll Ayr 1658	*
231	John Guillieland	6. 4. 1658	Ayr	M	U	Proc.	Misc	JC26/25 Port.Roll Ayr 1658	*
232	Jonnet Boyd	6. 4. 1658	Ayr	F	U	Proc.	Misc	JC26/25 Port.Roll Ayr 1658	*
233	Jonnet Wilsoune	6. 4. 1658	Ayr	F	U	Proc.	Misc	JC26/25 Port.Roll Ayr 1658	*
234	Jonet Grahame	6. 4. 1658	Ayr	F	U	Proc.	Misc	JC26/25 Port.Roll Ayr 1658	*

HIGH COURT OF JUSTICIARY									
No.	Name	Date	Place	Sex	Mar. Stat	Trial Stat	Fate	Source	New Case
235	Bessie Wodsyde	6. 4. 1658	Ayr	F	U	Proc.	Misc	JC26/25 Port.Roll Ayr 1658	*
236	Heline Thome	6. 4. 1658	Ayr	F	U	Proc.	Misc	JC26/25 Port.Roll Ayr 1658	*
237	Cristian Meving	6. 4. 1658	Ayr	F	W	Proc.	Misc	JC26/25 Port.Roll Ayr 1658	*
238	Agnes Wallace	6. 4. 1658	Ayr	F	W	Proc.	Misc	JC26/25 Port.Roll Ayr 1658	*
239	Annabell Gottray	6. 4. 1658	Ayr	F	W	Proc.	Misc	JC26/25 Port.Roll Ayr 1658	*
240	Jonnet Tait	6. 4. 1658	Ayr Craigie	F	U	Proc.	Misc	JC26/25 Port.Roll Ayr 1658	*
241	Marion Symsone	6. 4. 1658	Ayr Craigie	F	U	Proc.	Misc	JC26/25 Port.Roll Ayr 1658	*
242	Agnes Robeson	6. 4. 1658	Ayr Craigie	F	U	Proc.	Misc	JC26/25 Port.Roll Ayr 1658	*
243	Jonnet Murdock	6. 4. 1658	Ayr Craigie	F	U	Proc.	Misc	JC26/25 Port.Roll Ayr 1658	*
244	Jonnet Symson	6. 4. 1658	Ayr Craigie	F	U	Proc.	Misc	JC26/25 Port.Roll Ayr 1658	*
245	Agnes Wasoune	6. 4. 1658	Ayr Craigie	F	U	Proc.	Misc	JC26/25 Port.Roll Ayr 1658	*
246	John McKie	6. 4. 1658	Ayr Craigie	M	U	Proc.	Misc	JC26/25 Port.Roll Ayr 1658	*
247	Cristian Huntar	6. 4. 1658	Ayr Craigie	F	U	Proc.	Misc	JC26/25 Port.Roll Ayr 1658	*

HIGH COURT OF JUSTICIARY									
No.	Name	Date	Place	Sex	Mar. Stat	Trial Stat	Fate	Source	New Case
248	Margaret Patoune	6. 4. 1658	Ayr	F	W	Proc.	Misc	JC26/25 Port.Roll Ayr 1658	*
249	Johne Walker	6. 4. 1658	Ayr	M	U	Proc.	Misc	JC26/25 Port.Roll Ayr 1658	*
250	Jonet Hamiltoune	6. 4. 1658	Ayr	F	W	Proc.	Misc	JC26/25 Port.Roll Ayr 1658	*
251	Violat Guillieland	6. 4. 1658	Ayr	F	W	Proc.	Misc	JC26/25 Port.Roll Ayr 1658	*
252	Margaret Cumyngham	6. 4. 1658	Ayr	F	W	Proc.	Misc	JC26/25 Port.Roll Ayr 1658	*
253	Margaret Allan	6. 4. 1658	Ayr	F	M	Proc.	Misc	JC26/25 Port.Roll Ayr 1658	*
254	Margat Laurymer	6. 4. 1658	Ayr	F	M	Proc.	Misc	JC26/25 Port.Roll Ayr 1658	*
255	Elspeth Cuninghame	6. 4. 1658	Ayr	F	U	Proc.	Misc	JC26/25 Port.Roll Ayr 1658	*
256	Jonnet Slowland	6. 4. 1658	Ayr	F	U	Proc.	Misc	JC26/25 Port.Roll Ayr 1658	*
257	Jonnett Sauer	6. 4. 1658	Ayr	F	U	Proc.	Misc	JC26/25 Port.Roll Ayr 1658	*
258	Marion Millikene	-. 4. 1658	Ayr Craigie	F	U	Proc.	Misc	JC26/25 Port.Roll Ayr 1658	*
259	Johne Laurie	-. 4. 1658	Ayr Craigie	M	U	Proc.	Misc	JC26/25 Port.Roll Ayr 1658	*
260	Hew Dunbar	-. 4. 1658	Ayr Craigie	M	U	Proc.	Misc	JC26/25 Port.Roll Ayr 1658	*

HIGH COURT OF JUSTICIARY									
No.	Name	Date	Place	Sex	Mar. Stat	Trial Stat	Fate	Source	New Case
261	Bessie Fullertoun	-. 4. 1658	Ayr	F	W	Proc.	Misc	JC26/25 Port.Roll Ayr 1658	*
262	Issobell Hendersone	-. 4. 1658	Ayr	F	W	Proc.	Misc	JC26/25 Port.Roll Ayr 1658	*
263	Agnes Nemo	6. 7. 1658	Edinburgh Libberton	F	M	Proc.	NK.	JC26/ 251	*
264	Katharine Keg	22. 7. 1658	Alloa	F	U	Men.	NK.	JC26/ 26D1	*
265	Barbara Erskin	22. 7. 1658	Alloa Cambus	F	U	Men.	NK.	JC26/ 26	*
266	Bessie Harla	22. 7. 1658	Alloa	F	U	Men.	NK.	JC26/ 26D1	*
267	Katharine Wightman	22. 7. 1658	Alloa	F	U	Men.	NK.	JC26/ 26D1	*
268	Elizabeth Crokat	22. 7. 1658	Alloa	F	U	Men.	NK.	JC26/ 26D1	*
269	Jonet Meason	22. 7. 1658	Alloa	F	U	Men.	NK.	JC26/ 26D1	*
270	Janet Reid	22. 7. 1658	Alloa	F	U	Proc.	NK.	JC26/ 26	*
271	James Kirk	22. 7. 1658	Alloa	M	U	Proc.	NK.	JC26/ 26D1	
272	James Hudstoun	22. 7. 1658	Alloa	M	U	Proc.	NK.	JC26/ 26D1	
273	Jonet Millar	22. 7. 1658	Alloa Tullibodie	F	U	Proc.	NK.	JC26/ 26D1	
274	Katharine Rany	3. 8. 1658	Alloa	F	U	T	Ex.	JC26/ 26D	
275	Bessie Paton	3. 8. 1658	Alloa	F	U	T	Ex.	JC26/ 26D	
276	Jonet Black	3. 8. 1658	Alloa	F	U	T	Ex.	JC26/ 26D	

HIGH COURT OF JUSTICIARY									
No.	Name	Date	Place	Sex	Mar. Stat	Trial Stat	Fate	Source	New Case
277	Margaret Tailyeor	3. 8. 1658	Alloa	F	U	T	Ex.	JC26/ 26D	
278	Margaret Dempherstoun	– – 1658	Alloa	F	U	Proc.	NK.	Spott. Misc.V2 p.68	
279	Elspit Blak	– – 1658	Alloa	F	U	Proc.	NK.	Spott. Misc.V2 p.68	
280	Margaret Duchal	– – 1658	Alloa	F	U	Proc.	NK.	Spott. Misc.V2 p.68	
281	Jonet Flowan	– – 1658	Ayr ?	F	U	Proc.	NK.	JC26/25	*
282	Elspeth Cunningham	– – 1658	Ayr ?	F	U	Proc.	NK.	JC26/ 25	*
283	Barbara Erskin	– – 1658	Alloa	F	U	Proc.	NK.	Spott. Misc.V2 p.68	
284	Kathren Blak	– – 1658	Alloa	F	U	Proc.	NK.	Spott. Misc.V2 p.68	
285	Marion Lewars	– – 1658	Richorne	F	U	Proc.	NK.	PROC. S.R.O. List	*
286	Margaret Beverage	– – 1658	Dysart	F	M	Proc.	NK.	PROC. S.R.O. List	*
287	Janet Steil	– – 1658	Ayr	F	U	Proc.	Misc	PROC. S.R.O. List	*
288	Wallas	– – 1658	Ayr	U	U	Proc.	NK.	PROC. S.R.O. List	*
289	Marrion Wilsoune	23. 1. 1659	Stenton E Lothian	F	U	Men.	Ex.	JC26/ 26 C	*
290	Isobel Kemp	23. 1. 1659	Stenton E Lothian	F	U	Men.	Ex.	JC26/ 26 C	*

HIGH COURT OF JUSTICIARY										
No.	Name	Date	Place	Sex	Mar. Stat	Trial Stat	Fate	Source	New Case
291	Jonet Wood	8. 2. 1659	Dunbar Stenton ?	F	U	Proc.	Acqu	JC26/ 26	*
292	Janet Miller	25. 2. 1659	Stirling	F	U	Proc.	NK.	JC26/ 26	*
293	Margaret Gourley	25. 2. 1659	Stirling	F	U	Proc.	NK.	JC26/ 26	*
294	Helen Heriot	1. 3. 1659	Stentoune	F	U	T	Ex.	JC26/ 26C	
295	Alleson Fermor	1. 3. 1659	Stentoune	F	U	T	Ex.	JC26/ 26C	
296	Marion Angus	1. 3. 1659	Stentoune	F	U	T	Ex.	JC26/ 26C	
297	Jean Sydserff	1. 3. 1659	Stentoune	F	U	T	Ex.	JC26/ 26C	
298	Bessie Lacost	1. 3. 1659	Stentoune	F	U	T	Ex.	JC26/ 26C	
299	Janet Wood	11. 3. 1659	Torine Stenton	F	U	Men.	NK.	JC26/ 26 C	*
300	Margaret Harvie	16. 3. 1659	Stirling	F	U	Proc.	Misc.	JC26/ 26	*
301	Issobell Bennet	22. 3. 1659	Stirling	F	M	Proc.	NK.	JC26/ 26	*
302	Bessie Stevenson	22. 3. 1659	Stirling	F	W	Proc.	NK.	JC26/ 26	*
303	Helline Cuming	2. 4. 1659	Stenton E Lothian	F	U	Proc.	Misc	JC26/ 26	*
304	Jonnet Man	2. 4. 1659	Stenton E Lothian	F	S	Proc.	Misc	JC26/ 26	*
305	Isable Bennet	8. 4. 1659	Roxburgh	F	U	Proc.	NK.	JC26/ 26	*
306	Martha	27. 4. 1659	Tranent Preston	F	U	Men.	NK.	JC26/26 (9)	*
307	Martha Butter	27. 4. 1659	Salt Preston-pans	F	M	Men.	NK	JC26/ 26 (9)	*

HIGH COURT OF JUSTICIARY									
No.	Name	Date	Place	Sex	Mar. Stat	Trial Stat	Fate	Source	New Case
308	Cristian Cranstoun	27. 4. 1659	Tranent	F	U	Proc.	NK.	JC26/ 26 (5)	*
309	B Cochrane	27. 4. 1659	Tranent	F	U	Proc.	NK.	JC26/ 26 (7)	*
310	Elspeth Colvill	27. 4. 1659	Tranent W Port Edin	F	M	Men.	Ex.	JC26/ 26 (1)	*
311	Jonet Balfour	27. 4. 1659	Tranent	F	W	Men.	NK.	JC26/ 26 (1)	*
312	Elspeth Robertson	27. 4. 1659	Tranent	F	M	Men.	NK.	JC26/ 26 (1)	*
313	Meg Maitland	27. 4. 1659	Tranent	F	U	Men.	Ex.	JC26/ 26 (7)	*
314	Cristian Harper	27. 4. 1659	Tranent	F	U	Men.	Misc	JC26/ 26 (7)	*
315	Issobel Home	27. 4. 1659	Tranent	F	W	Men.	NK.	JC26/ 26 (7)	*
316	Hellen Fleck	27. 4. 1659	Tranent	F	U	Men.	Misc	JC26/ 26 (7)	*
317	Katharine Gibsone	-. 4. 1659	Tranent	F	U	Men.	NK.	JC26/ 26 (8)	*
318	Martha Hall	-. 4. 1659	Tranent	F	U	Men.	NK.	JC26/ 26 (8)	*
319	Thomas Thompson	-. 4. 1659	Tranent Preston	M	U	Men.	NK.	JC26/ 26 (8)	*
320	Agnes Thomson	-. 4. 1659	Tranent	F	U	Men.	NK.	JC26/ 26 (8)	*
321	Marioun Lowrie	-. 4. 1659	Tranent	F	M	Men.	NK.	JC26/ 26 (8)	*
322	Katharine Gray	-. 4. 1659	Tranent	F	U	Men.	NK.	JC26/ 26 (8)	*
323	Margaret Robertson	-. 4. 1659	Tranent	F	M	Men.	NK.	JC26/ 26 (1)(9)	*
324	Helen Gibson	-. 4. 1659	Tranent	F	M	Men.	NK.	JC26/ 26 (9)	*

HIGH COURT OF JUSTICIARY									
No.	Name	Date	Place	Sex	Mar. Stat	Trial Stat	Fate	Source	New Case
325	Lancelot Crictoun	-. 4. 1659	Tranent	M	M	Men.	NK.	JC26/ 26 (9)	*
326	Grissel Fleck	-. 4. 1659	Tranent	F	M	Men.	NK.	JC26/ 26 (9)	*
327	Marion Gray	-. 4. 1659	Tranent	F	M	Men.	NK.	JC26/ 26 (1)	*
328	Elspeth Fouller	-. 4. 1659	Tranent	F	W	Proc.	Misc	JC26/ 26 (1)	*
329	Helen Wilson	3. 5. 1659	Tranent	F	W	T	Ex.	JC26/ 26	
330	Jonet Thomson	3. 5. 1659	Tranent	F	M	T	Ex.	JC26/ 26	
331	Cristian Cranstoun	3. 5. 1659	Tranent	F	W	T	Ex.	JC26/ 26	
332	Barbara Cochran	3. 5. 1659	Tranent	F	W	T	Ex.	JC26/ 26	
333	John Douglas	3. 5. 1659	Tranent	M	U	T	Ex.	JC26/ 26	
334	Marioun Lynn	3. 5. 1659	Tranent	F	W	T	Ex.	JC26/ 26	
335	Marion Logan	3. 5. 1659	Tranent	F	U	T	Ex.	JC26/ 26	
336	Mareone Guild	3. 5. 1659	Tranent	F	M	T	Ex.	JC26/ 26	
337	Janet Crooks	3. 5. 1659	Tranent	F	U	T	Ex.	JC26/ 26	
338	Elspeth Black	1. 6. 1659	Stirling Alloway	F	M	Proc.	Misc	JC26/ 26	*
339	Katharine Black	-. 7. 1659	Alloa	F	M	Proc.	NK.	JC26/ 26	
340	Janet Tucidie	- - 1659	Corstor-phine	F	U	Men.	NK.	JC26/ 26 3	*
341	Janet Watson	- - 1659	Tranent	F	U	Men.	NK.	JC26/ 26 (3)(5)	*

HIGH COURT OF JUSTICIARY									
No.	Name	Date	Place	Sex	Mar. Stat	Trial Stat	Fate	Source	New Case
342	Isobell Keir	- - 1659	Stirling	F	U	Proc.	Misc	JC26/ 26	*
343	Helen Simbeard	- - 1659	Tranent	F	U	Proc.	NK.	JC26/ 26 (10)	*
344	Katharine Gray	- - 1659	Tranent	F	U	Proc.	NK.	JC26/ 26(1)(5)	*
345	Anna Nisbit	- - 1659	Tranent Elphinstone	F	U	Men.	NK.	JC26/ 26(7)	*
346	Magdalen Blair	- - 1659	Stirling	F	S	Proc.	Misc	JC26/ 26	*
347	Barbara Erskin	- - 1659	Stirling	F	U	Proc.	Misc	JC26/ 26	
348	Elizabeth Crocker	- - 1659	Stirling	F	U	Proc.	Misc	JC26/ 26	
349	James Kirk	- - 1659	Stirling	M	U	Proc.	Misc	JC26/ 26	
350	Marioun Yool	- - 1660	Tranent	F	U	Men.	NK.	JC26/ 26(4)	*
351	Elspeth Mowat	29. 6. 1661	Liberton	F	M	Proc.	Acqu	JC/26/ 27	*
352	Jonet Hewat	29. 6. 1661	Liberton	F	U	Proc.	NK.	JC/26/ 27	*
353	Janet Allane	-. 6. 1661	Edinburgh Holyrood	F	U	Proc.	Ex.	Dal.pp. 626;640	
354	Margaret Wyllie	5. 7. 1661	Edinburgh	F	U	T	Misc	JC2/ 10P2	
355	Jean Brown	5. 7. 1661	Edinburgh?	F	U	T	Misc	JC2/ 10P2	
356	Bessie Moffat	16. 7. 1661	Dalkeith	F	M	Proc.	NK.	JC26/ 27/1	
357	Jonet Watsone	16. 7. 1661	Dalkeith	F	U	Proc.	NK.	JC26/ 27/1	
358	Jean Howison	25. 7. 1661	Ormeston Neqtoun	F	U	Proc.	NK.	JC26/ 27	

HIGH COURT OF JUSTICIARY									
No.	Name	Date	Place	Sex	Mar. Stat	Trial Stat	Fate	Source	New Case
359	Margaret Steivinstene	25. 7. 1661	Ormeston	F	U	Proc.	NK.	JC26/ 27	*
360	Janet Daill	29. 7. 1661	Moffat	F	U	Proc.	NK.	JC/26/27 /Muffet B.R. Jul. 29 1661	*
361	Thomas Wilson	29. 7. 1661	Moffat	M	U	Proc.	NK.	JC/26/27 /Muffet B.R. Jul. 29 1661	*
362	Janet Daill	29. 7. 1661	Mussel- burgh	F	M	T	Ex.	JC26	*
363	Agnes Loch	29. 7. 1661	Mussel- burgh	F	M	T	Ex.	JC2/10 JC26	
364	David Johnston	29. 7. 1661	Mussel- burgh	M	U	T	Ex.	JC2/10 JC26	
365	Janet Lyle	29. 7. 1661	Mussel- burgh Edistoun	F	W	T	Ex.	JC2/10 JC26	*
366	Margaret Rammage	29. 7. 1661	Mussel- burgh	F	U	T	Ex.	JC26/27 JC2/10	*
367	Isobell Brand	31. 7. 1661	Dudding- ston	F	U	Proc.	NK.	JC/26/ 27	*
368	Agnes Barhill	31. 7. 1661	Dudding- ton	F	U	Proc.	NK.	JC/26/ 27	*
369	Janet Paistoun	-. 7. 1661	Dalkeith	F	M	Proc.	NK.	JC26/27/ 1	
370	Marion Greinlaw	-. 7. 1661	Ormeston Sunisyd	F	U	Proc.	NK.	JC26/27	
371	Katerine Hunter	3. 8. 1661	Dalkeith	F	U	Proc.	Acqu	JC26/27/ 1	
372	Elspet Graham	3. 8. 1661	Dalkeith	F	M	T	Ex.	JC26/27/ 1 JC2/11	
373	Issobell Fergussone	3. 8. 1661	Dalkeith Newbattle	F	U	T	Ex.	JC2/11 JC26/ 27/1	

HIGH COURT OF JUSTICIARY									
No.	Name	Date	Place	Sex	Mar. Stat	Trial Stat	Fate	Source	New Case
374	Marjory Wilson	3. 8. 1661	Dalkeith Newbattle	F	U	T	Ex.	JC26/ 27/1	
375	Christiane Wilsone	3. 8. 1661	Dalkeith Newbattle	F	U	T	Ex.	JC26/27 JC26/ 27/1	
376	Christian Patersone	3. 8. 1661	Dalkeith Newbattle	F	W	T	Ex.	JC26/ 27/1 JC2/11	
377	Beatrix Leslie	3. 8. 1661	Dalkeith Newbattle	F	W	T	Ex.	JC26/ 27	
378	Agnes Pogavie	7. 8. 1661	Edinburgh Liberton	F	U	T	Ex.	JC26/ 27	
379	Bessie Wilson	7. 8. 1661	Edinburgh Liberton	F	U	T	Ex.	JC26/ 27	
380	Elspett Blackie	7. 8. 1661	Edinburgh Liberton	F	U	T	Ex.	JC26/ 27	
381	Thomas Black	7. 8. 1661	Edinburgh Liberton	M	U	T	Ex.	JC26/ 27	
382	Margaret Bryson	7. 8. 1661	Edinburgh Liberton	F	M	T	Ex.	JC26/ 27	
383	Janet Gibson	7. 8. 1661	Edinburgh Liberton	F	U	T	Ex.	JC26/ 27	
384	Issobell Dodis	7. 8. 1661	Liberton Dudding-ston	F	U	Proc.	Acqu	JC/26/ 27	*
385	Janet Hall	7. 8. 1661	Liberton Dudding-ston	F	U	Proc.	Acqu	JC/26/ 27	*
386	Margaret Burton	7. 8. 1661	Liberton Dudding-ston	F	U	Proc.	Acqu	JC/26/ 27	*
387	Marjorie Fairwell	10. 8. 1661	Dudding-ston	F	U	Proc.	NK.	JC/26/ 27/8-9	
388	Issobel Broun	10. 8. 1661	Dudding-ston	F	U	Proc.	NK.	JC/26/ 27	*

HIGH COURT OF JUSTICIARY									
No.	Name	Date	Place	Sex	Mar. Stat	Trial Stat	Fate	Source	New Case
389	Issobell Robiesone	10. 8. 1661	Dudding-ston	F	U	Proc.	Acqu	JC/26/27	*
390	Jonet Ker	20. 8. 1661	Dalkeith	F	U	T	Ex.	JC26/27 JC10 p.21F	
391	Hele Casse ? Helen Casse?	20. 8. 1661	Dalkeith Dudding-ston	F	M	T	Ex.	JC26/27 8-9 JC2/10 p.218	
392	Jonet Miller	20. 8. 1661	Dalkeith	F	U	T	Acqu	JC2/10 p.218 JC2/10 p.2 JC26/27	
393	Margaret Hutchison	20. 8. 1661	Dalkeith Dudding-ston	F	M	T	Acqu	JC26/27 8-9 JC10 p.21F	
394	Isobal Ramsay	20. 8. 1661	Dalkeith	F	U	T	Ex.	JC2/10 p.21F JC26/27 8-9?	
395	Issobel F	20. 8. 1661	Dalkeith	F	U	T	NK.	JC26/26/1	*
396	Bessie Flinker	-. 8. 1661	Liberton Dudding-ston	F	U	Proc.	Acqu	JC/26/27	*
397	Issobel Ker	-. 8. 1661	Dalkeith	F	U	Proc.	Acqu	JC26/27/1	
398	Janet Blackie	-. 8. 1661	Dalkeith	F	U	Proc.	NK.	JC26/27/1	*
399	Margaret Grieve	4. 9. 1661	Stennar	F	U	T	Acqu	JC2/11	
400	Margaret Porteous	4. 9. 1661	Edinburgh Liberton	F	W	T	Acqu	JC2/11 JC26/27	*
401	Margaret Hutchison	10. 9. 1661	Dalkeith Dudding-ston	F	M	T	Ex.	JC26/27 8-9 JC10 p.21F	

HIGH COURT OF JUSTICIARY									
No.	Name	Date	Place	Sex	Mar. Stat	Trial Stat	Fate	Source	New Case
402	Janet Cock	10. 9. 1661	Dalkeith	F	M	T	Acqu	JC2/ 11	
403	Jonet Miller	-. 9. 1661	Kirkliston	F	U	Proc.	NK.	JC/26/ 27	*
404	Janet Cock	11.11. 1661	Dalkeith	F	M	T	Ex.	JC2/ 11	
405	Margaret Allan	14.11. 1661	Dudding-ston Newhall	F	M	T	NCP	JC2/ 11 JC26/27	
406	Jean Cock	-.11. 1661	Dalkeith	F	U	T	Ex.	JC2/ 11	*
407	Effie Pothif	- - 1661	Liberton	F	M	Men.	NK.	JC26/ 27	*
408	Robert Wir's Wife	- - 1661	Liberton	F	M	Men.	NK.	JC26/ 27	*
409	Jon Ramsay	- - 1661	Ormeston	M	U	Proc.	NK.	JC26/ 27 ?	*
410	Isabel Dodds	- - 1661	Mussel-burgh	F	U	Proc.	Misc	PROC. SRO List	*
411	Jonet Ewart	- - 1661	Gilmerton	F	U	Proc.	NK.	JC/26/ 27/8.9	*
412	Janet Coldane	- - 1661	Dalkeith	F	U	Proc.	NK.	PROC. SRO List	*
413	Jeane Gaylol	- - 1661		F	U	Proc.	NK.	JC26/ 27	*
414	Thomas Black	- - 1661	Gilmerton	M	U	Proc.	NK.	JC26/ 27	
415	Helen Mathie	- - 1661	Liberton Dudding-ston	F	U	Men.	NK.	JC/26/ 27	*
416	Janet Pumphersone	- - 1661	Liberton Dudding-ston	F	U	Men.	NK.	JC/26/ 27	*
417	Jean Mathie	- - 1661	Liberton Dudding-ston	F	U	Men.	NK.	JC/26/ 27	*

HIGH COURT OF JUSTICIARY									
No.	Name	Date	Place	Sex	Mar. Stat	Trial Stat	Fate	Source	New Case
418	Margaret Broun	- - 1661	Liberton Dudding-ston	F	U	Men.	NK.	JC/26/ 27	*
419	Helen Spears	- - 1661	Gilmerton?	F	U	Men.	NK.	JC/26/ 27	*
420	Janet Robison	- - 1661	Gilmerton?	F	U	Men.	NK.	JC/26/ 27	*
421	Margaret Brunton	- - 1661	Dalkeith	F	U	Men.	NK.	JC/26/ 27	*
422	Elspeth Chib	- - 1661	Liberton	F	U	Men.	NK.	JC/26/ 27	*
423	Agnes Brown	- - 1661	Liberton	F	U	Men.	NK.	JC/26/ 27	*
424	Cristine Bell	- - 1661	Liberton	F	U	Men.	Ex.	JC/26/ 27	*
425	Bessie Nicoson	- - 1661	Liberton	F	U	Men.	Ex.	JC/26/ 27	*
426	Cuthbert Wynd	- - 1661	Liberton	M	U	Men.	Ex.	JC/26/ 27	*
427	Margret Waldon	- - 1661	Liberton	F	U	Men.	Ex.	JC/26/ 27	*
428	Marin Coran	- - 1661	Liberton	F	U	Men.	NK.	JC/26/ 27	*
429	Agnes Cowie	- - 1661	Liberton	F	U	Men.	Ex.	JC/26/ 27	*
430	Margaret Indrie	- - 1661	Liberton	F	U	Men.	Ex.	JC26/ 27	*
431	Agnes Williamson	27. 1. 1662	Samuel-ston E.Lothian	F	M	T	Acqu	JC/2/ 10/11 JC26	
432	James Welsh	17. 4. 1662	Samuel-ston E.Lothian	M	U	T	NCP	JC/26/ 28	
433	Margaret Wilsone	-. 4. 1662	Auldearn	F	U	Men.	NK.	Pit.V3 pp.616 -618	

HIGH COURT OF JUSTICIARY									
No.	Name	Date	Place	Sex	Mar. Stat	Trial Stat	Fate	Source	New Case
434	Bessie Wilson	-. 4. 1662	Auldearn	F	U	Men.	NK.	Pit.V3 pp.616 -618	
435	Bessie Friece	-. 4. 1662	Auldearn	F	U	Men.	NK.	Pit.V3 pp.616 -618	
436	Issobel Friece	-. 4. 1662	Auldearn	F	U	Men.	NK.	Pit.V3 pp.616 -618	
437	Elspet Makhomie	-. 4. 1662	Auldearn	F	U	Men.	NK.	Pit.V3 pp.616 -618	
438	Mariorie Man	-. 4. 1662	Auldearn	F	U	Men.	NK.	Pit.V3 pp.616 -618	
439	Archibald Man	-. 4. 1662	Auldearn	M	M	Men.	NK.	Pit.V3 pp.616 -618	
440	Bessie Hay	-. 4. 1662	Auldearn	F	U	Men.	NK.	Pit.V3 pp.616 -618	
441	Mariore Taylor	-. 4. 1662	Auldearn	F	U	Men.	NK.	Pit.V3 pp.616 -618	
442	Elspet Nishie	-. 4. 1662	Auldearn	F	U	Men.	NK.	Pit.V3 pp.616 -618	
443	Elspet Makbeith	-. 4. 1662	Auldearn	F	U	Men.	NK.	Pit.V3 pp.616 -618	
444	Janet Burnet	-. 4. 1662	Auldearn	F	U	Men.	NK.	Pit.V3 pp.616 -618	
445	Barbara Friece	-. 4. 1662	Auldearn	F	U	Men.	NK.	Pit.V3 pp.616 -618	
446	Margaret Brodie	-. 4. 1662	Auldearn	F	U	Men.	NK.	Pit.V3 pp.616 -618	

HIGH COURT OF JUSTICIARY									
No.	Name	Date	Place	Sex	Mar. Stat	Trial Stat	Fate	Source	New Case
447	Agnes Grant	-. 4. 1662	Auldearn	F	U	Men.	NK.	Pit.V3 pp.616 -618	
448	Walter Ledy	-. 4. 1662	Auldearn	M	U	Men.	NK.	Pit.V3 pp.616 -618	
449	Margret Hucheons	-. 4. 1662	Auldearn	F	U	Men.	NK.	Pit.V3 pp.616 -618	
450	Bessie Hutcheons	-. 4. 1662	Auldearn	F	U	Men.	NK.	Pit.V3 pp.616 -618	
451	Elspet Falconer	-. 4. 1662	Auldearn	F	U	Men.	NK.	Pit.V3 pp.616 -618	
452	Bessie Young	-. 4. 1662	Auldearn	F	U	Men.	NK.	Pit.V3 pp.616 -618	
453	Issobel Nicoll	-. 4. 1662	Auldearn	F	U	Men.	NK.	Pit.V3 pp.616 -618	
454	Alexander Bell	-. 4. 1662	Auldearn	M	U	Men.	NK.	Pit.V3 pp.616 -618	
455	Bessie Peterkin	-. 4. 1662	Auldearn	F	U	Men.	NK.	Pit.V3 pp.616 -618	
456	Janet Smith	-. 4. 1662	Auldearn	F	U	Men.	NK.	Pit.V3 pp.616 -618	
457	Agnes Brodie	-. 4. 1662	Auldearn	F	U	Men.	NK.	Pit.V3 pp.616 -618	
458	Elspet Gilbert	-. 4. 1662	Auldearn	F	U	Men.	NK.	Pit.V3 pp.616 -618	
459	Allexander Ledy	-. 4. 1662	Auldearn	M	U	Men.	NK.	Pit.V3 pp.616 -618	

HIGH COURT OF JUSTICIARY									
No.	Name	Date	Place	Sex	Mar. Stat	Trial Stat	Fate	Source	New Case
460	Kylie	-. 4. 1662	Auldearn	U	U	Men.	NK.	Pit.V3 pp.616 -618	
461	Mariorie Dunbar	-. 4. 1662	Auldearn	F	U	Men.	NK.	Pit.V3 pp.616 -618	
462	Janet Man	-. 4. 1662	Auldearn	F	M	Men.	NK.	Pit.V3 pp.616 -618	
463	Allexander Sheipheard	-. 4. 1662	Auldearn	M	M	Men.	NK.	Pit.V3 pp.616 -618	
464	Grisall Sinklar	-. 4. 1662	Auldearn	F	M	Men.	NK.	Pit.V3 pp.616 -618	
465	John Robertson	-. 4. 1662	Auldearn	M	M	Men.	NK.	Pit.V3 pp.616 -618	
466	Elspet Lair	-. 4. 1662	Auldearn	F	U	Men.	NK.	Pit.V3 pp.616 -618	
467	Janet Finlay	-. 4. 1662	Auldearn	F	M	Men.	NK.	Pit.V3 pp.616 -618	
468	Allexander Elder	-. 4. 1662	Auldearn	M	M	Men.	NK.	Pit.V3 pp.616 -618	
469	Elspet Chisolme	-. 4. 1662	Auldearn	F	U	Men.	NK.	Pit.V3 pp.616 -618	
470	Agnes Torrie	-. 4. 1662	Auldearn	F	U	Men.	NK.	Pit.V3 pp.616 -618	
471	Witch Bandon	30. 9. 1662	Auldearn	F	U	T	NK.	Brodie p.274	
472	Helen Inglis	- - 1662	Auldearn	F	U	Men.	NK.	Pit.V3 pp.616 -618	

HIGH COURT OF JUSTICIARY									
No.	Name	Date	Place	Sex	Mar. Stat	Trial Stat	Fate	Source	New Case
473	Keathren Sowter	- - 1662	Auldearn	F	U	Men.	Ex.	Pit.V3 p.618	
474	Jonet Blyth	- - 1662	Haddington	F	U	Men.	NK.	JC26/ 28	*
475	Marion Lindsay	- - 1662	Haddington	F	U	Men.	NK.	JC26/ 28	*
476	Jonet Todry	- - 1662	Haddington	F	U	Men.	NK.	JC26/ 28	*
477	Wife of Richard Gulvitas	- - 1662	Haddington	F	M	Men.	NK.	JC26/ 28	*
478	Barbara Conglitoun	- - 1662	Haddington	F	U	Men.	NK.	JC26/ 28	*
479	Violet Nymmo	- - 1662	Haddington	F	U	Men.	NK.	JC26/ 28	*
480	Bessie D	- - 1662	Haddington	F	U	Men.	NK.	JC26/ 28	*
481	Agne Bapae	- - 1662	Skinner-sood	F	U	Men.	NK.	JC26/ 28	*
482	Walter Dykis	- - 1662	Haddington	M	U	Men.	NK.	JC26/ 28	*
483	Jonet Watson	- - 1662	Haddington	F	U	Men.	NK.	JC26/ 28	*
484	William Martin	- - 1662	Haddington	M	U	Men.	NK.	JC26/ 28	*
485	Edward Dickson	- - 1662	Haddington	M	U	Men.	NK.	JC26/ 28	*
486	Helen Birks	- - 1662	Haddington	F	U	Men.	NK.	JC26/ 28	*
487	Jonet Dewar	- - 1662	Haddington	F	M	Men.	NK.	JC26/ 28	*
488	Marion Raeburn	- - 1662	Haddington	F	M	Men.	NK.	JC26/ 28	*
489	Nicoll Wadie	- - 1662	Haddington	M	M	Men.	NK.	JC26/ 28	*

HIGH COURT OF JUSTICIARY									
No.	Name	Date	Place	Sex	Mar. Stat	Trial Stat	Fate	Source	New Case
490	Marion Broun	- - 1662	Samuel-ston	F	M	Men.	NK.	JC/26/28	*
491	Helen Reid	- - 1662	Samuel-ston	F	M	Men.	NK.	JC/26/28	
492	Patrick Meikle	- - 1662	Samuel-ston	M	M	Men.	NK.	JC/26/28	
493	Margaret Blak	- - 1662	Samuel-ston	F	M	Men.	NK.	JC/26/28	
494	John Homme	- - 1662	Samuel-ston	M	M	Men.	NK.	JC/26/28	
495	Jon Bartleman	- - 1662	Samuel-ston	M	M	Men.	NK.	JC/26/28	*
496	George Scherswood	- - 1662	Samuel-ston	M	M	Men.	NK.	JC/26/28	*
497	Christian Deans	- - 1662	Samuel-ston	F	U	Men.	NK.	JC/26/28	
498	Agnes Williamson	- - 1662	Samuel-ston	F	U	Men.	NK.	JC/26/28	
499	God-daughter of T Finlasoun	- - 1662	E.Lothian	F	U	Men.	NK.	JC26/28	*
500	Mirrilies	- - 1662	E.Lothian	U	U	Men.	NK.	JC26/28	*
501	Jon Kincaid	- - 1662	E.Lothian	M	U	Men.	NK.	JC26/28	
502	Robesonis	- - 1662	E.Lothian Nisbet	U	U	Men.	NK.	JC26/28	*
503	Marion Stevinstoun	- - 1662	E.Lothian Nisbet	F	U	Men.	NK.	JC26/28	*
504	Wife of W Finlasoun	- - 1662	E.Lothian	F	M	Men.	NK.	JC26/28	*
505	Wife of Thomas Finlason	- - 1662	Over-salking	F	M	Men.	NK.	JC26/28	*
506	Thomas Finlason	- - 1662	Over-salking	M	M	Men.	NK.	JC26/28	*

HIGH COURT OF JUSTICIARY									
No.	Name	Date	Place	Sex	Mar. Stat	Trial Stat	Fate	Source	New Case
507	Alexander Huntar	- - 1662	E.Lothian Salving	M	U	Men.	NK.	JC/26/ 28	*
508	Narriles Smith	- - 1662	E.Lothian Salving	U	U	Men.	NK.	JC/26/ 28	*
509	Wife of Archibald Baird	- - 1662	E.Lothian Blans	F	M	Men.	NK.	JC/26/ 28	*
510	Archibald Baird	- - 1662	E.Lothian Blans	M	M	Men.	NK.	JC/26/ 28	*
511	Beigis Sandeson	- - 1662	Samuel-ston	F	U	Men.	NK	JC/26/ 28	*
512	Christian Deanes	- - 1662	Samuel-ston	F	M	Men.	NK.	JC/26/ 28	
513	Agnes Spens	- - 1662	Samuel-ston	F	U	Men.	NK.	JC/26/ 28	*
514	Helen Trottar	- - 1662	Samuel-ston	F	U	Men.	NK.	JC/26/ 28	*
515	Issobell Cathie	- - 1662	Samuel-ston	F	U	Men.	NK.	JC/26/ 28	
516	Jonet Wast	- - 1662	Samuel-ston	F	M	Men.	NK.	JC/26/ 28	
517	Patrick Cathie	- - 1662	Samuel-ston	M	M	Men.	NK.	JC/26/ 28	
518	Susanna Bannyntyne	- - 1662	Samuel-ston	F	U	Men.	NK.	JC/26/ 28	
519	Issobell Stillie	- - 1662	Samuel-ston	F	U	Men.	NK.	JC/26/ 28	
520	Christian Blaik	- - 1662	Samuel-ston	F	M	Men.	NK.	JC/26/ 28	
521	Nicoll Stillie	- - 1662	Samuel-ston	M	M	Men.	NK.	JC/26/	
522	Jonet Kempe	- - 1662	Samuel-ston	F	U	Men.	NK.	JC/26/ 28	
523	Margaret Paterson	- - 1662	Samuel-ston	F	U	Men.	NK.	JC/26/ 28	*

HIGH COURT OF JUSTICIARY

No.	Name	Date	Place	Sex	Mar. Stat	Trial Stat	Fate	Source	New Case
524	Elspeth Tailyeor	- - 1662	Samuel-ston	F	U	Men.	NK.	JC/26/28	
525	Anna Pilmore	- - 1662	Samuel-ston	F	M	Men.	NK.	JC/26/28	
526	David Meikle	- - 1662	Samuel-ston	M	M	Men.	NK.	JC/26/28	*
527	Issobell Thomsen	- - 1662	Samuel-ston	F	U	Men.	NK.	JC/26/28	*
528	Jeane Kirkwood	- - 1662	Samuel-ston	F	M	Men.	NK.	JC/26/28	*
529	Robert Scot	- - 1662	Samuel-ston	M	M	Men.	NK.	JC/26/28	*
530	Jonet Robeson	- - 1662	Samuel-ston	F	U	Men.	NK.	JC/26/28	*
531	Anna Hunter	- - 1662	Nedla E.Lothian	F	M	Men.	NK.	JC/26/28	*
532	Guidfellow	- - 1662	E.Lothian	F	M	Men.	NK.	JC/26/28	*
533	Robert Capae	- - 1662	Hogel E.Lothian	M	M	Men.	NK.	JC/26/28	*
534	Wife of George Sandie	- - 1662	E.Lothian	F	M	Men.	NK.	JC/26/28	*
535	Mamie Lamb	- - 1662	E.Lothian	F	M	Men.	NK.	JC/26/28	*
536	George Gledd	- - 1662	Winton E.Lothian	M	U	Men.	NK.	JC/26/28	*
537	Wife of Thomas Baylie	- - 1662	E.Lothian	F	M	Men.	NK.	JC/26/28	*
538	Wife of Alexander Bell	- - 1662	E.Lothian	F	M	Men.	NK.	JC/26/28	*
539	Marion Blaik	- - 1662	E.Lothian	F	U	Men.	NK.	JC/26/28	*
540	Bessie Thompson	- - 1662	Pentcait-land E.Lothian	F	U	Men.	NK.	JC/26/28	*

HIGH COURT OF JUSTICIARY									
No.	Name	Date	Place	Sex	Mar. Stat	Trial Stat	Fate	Source	New Case
541	Jonet Liddell	- - 1662	Pentcait-land E.Loth.	F	U	Men.	NK.	JC/26/ 28	*
542	Wife of Archibald Manners	- - 1662	E.Lothian	F	M	Men.	NK.	JC/26/ 28	*
543	Jonet Lowrie	- - 1662	E.Lothian	F	M	Men.	NK.	JC/26/ 28	*
544	Margaret Tailyeor	- - 1662	E.Lothian	F	U	Men.	NK.	JC/26/ 28	*
545	Jeane Manner	- - 1662	E.Lothian	F	U	Men.	NK.	JC/26/ 28	*
546	Jeane Foster	- - 1662	E.Lothian	F	U	Men.	NK.	JC/26/ 28	*
547	Jeane Dikson	- - 1662	E.Lothian	F	M	Men.	NK.	JC/26/ 28	*
548	Elspeth Fermor	- - 1662	E.Lothian	F	U	Men.	NK.	JC/26/ 28	*
549	Jean Daglas	- - 1662	E.Lothian	F	U	Men.	NK.	JC/26/ 28	*
550	Marion Dikson	- - 1662	E.Lothian	F	U	Men.	NK.	JC26/ 28	*
551	Margaret Edington	- - 1662	E.Lothian	F	U	Men.	NK.	JC26/ 28	
552	Marion Wood	- - 1662	E.Lothian	F	U	Men.	NK.	JC26/ 28	
553	Christian Wilson	- - 1662	E.Lothian	F	U	Men.	NK.	JC26/ 28	
554	Margaret Fulkhart	- - 1662	E.Lothian	F	U	Men.	NK.	JC26/ 28	*
555	John Task	- - 1662	East-barne	M	U	Men.	NK.	JC26/ 28	*
556	Jeane Martin	- - 1662	Dunbar	F	U	Men.	NK.	JC26/ 28	*

HIGH COURT OF JUSTICIARY									
No.	Name	Date	Place	Sex	Mar. Stat	Trial Stat	Fate	Source	New Case
557	Jean Kerse	- - 1662	E.Lothian	F	M	Men.	NK.	JC26/28	*
558		- - 1662	Broks-burne	F	U	Men.	NK.	JC26/28	*
559	Janet Symson	- - 1662	Samuel-ston	F	U	Men.	NK.	JC26/28	*
560	Bessie Lamb	- - 1662	E.Lothian	F	U	Men.	NK.	JC26/28	*
561	Jon Russell	- - 1662	E.Lothian Nisbet	M	U	Men.	NK.	JC26/28	*
562	Jon Lyil	- - 1662	E.Lothian Boigis	M	U	Men.	NK.	JC26/28	*
563	Wife of Thomas Hay	- - 1662	Wintoun	F	M	Men.	NK.	JC26/28	*
564	Thomas Hay	- - 1662	Wintoun	M	M	Men.	NK.	JC26/28	*
565	Marion Cumming	- - 1662	E.Lothian	F	U	Men.	NK.	JC26/28	*
566	George Binnie	- - 1662	Stenton	M	U	Men.	NK.	JC26/28	*
567	George Lacost	- - 1662	E.Lothian Newmyln	M	U	Men.	NK.	JC26/28	*
568	Helen Nicolson	- - 1662	E.Lothian	F	M	Men.	NK.	JC26/28	*
569	David Schankis	- - 1662	E.Lothian	M	U	Men.	NK.	JC26/28	*
570	Wife of Pipper	- - 1662	Saltoun E.Lothian	F	M	Men.	NK.	JC26/28	*
571	Pipper	- - 1662	Saltoun E.Lothian	M	M	Men.	NK.	JC26/28	*
572	Neving	- - 1662	Saltoun E.Lothian	F	M	Men.	NK.	JC26/28	*
573	George Lacost	- - 1662	Saltoun E.Lothian	M	M	Men.	NK.	JC26/28	*

HIGH COURT OF JUSTICIARY									
No.	Name	Date	Place	Sex	Mar. Stat	Trial Stat	Fate	Source	New Case
574	Barbara Drummond	20.12. 1664	Kilbride	F	M	T	Acqu	JC/2/ 10	
575	Marie Nian Innes Vic Coull	– – 1669		F	U	Proc.	NK.	PROC. SRO List	*
576	Major Thomas Weir	6. 4. 1670	Edinburgh	M	U	T	Ex.	JC2/ 13	
577	Jean Weir	6. 4. 1670	Edinburgh	F	U	T	Ex.	JC2/ 13	
578	Mary Man Innes Du Doul	1. 6. 1670	Skye Sleat	F	U	T	Acqu	JC2/ 13	
579	Cristian Brake	–.11. 1670	Aberdeen	F	U	Proc.	NK.	JC26/ 40	*
580	James Anderson	–.11. 1670	Aberdeen	M	U	Proc.	NK.	JC26/ 40	*
581	Janet Anderson	–.11. 1670	Aberdeen	F	W	Proc.	NK.	JC26/ 40	*
582	Jeane Laying	–.11. 1670	Aberdeen	F	U	Proc.	NK.	JC26/ 40	*
583	Helen George	6. 5. 1671	Aberdeen	F	M	Proc.	NK.	JC26/38 ABN.Roll 1671	*
584	Jean Ross	6. 5. 1671	Aberdeen	F	U	Proc.	NK.	JC26/38 ABN.Roll 1671	*
585	Geilles Burnett	9. 5. 1671	Aberdeen	F	M	T	Acqu	JC26/40 JC26/38 ABN.Roll 1671	*
586	Helen Symen	10. 5. 1671	Aberdeen	F	U	Proc.	NK.	JC26/38/ 40 ABN. Roll	*
587	Christian Foord	10. 5. 1671	Aberdeen	F	U	Proc.	Acqu	JC26/38 ABN.Roll 1671	*
588	Elspeth Thomsone	15. 5. 1671	Dumfries	F	U	T	Ex.	JC26/ 38	

HIGH COURT OF JUSTICIARY									
No.	Name	Date	Place	Sex	Mar. Stat	Trial Stat	Fate	Source	New Case
589	Janet McMuldritchie	15. 5. 1671	Dumfries	F	U	T	Ex.	JC26/ 38	
590	Andrew Laidly	3. 7. 1671	Jedburgh Edinburgh	M	U	T	Acqu	JC2/ 13	
591	Mary Sommerveil	10. 7. 1671	Jedburgh Edinburgh	F	U	T	Acqu	JC2/ 13	
592	George Guislet	10. 7. 1671	Jedburgh	M	U	T	Acqu	JC2/ 13	
593	John Scott	24. 7. 1671	Leith	M	U	T	Acqu	JC2/ 13	
594	Jonet Miller	– – 1671	Dumfries	F	U	Men.	Ex.	JC26/ 38	*
595	Helen Sumner	– – 1671	Aberdeen	F	U	Proc.	NK.	JC26/ 38 ABN Roll 1671	*
596	James Beverley	– – 1671	Aberdeen	M	U	Proc.	NK.	JC26/ 38/41? PROC. SRO List	*
597	Duplicates	594							
598	Grissel McIlney	– – 1671	Dumfries	F	U	Proc.	NK.	JC26/ 38	*
599	Bessie Paine	– – 1671	Dumfries?	F	U	Proc.	NK.	JC26/ 38	*
600	Elspeth Thomson	– – 1671	Banff	F	U	Proc.	NK.	JC26/41 Banff Roll 1671	*
601	Christian Morison	5. 2. 1672	Stirling	F	U	T	Misc	JC2/ 13	
602	Margaret McGuffock	15. 7. 1672	Kirkcud-bright	F	U	T	Misc	JC2/ 13	
603	Grissell Rae	15. 7. 1672	Kirkcud-bright	F	U	T	Misc	JC2/ 13	
604	Jonet Howat	15. 7. 1672	Kirkcud-bright	F	U	T	Misc	JC2/ 13	

HIGH COURT OF JUSTICIARY									
No.	Name	Date	Place	Sex	Mar. Stat	Trial Stat	Fate	Source	New Case
605	Mary Ncthomas	16.10. 1673	Rothesay	F	U	T	Ex.	Argyll J.Rec. V1 p.21	*
606	Janet McNicol	16.10. 1673	Rothesay	F	U	T	Ex.	Hew.V2 pp.262 -263	
607	Margaret Clerk	4. 6. 1674	Seatoun of Cullen	F	M	T	Acqu	JC2/14 p.181F	
608	Margaret Clerk	4. 6. 1674	Seton of Cullen	F	M	T	Acqu	J.C.Rec. Edin. V2 p.269	
609	Agnes Hendrie	9. 7. 1675	Culross	F	W	T	Ex.	JC/24	
610	Jonet Hendrie	9. 7. 1675	Culross	F	W	T	Ex.	JC/14	
611	Issobell Inglis	9. 7. 1675	Culross	F	W	T	Ex.	JC/14	
612	Katherine Sands	9. 7. 1675	Culross	F	M	T	Ex.	JC2/ 14	
613	Christian Hoggen	13. 1. 1678	Mid-lothian Crichton	U	U	T	Acqu	JC2/ 15	*
614	Helen Forrester	13. 6. 1678	Crighton	F	U	T	NK.	Dalyell p.570	
615	Margaret Smaill	13. 9. 1678		F	U	T	NK.	Dalyell p.555,623	
616	Margaret Douglas	13. 9. 1678		F	U	T	NK.	Dalyell p.575	
617	Helen Forrester	13. 9. 1678	Mid-lothian Crichton	F	U	T	Ex.	JC2/ 15	
618	Barbara Veitch	13. 9. 1678	Mid-lothian Crichton	F	U	Men.	NK.	JC2/ 15	*
619	Margaret Douglas	13. 9. 1678	Mid-lothian Crichton	F	U	T	Ex.	JC2/ 15	

HIGH COURT OF JUSTICIARY									
No.	Name	Date	Place	Sex	Mar. Stat	Trial Stat	Fate	Source	New Case
620	Margaret Smaill	13. 9. 1678	Mid-lothian Crichton	F	U	T	Ex.	JC2/ 15	
621	Grissell Walker	13. 9. 1678	Paiston	F	M	T	Misc	JC2/ 15	*
622	Marion Campbell	13. 9. 1678	Paiston	F	M	T	Misc	JC2/ 15	*
623	Gideon Penman	13. 9. 1678	Paiston	M	U	Proc.	Misc	JC2/ 15	
624	Sarah Cranston	13. 9. 1678	Paiston	F	U	Men.	NK.	JC2/ 15	*
625	Katherine Halyday	13. 9. 1678	Paiston	F	U	Men.	NK.	JC2/ 15	*
626	Janet Burton	13. 9. 1678	Paiston	F	U	Men.	NK.	JC2/ 15	*
627	Isobel Shand	13. 9. 1678	Paiston	F	U	T	Ex.	JC2/ 15	*
628	Margaret Lowis	13. 9. 1678	Paiston	F	U	T	Ex.	JC2/ 15	*
629	Agnes Thomson	13. 9. 1678	Paiston	F	U	T	Misc	JC2/ 15	*
630	Elspeth Knox	13. 9. 1678	Paiston	F	U	T	Misc	JC2/ 15	*
631	Elizabeth Wood	13. 9. 1678	Paiston	F	U	T	Misc	JC2/ 15	*
632	Margaret Russel	13. 9. 1678	Paiston	F	U	T	Misc	JC2/ 15	*
633	James Campbell	13. 9. 1678	Paiston	M	U	T	Misc	JC2/ 15	*
634	Margaret Anderson	13. 9. 1678	Paiston	F	W	T	Misc	JC2/ 15	*
635	Margaret Dalgleish	13. 9. 1678	Paiston	F	M	T	Misc	JC2/ 15	*
636	Isobell Eliot	13. 9. 1678	Paiston Templehill	F	U	T	Ex.	JC2/ 15	

HIGH COURT OF JUSTICIARY									
No.	Name	Date	Place	Sex	Mar. Stat	Trial Stat	Fate	Source	New Case
637	Helen Laying	13. 9. 1678	Paiston	F	W	T	Ex.	JC2/ 15	
638	Margaret Dods	13. 9. 1678	Paiston	F	U	T	Ex.	JC2/ 15	
639	Marion Veitch	13. 9. 1678	Paiston	F	M	T	Ex.	JC2/ 15	
640	Margaret Sonnes	4.11. 1678		F	U	T	NK.	Dalyell p.555	
641	Bessie Gourdie	4.11. 1678	Mid-lothian Fala	F	U	T	Ex.	JC2/ 15	*
642	Margaret Sonns	4.11. 1678	Mid-lothian Fala	F	U	T	Ex.	JC2/ 15	*
643	Agnes Somerville	4.11. 1678	Mid-lothian Fala	F	U	T	Ex.	JC2/ 15	*
644	Elspeth Cheuslie	- - 1679	Preston-pans	F	U	Proc.	NK.	JC2/ 15	*
645	Nicholas Buchanan	5. 1. 1680	Croy	M	U	T	Acqu	JC2/ 15	*
646	Bessie Gibb	19. 1. 1680	Bo'ness	F	M	Proc.	Acqu	JC2/ 15	*
647	Margaret Whyte	27. 3. 1680	Bo'ness	F	M	T	Acqu	JC2/ 15	*
648	Elizabeth Hutcheson	27. 3. 1680	Bo'ness	F	U	T	Acqu	JC2/ 15	*
649	Elizabeth Scotland	27. 3. 1680	Bo'ness	F	U	T	Acqu	JC2/ 15	*
650	Margaret Comb	27. 3. 1680	Bo'ness	F	U	T	Acqu	JC2/ 15	*
651	Agnes Stewart	27. 3. 1680	Bo'ness	F	U	T	Acqu	JC2/ 15	*
652	Janet Robertson	- - 1681	Stanhous	F	U	Proc.	NK.	PROC. S.R.O. List	*

HIGH COURT OF JUSTICIARY									
No.	Name	Date	Place	Sex	Mar. Stat	Trial Stat	Fate	Source	New Case
653	Jonet Losk	-. 5. 1683	Ayr	F	W	Proc.	Acqu	JC26/64 Ayr Port. Roll May 1683	*
654	Hopkin	-. 5. 1683	Ayr	F	M	Proc.	Acqu	JC26/64 Ayr Port. Roll May 1683	*
655	Janet Fisher	-. 5. 1683	Ayr	F	M	Proc.	Acqu	JC26/64 Ayr Port. Roll May 1683	*
656	Helen Wilson	-. 5. 1683	Ayr	F	W	Proc.	Acqu	JC26/64 Ayr Port. Roll May 1683	*
657	Joan Graham	-. 5. 1683	Ayr	F	U	Proc.	Acqu	JC26/64 Ayr Port. Roll May 1683	*
658	Marion McRae	-. 5. 1683	Ayr	F	U	Proc.	Acqu	JC26/64 Ayr Port. Roll May 1683	*
659	Issabell Reid	-. 5. 1683	Ayr	F	U	Proc.	Acqu	JC26/64 Ayr Port. Roll May 1683	*
660	Catharin Lorimer	-. 5. 1683	Ayr	F	M	Proc.	Acqu	JC26/64 Ayr Port. Roll May 1683	*
661	John Hislop	10. 7. 1683	Edinburgh	M	U	Proc.	Acqu	JC26/62 JC26/65 Edin. Port.Rolls	*
662	Jean Gray	10. 7. 1683	Edinburgh	F	M	Proc.	Acqu	JC26/62 JC26/65 Edin. Port.Rolls	*

HIGH COURT OF JUSTICIARY									
No.	Name	Date	Place	Sex	Mar. Stat	Trial Stat	Fate	Source	New Case
663	Margaret Logan	10. 7. 1683	Edinburgh	F	W	Proc.	Acqu	JC26/62 JC26/65 Edin. Port.Rolls	*
664	Isobell Hislop	10. 7. 1683	Edinburgh	F	W	Proc.	Ex.	JC26/62 JC26/65 Edin. Port.Rolls	*
665	Marion Hislop	10. 7. 1683	Edinburgh	F	M	Proc.	Acqu	JC26/62 JC26/65 Edin. Port.Rolls	*
666	Jennet Broun	- - 1683	Dumfries	F	U	Proc.	NK.	JC26/ 63	*
667	John Black	- - 1683	Berwick	M	U	Proc.	NK.	JC26/62 Ber.Port. Roll 1683	*
668	Elizabeth Heswith	- - 1683	Stirling	F	U	Proc.	NK.	JC26/65 Perth Port.Roll 1683	*
669	Margaret Wilkin	- - 1683	Annan	F	M	Proc.	NK.	JC26/25 Annan-dale Roll 1683	*
670	Elizabeth Anderson	-. 5. 1699	Glasgow	F	U	Men.	NK.	JC26/ 81/D9	*
671	Gean Hadron	-. 5. 1699	Glasgow	F	W	Proc.	Acqu	JC26/ 81/D9	*
672	Elspeth Wood	-. 5. 1699	Glasgow	F	W	Proc.	Acqu	JC26/ 81/D9	*
673	John Glass	-. 5. 1700	Ross-shire Killernan	M	M	T	Acqu	JC3/D1/ 66-67 JC26/81/ D3	
674	Agnes Snyp	-. 5. 1700	Glasgow	F	M	T	Acqu	JC3/D1/ 89 JC26 /81/D9	*

HIGH COURT OF JUSTICIARY									
No.	Name	Date	Place	Sex	Mar. Stat	Trial Stat	Fate	Source	New Case
675	Jannet Laing	-. 5. 1700	Glasgow	F	M	T	Acqu	JC3/D1/ 89 JC26 /81/D9	*
676	Jean Ross	-. 5. 1700	Glasgow	F	U	T	Acqu	JC3/D1/ 89 JC26 /81/D9	*
677	Jean Whythill	-. 5. 1700	Glasgow	F	M	T	Acqu	JC26/81 /D9 JC3 /D1/89	*
678	Margaret Duncan	-. 5. 1700	Glasgow	F	W	T	Acqu	JC26/81 /D9 JC3 /D1/89	*
679	John Paterson	-. 5. 1700	Glasgow	M	U	T	Acqu	JC26/81 /D9 JC3 /D1/89	*
680	Jannet Boyd	-. 5. 1700	Glasgow	F	U	T	Acqu	JC26/81 /D9 JC3 /D1/89	*
681	Alexander Lyle	-. 5. 1700	Glasgow	M	U	T	Acqu	JC3/D1 /89 JC26 /81/D9	*
682	Bessie Cochran	-. 5. 1700	Glasgow	F	W	T	Acqu	JC3/D1/ 89 JC26 /81/D9	*
683	Margaret Alexander	-. 5. 1700	Glasgow	F	U	T	Acqu	JC3/D1/ 89 JC26 /81/D9	*
684	Elspeth Tarbat	-. 5. 1700	Glasgow	F	M	T	Acqu	JC3/D1/ 89 JC26 /81/D9	*
685	Jean Woodrow	-. 5. 1700	Glasgow	F	W	T	Acqu	JC3/D1/ 89 JC26 /81/D9	*
686	Jean Drummond	-. 5. 1700	Glasgow	F	M	T	Acqu	JC3/D1/ 89 JC26 /81/D9	*
687	Bessie Little	-. 5. 1700	Glasgow	F	M	T	Acqu	JC3/D1/ 89 JC26 /81/D9	*

HIGH COURT OF JUSTICIARY									
No.	Name	Date	Place	Sex	Mar. Stat	Trial Stat	Fate	Source	New Case
688	Annabill Reid	-. 5. 1700	Glasgow	F	M	T	Acqu	JC3/D1/ 89 JC26 /81/D9	*
689	Isobell Houston	-. 5. 1700	Glasgow	F	M	T	Acqu	JC3/D1/ 89 JC26 /81/D9	*
690	Mary Morisone	-. 5. 1700	Glasgow	F	M	T	Acqu	JC26/81 /D9 JC3/D1/ 87-88 JC26/81 /D2	*
691	John Dougall	-. 5. 1700	Glasgow	M	U	T	Acqu	JC26/81 /D9 JC3 /D1/89	*
692	Anna Hill	-. 5. 1700	Glasgow	F	U	T	Acqu	JC26/81 /D9 JC3 /D1/89	*
693	Jean Gilmore	-. 5. 1700	Glasgow	F	M	T	Acqu	JC26/81 D9 JC3 /D1/89	*
694	Janet Robertson	-. 5. 1700	Glasgow	F	M	T	Acqu	JC26/81 D9 JC3/ D1/89	*
695	Jannet Gentleman	-. 5. 1700	Glasgow	F	M	T	Acqu	JC26/81 /D9 JC3 /D1/89	*
696	Marion Ure	-. 5. 1700	Glasgow	F	W	T	Acqu	JC26/81 /D9 JC3 /D1/89	*
697	Janit Dougan	-.10. 1708	Dumfries Partoun	F	U	Proc.	NK.	JC26/86 /D/250	*
698	Adam Black	-.10. 1708	Dumfries Larnanadie	M	U	Proc.	NK.	JC26/86 /D/250	*
699	Agnes Currie	21.11. 1708	Perth Torrie-burn	F	U	Proc.	NK.	JC26/86 /D/245 JC26/86 /D/228	*
700	Janet Hairstains	3. 5. 1709	Galloway	F	U	T	Acqu	Dalyell p.630	

HIGH COURT OF JUSTICIARY									
No.	Name	Date	Place	Sex	Mar. Stat	Trial Stat	Fate	Source	New Case
701	Elspeth Rule	3. 5. 1709	Dumfries	F	U	T	NCP	Arnot, pp.411 -412	
702	James Davidson	- - 1709	Water-haugh	M	U	Proc.	NK.	PROC. D/348	*
704	Elspeth Wood	- - 1709	Over-gurrock	F	W	Proc.	Acqu	PROC. D/469	*
705	Christian Bonn	- - - -	Clune	F	U	Proc.	NK.	JC27/ 10 Paper 9	*
706	Marion Tailyour	- - - -	Bryhainye	F	W	Proc.	NK.	JC27/ 10	*
707	Giddoch Boyne McAlester	- - - -	Anthuabey-thane	U	U	Proc.	NK.	JC27/ 10	*
708	Bornlie	- - - -	Flenes Moir	F	U	Proc.	NK.	JC27/ 10 Papers 8-9	*

CIRCUIT COURT CASES									
No.	Name	Date	Place	Sex	Mar. Stat	Trial Stat	Fate	Source	New Case
709		- - 1652		U	U	T	Acqu	Whit. p.545	
710		- - 1652		U	U	T	Acqu	Whit. p.545	
711		- - 1652		U	U	T	Acqu	Whit. p.545	
712		- - 1652		U	U	T	Acqu	Whit. p.545	
713		- - 1652		U	U	T	Acqu	Whit. p.545	
714		- - 1652		U	U	T	Acqu	Whit. p.545	
715		- - 1652		U	U	T	Acqu	Whit. p.545	
716		- - 1652		U	U	T	Acqu	Whit. p.545	
717		- - 1652		U	U	T	Acqu	Whit. p.545	
718		- - 1652		U	U	T	Acqu	Whit. p.545	
719		- - 1652		U	U	T	Acqu	Whit. p.545	
720		- - 1652		U	U	T	Acqu	Whit. p.545	
721		- - 1652		U	U	T	Acqu	Whit. p.545	
722		- - 1652		U	U	T	Acqu	Whit. p.545	
723		- - 1652		U	U	T	Acqu	Whit. p.545	
724		- - 1652		U	U	T	Acqu	Whit. p.545	
725		- - 1652		U	U	T	Acqu	Whit. p.545	

CIRCUIT COURT CASES									
No.	Name	Date	Place	Sex	Mar. Stat	Trial Stat	Fate	Source	New Case
726		- - 1652		U	U	T	Acqu	Whit. p.545	
727		- - 1652		U	U	T	Acqu	Whit. p.545	
728		- - 1652		U	U	T	Acqu	Whit. p.545	
729		- - 1652		U	U	T	Acqu	Whit. p.545	
730		- - 1652		U	U	T	Acqu	Whit. p.545	
731		- - 1652		U	U	T	Acqu	Whit. p.545	
732		- - 1652		U	U	T	Acqu	Whit. p.545	
733		- - 1652		U	U	T	Acqu	Whit. p.545	
734		- - 1652		U	U	T	Acqu	Whit. p.545	
735		- - 1652		U	U	T	Acqu	Whit. p.545	
736		- - 1652		U	U	T	Acqu	Whit. p.545	
737		- - 1652		U	U	T	Acqu	Whit. p.545	
738		- - 1652		U	U	T	Acqu	Whit. p.545	
739		- - 1652		U	U	T	Acqu	Whit. p.545	
740		- - 1652		U	U	T	Acqu	Whit. p.545	
741		- - 1652		U	U	T	Acqu	Whit. p.545	
742		- - 1652		U	U	T	Acqu	Whit. p.545	

CIRCUIT COURT CASES									
No.	Name	Date	Place	Sex	Mar. Stat	Trial Stat	Fate	Source	New Case
743		- - 1652		U	U	T	Acqu	Whit. p.545	
744		- - 1652		U	U	T	Acqu	Whit. p.545	
745		- - 1652		U	U	T	Acqu	Whit. p.545	
746		- - 1652		U	U	T	Acqu	Whit. p.545	
747		- - 1652		U	U	T	Acqu	Whit. p.545	
748		- - 1652		U	U	T	Acqu	Whit. p.545	
749		- - 1652		U	U	T	Acqu	Whit. p.545	
750		- - 1652		U	U	T	Acqu	Whit. p.545	
751		- - 1652		U	U	T	Acqu	Whit. p.545	
752		- - 1652		U	U	T	Acqu	Whit. p.545	
753		- - 1652		U	U	T	Acqu	Whit. p.545	
754		- - 1652		U	U	T	Acqu	Whit. p.545	
755		- - 1652		U	U	T	Acqu	Whit. p.545	
756		- - 1652		U	U	T	Acqu	Whit. p.545	
757		- - 1652		U	U	T	Acqu	Whit. p.545	
758		- - 1652		U	U	T	Acqu	Whit. p.545	
759		- - 1652		U	U	T	Acqu	Whit. p.545	

CIRCUIT COURT CASES									
No.	Name	Date	Place	Sex	Mar. Stat	Trial Stat	Fate	Source	New Case
760		- - 1652		U	U	T	Acqu	Whit. p.545	
761		- - 1652		U	U	T	Acqu	Whit. p.545	
762		- - 1652		U	U	T	Acqu	Whit. p.545	
763		- - 1652		U	U	T	Acqu	Whit. p.545	
764		- - 1652		U	U	T	Acqu	Whit. p.545	
765		- - 1652		U	U	T	Acqu	Whit. p.545	
766		- - 1652		U	U	T	Acqu	Whit. p.545	
767		- - 1652		U	U	T	Acqu	Whit. p.545	
768		- - 1652		U	U	T	Acqu	Whit. p.545	
769	Elspet Sckogie	- - 1654	Couper	F	U	Proc.	Acqu	JC37/ 1	*
770	Andro McGibbone	13. 8. 1655	Inver- ness	M	U	T	Misc	JC10/ 2	*
771	Malcolm McConel	13. 8. 1655	Inver- ness	M	U	Proc.	NCP	JC10/ 2	*
772	Issobell Sesbie	27. 8. 1655	Perth	F	U	T	Acqu	JC10/2 Perth Roll	*
773	Elspeth Scrogie	27. 8. 1655	Perth	F	U	T	NK.	JC10/ 2	*
774	Gilbert Mowat	- - 1655	Caithness Wick	M	M	Proc.	NK.	JC17/1 C'ness Fug. List	*
775	Patrick Barnett	- - 1655	Perth Balbugie	M	U	Proc.	NK.	JC17/1 Perth Fug.List	*

CIRCUIT COURT CASES									
No.	Name	Date	Place	Sex	Mar. Stat	Trial Stat	Fate	Source	New Case
776	Bessie Andro	- - 1655	Caithness Wick	F	U	Proc.	NK.	JC17/1 C'ness Fug. Roll	*
777	Agnes Gune	- - 1655	Caithness Wick	F	U	Proc.	NK.	JC17/1 C'ness Fug. Roll	*
778	Jonnet Dow	- - 1655	Caithness Wick	F	M	Proc.	NK.	JC17/1 C'ness Fug. Roll.	*
779	Marshall Sutherland	- - 1655	Caithness Nether-land	M	U	Proc.	NK.	JC17/1 C'ness Fug. Roll	*
780	Adam Barnie	- - 1655	Caithness Keyse	M	U	Proc.	NK.	JC17/1 C'ness Fug. Roll	*
781	Marione Kenoch	- - 1655	Caithness Papryo	F	U	Proc.	NK.	JC17/1 C'ness Fug. Roll	*
782	John Harper	- - 1655	Caithness Wick	M	U	Proc.	NK.	JC17/1 C'ness Fug. Roll	*
783	William McAngus	- - 1655	Suther-land Clyne	M	U	Proc.	Acqu	JC17/1 S'land Fug. List	*
784	Thomas MrGillie Lukell	- - 1655	Sutherland Clyne	M	U	Proc.	Acqu	JC17/1 S'land Fug. List	*
785	Margaret Nakoch	- - 1655	Caithness Wick	F	U	Proc.	NK.	JC17/1 C'ness Fug. Roll	*

CIRCUIT COURT CASES									
No.	Name	Date	Place	Sex	Mar. Stat	Trial Stat	Fate	Source	New Case
786	Gretchach Unchach	- - 1655	Caithness Wick	F	U	Proc.	NK.	JC17/1 C'ness Fug. Roll	*
787	Henrie Lyell	- - 1655	Caithness Wick	M	U	Proc.	NK.	JC17/1 C'ness Fug. List	*
788	Donald McChereich	- - 1655	Suther-land Currell	M	U	Proc.	Acqu	JC17/1 S'land Fug. List	*
789	Agnes Pryde	27. 8. 1656	Perth	F	U	T	Acqu	JC10/2 Perth Roll	*
790	Bessie Neveing	31. 3. 1658	Renfrew	F	U	T	NK.	JC10/2	*
791	Bessie Neveing	2. 4. 1658	Lanark	F	U	T	Misc	JC10/2	*
792	Isobell Henderson	6. 4. 1658	Ayr	F	W	T	NK.	JC10/2	*
793	Janet Ross	6. 4. 1658	Ayr	F	U	T	NK.	JC10/2	*
794	Wallace	6. 4. 1658	Ayr	U	U	T	NK.	JC10/2	*
795	Jonet Slobane	6. 4. 1658	Ayr	F	U	T	NK.	JC10/2	*
796	Jonet Steik	6. 4. 1658	Ayr	F	U	T	NK.	JC10/2	*
797	Elspeth Cunningham	6. 4. 1658	Ayr	F	U	T	Misc	JC10/2	*
798	Jannett Sawes	7. 4. 1658	Ayr	F	U	T	Ex.	JC10/2	
799	Katharine Clacherty	9. 4. 1658	Kirkcud-bright	F	U	T	Ex.	JC10/2	*
800	Jonet Miller	9. 4. 1658	Dumfries	F	U	T	Ex.	JC10/2	*

CIRCUIT COURT CASES									
No.	Name	Date	Place	Sex	Mar. Stat	Trial Stat	Fate	Source	New Case
801	Marione Lewers	9. 4. 1658	Kirkcud-bright	F	U	T	Acqu	JC10/ 2	*
802	Jonet Salber	23. 4. 1658	Ayr	F	U	T	Ex.	JC10/ 2	*
803	Magdalen Blair	22. 3. 1659	Stirling	F	U	T	Acqu	JC10/ 2	*
804	Issobell Bennet	22. 3. 1659	Stirling	F	U	T	NCP	JC10/ 2	*
805	Bessie Stevinson	22. 3. 1659	Stirling	F	U	T	Ex.	JC10/ 2	
806	Katharine Blak	23. 3. 1659	Stirling	F	U	T	NCP	JC10	*
807	Issobel Ker	23. 3. 1659	Stirling	F	U	T	Acqu	JC10	*
808	Elspeth Crocket	23. 3. 1659	Stirling	F	U	T	NCP	JC10	*
809	Elizabeth Black	23. 3. 1659	Stirling	F	U	T	NCP	JC10	*
810	Janet Miller	23. 3. 1659	Stirling	F	U	T	NK.	JC10	*
811	Margaret Gourley	23. 3. 1659	Stirling	F	U	T	Acqu	JC10/	*
812	James Kirk	23. 3. 1659	Stirling	M	U	T	Acqu	JC10	*
813	Margaret Harvie	27. 3. 1659	Stirling	F	U	T	Acqu	JC10	*
814	Barbara Erskine	27. 3. 1659	Stirling	F	U	T	Acqu	JC10/	*
815	Janet Slowane	29. 3. 1659	Ayr	F	U	T	Acqu	JC10/ 2	*
816	Elspeth Cunninghame	30. 3. 1659		F	U	T	Ex.	JC10/ 2	*
817	Barbara Cunninghame	30. 3. 1659	Ayr	F	U	T	Acqu	JC10/ 2	*

CIRCUIT COURT CASES									
No.	Name	Date	Place	Sex	Mar. Stat	Trial Stat	Fate	Source	New Case
818	Barbara Cunninghame	30. 3. 1659	Ayr	F	U	T	NK.	JC10	*
819	Jean Thomson	2. 4. 1659	Dumfries	F	U	T	Ex.	JC10/ 2	*
820	Margaret Clerk	2. 4. 1659	Dumfries	F	U	T	Ex.	JC10/ 2	*
821	Janet McGown	2. 4. 1659	Dumfries	F	U	T	Ex.	JC10/ 2	*
822	Bigis Cairnes	2. 4. 1659	Dumfries	F	U	T	Ex.	JC10/ 2	*
823	Jannet Corsan	4. 4. 1659	Dumfries	F	U	T	Ex.	JC10/ 2	
824	Agnes Clark	4. 4. 1659	Dumfries	F	U	T	Ex.	JC10/ 2	*
825	Jennat McKnight	4. 4. 1659	Dumfries	F	U	T	Ex.	JC10/ 2	*
826	Jennat Callen	4. 4. 1659	Dumfries	F	U	T	Ex.	JC10/ 2	
827	Helen Moorheid	4. 4. 1659	Dumfries	F	U	T	Ex.	JC10/ 2	
828	Helen Tait	5. 4. 1659	Dumfries	F	U	T	Acqu	JC10/ 2	
829	Jonet Slowane	6. 4. 1659	Ayr	F	U	T	Misc	JC10/ 2	*
830	Katharine Russell	30. 3. 1671	Anford	F	U	T	NK.	JC10/ 3	*
831	Jean Rosse	30. 3. 1671	Anford	F	U	T	NK.	JC10/ 3	*
832	Helen George	30. 3. 1671	Inverary	F	M	T	NK.	JC2/3	*
833	Margaret Durie	30. 3. 1671	Aberdeen Filtue	F	U	T	NK.	JC10/ 3	*
834	Elspeth Thomson	3. 4. 1671	Banff Fortrie	F	U	T	NK.	JC10/ 3	*

CIRCUIT COURT CASES									
No.	Name	Date	Place	Sex	Mar. Stat	Trial Stat	Fate	Source	New Case
835	Margaret Jonking	6. 4. 1671	Elgin	F	M	T	NK.	JC10/3	*
836	Elspeth Dason	15. 4. 1671	Ross-shire	F	U	T	NK.	JC10/3	*
837	Grissel Grot	15. 4. 1671	Ross-shire	F	U	T	NK.	JC10/3	*
838	Elspeth Thomson	15. 4. 1671	Dumfries	F	U	T	Ex.	JC10/3	
839	Alex Grant	15. 4. 1671	Ross-shire	M	U	T	NK.	JC10/3	*
840	Jean Rutherd	24. 4. 1671	Jedburgh	F	M	T	NK.	JC10/3	*
841	Elspeth Wood	24. 4. 1671	Jedburgh	F	U	T	Misc	JC10/3	*
842	George Guislet	24. 4. 1671	Jedburgh	M	U	T	NK.	JC10/3	
843	Marie Somerveill	24. 4. 1671	Jedburgh	F	U	T	NK.	JC10/3	
844	Marion McCall	8. 5. 1671	Ayr	F	M	T	NCP	JC10/3	*
845	Geils Burnet	9. 5. 1671	Aberdeen	F	W	T	Acqu	JC10/3	*
846	Janet McMurdoch	15. 5. 1671	Dumfries	F	U	T	Ex.	JC10/3	
847	Christian Cechie	24. 5. 1671	Jedburgh	F	U	T	NK.	JC10/3	*
848	John Crisbie	24. 5. 1671	Jedburgh	M	U	T	NK.	JC10/3	*
849	Isobell Robison	24. 5. 1671	Jedburgh	F	U	T	NK.	JC10/3	*
850	William Bannerman	- - 1671	Elgin	M	U	T	NCP	JC10/3	*
851	William Stewart	8. 9. 1679	Stobo	M	U	T	Acqu	JC10/4	*

CIRCUIT COURT CASES									
No.	Name	Date	Place	Sex	Mar. Stat	Trial Stat	Fate	Source	New Case
852	James Russell	8. 9. 1679	Dreva	M	U	T	Acqu	JC10/4	*
853	Richard Halywall	8. 9. 1679	Selkirk	M	U	T	NK.	JC10/4	*
854	Jannet Hil	8. 9. 1679	North Leith	F	M	T	NK.	JC10/4	*
855	Bessie Ramsay	8. 9. 1679	Morton-hall	F	U	T	NK.	JC10/4	*
856	Katharin Smith	8. 9. 1679	Morton-hall	F	U	T	NK.	JC10/4	*
857	John Scott	8. 9. 1679	Leith	M	U	T	NK.	JC10/4	*
858	Margaret Wightman	8. 9. 1679	Hadding-ton	F	U	T	Misc	JC10/4	*
859	Christian Lockhart	8. 9. 1679	Hadding-ton	F	U	T	Misc	JC10/4	*
860	Elspeth Chousley	8. 9. 1679	Hadding-ton	F	U	T	Acqu	JC10/4	*
861	Geils Harley	8. 9. 1679	Fisherawe	F	M	T	NK.	JC10/4	*
862	Marion Robertson	8. 9. 1679	Fisherawe	F	M	T	NK.	JC10/4	*
863	Issobell Hislope	8. 9. 1679	Crichton	F	W	T	NK.	JC10/4	*
864	Marion Hislop	8. 9. 1679	Crichton	F	M	T	NK.	JC10/4	*
865	Marg Logan	8. 9. 1679	Crichton	F	M	T	NK.	JC10/4	*
866	John Hislop	8. 9. 1679	Crichton	M	U	T	NK.	JC10/4	*
867	James Stewart	16.10. 1679	Stobo	M	U	T	Acqu	JC10/4	*
868	Christian Wilkieson	13. 3. 1708	Jedburgh Greenlaw	F	U	Proc.	NK.	D/249	*

CIRCUIT COURT CASES									
No.	Name	Date	Place	Sex	Mar. Stat	Trial Stat	Fate	Source	New Case
869	Marion Brown	5. 3. 1709	Kilmar-nock	F	U	Proc.	NK.	D/321	*
870	Margaret Clark	13. 5. 1709	Carkmuir	F	U	Proc.	NK.	D/386	*
871	Janet Watt	13. 5. 1709	Ball-gillo	F	U	Proc.	NK.	D/386	*
872	Nicolas Lawson	20. 5. 1709	Pitten-weam	M	M	Proc.	NK.	D/245 D/228 D/346	*
873	Bettie Laing	20. 5. 1709	Pitten-weam	F	U	Proc.	NK.	D/228 D/346 D/225	*

PRIVY COUNCIL CASES									
No.	Name	Date	Place	Sex	Mar. Stat	Trial Stat	Fate	Source	New Case
874	Katie	- - 1585	Edinburgh	F	U	Men.	NK.	Cal.V4 p.442	
875	Helene Elliot	16. 2. 1586	Jedburgh	F	U	Men.	NK.	R.P.C. V4 p.147	
876	Niniane Chirneyside	24. 5. 1591	Edinburgh	M	U	Men.	Misc	R.P.C. V4 pp.610: 614:624	
877	Jonnett Finlasoun	26. 7. 1597	Burntis-land	F	M	Men.	NK.	R.P.C. V5 pp.405 -406	
878	Issobell Douglas	2. 3. 1598	Dunkeld	F	M	Men.	Acqu	R.P.C. V5 p.448	*
879	Margaret Stewart	2. 3. 1598	Dunkeld	F	W	Men.	Acqu	R.P.C. V5 p.448	*
880	Robert Boyd	2. 3. 1598	Dunkeld	M	M	Men.	Acqu	R.P.C. V5 p.448	*
881	Marion Agnes Macause	9. 9. 1598	Perth	F	U	Men.	Ex.	R.P.C. V5 p.448	
882	Janet Robertson	9. 9. 1598	Perth	F	U	Men.	Ex.	R.P.C. V5 p.448	
883	Bessie Ireland	9. 9. 1598	Perth	F	U	Men.	Ex.	R.P.C. V5 p.448	
884	Margaret Hay	16.11. 1598	Lasswade	F	M	Com.	NK.	R.P.C. V5 p.495	
885	George Methven	2. 7. 1601	Methven's Coble	M	U	Men.	NK.	R.P.C. V6 p.264	
886	Hew Methven	2. 7. 1601	Methven's Coble	M	U	Men.	NK.	R.P.C. V6 p.264	

PRIVY COUNCIL CASES									
No.	Name	Date	Place	Sex	Mar. Stat	Trial Stat	Fate	Source	New Case
887	Patrick Lowrie	27. 7. 1605	Hailie	M	U	Men.	Ex.	R.P.C. V7 pp.67-68	
888	Issobell Falconner	29. 8. 1606	Eyemouth	F	M	Men.	Ex.	R.P.C. V7 pp.238 -239	
889		- - 1608	Brechin	F	U	Men.	Ex.	R.P.C. V7 p.605	
890	Jonet Drysdaill	18. 7. 1609	Inveresk	F	U	Men.	Misc	R.P.C. V8 pp.322; 701	
891	Gelis Johnston	20. 7. 1609	Mussell-burgh	F	W	Men.	NK.	R.P.C. V8 pp.328 -329	
892	Marioun Tailyeour	11. 6. 1611	Moray	F	U	Com.	NK.	R.P.C. V10 p.191	
893	Marjorie Mongomerie	11. 6. 1611	Moray	F	U	Com.	NK.	R.P.C. V10 p.191	
894	Issobell McKie	25. 8. 1611	Stirling	F	U	Com.	NK.	R.P.C. V11 p.224	
895	Katherine Cunynhame	4. 6. 1612	Mylne	F	M	Com.	NK.	R.P.C. V9 pp.387 -388	
896	Bessie Hendirson	4. 6. 1612	Kidlaw	F	U	Com.	NK.	R.P.C. V9 pp.387 -388	
897	Christian Grintoun	9.11. 1612	Dunbar	F	U	Com.	NK.	R.P.C. V9 pp.471 -472	*

PRIVY COUNCIL CASES									
No.	Name	Date	Place	Sex	Mar. Stat	Trial Stat	Fate	Source	New Case
898	Jonet Listar	2.12. 1612	Lothian Inner-weik	F	M	Com.	NK.	R.P.C. V9 p.500: V10 pp.4-5	
899	Jonnet Henrie	2.12. 1612	Lothian Scaitraw	F	M	Com.	NK.	R.P.C. V9 p.500 V10 pp.5;28	
900	Agnes Smyth	2.12. 1612	Lothian Scaitraw	F	W	Com.	NK.	R.P.C. V9 p.500 V10 pp.5;28	
901	Kathereine Vertie	2.12. 1612	Lothian Corhous	F	M	Com.	NK.	R.P.C. V9 p.500 V10 pp.4-5	
902	Janet Campbell	22.12. 1612	Perth	F	U	Com.	NK.	R.P.C. V9 p.522	
903	Robertson	22.12. 1612	Perth	U	U	Com.	NK.	R.P.C. V9 p.522	
904	Robert Allane	22.12. 1612	Lothian Dunbar	M	M	Com.	NK.	R.P.C. V9 p.522	
905	Katherine Hammiltoune	22.12. 1612	Lothian Dunbar	F	M	Com.	NK.	R.P.C. V9 p.522	
906	Spouse of Alexander Burghie	- - 1612	Lothian Dunbar	F	M	Com.	NK.	R.P.C. V9 p.500; V10 pp.4-5; 28	
907	Ewphame Young	4. 3. 1613	Cockburns-path	F	U	Com.	NK.	R.P.C. V10 p.5.	

PRIVY COUNCIL CASES									
No.	Name	Date	Place	Sex	Mar. Stat	Trial Stat	Fate	Source	New Case
908	Alisoun Denis	7. 4. 1613	Dunbar	F	U	Com.	NK.	R.P.C. V10 p.28	
909	Marjorie Lyell	8. 4. 1613	Jedburgh	F	U	Com.	NK.	R.P.C. V10 p.29	
910	Marioun Hendirsoun	8. 4. 1613	Jedburgh	F	U	Com.	NK.	R.P.C. V10 p.29	
911	Mary Elliot	8. 4. 1613	Jedburgh	F	W	Com.	NK.	R.P.C. V10 p.29	
912	Margaret Reoch	10. 6. 1613	Aberdeen	F	U	Com.	NK.	R.P.C. V10 p.76	
913	Annas Erskine	22. 6. 1613	Perth-shire	F	U	Com.	Ex.	R.P.C. V10 p.180	
914	Helene Erskine	22. 6. 1613	Perth-shire	F	U	Com.	NCP	R.P.C. V10 p.180	
915	Gilbert Campbell	1.12. 1613	Perth-shire	M	U	Com.	NK.	R.P.C. V10 p.180	
916	George Kirk	1.12. 1613	Perth-shire	M	U	Com.	NK.	R.P.C. V10 p.180	
917	Issobell Erskine	1. 12. 1613	Perth-shire	F	U	Com.	Ex.	R.P.C. V10 p.180	
918	Johnne Kirk	1.12. 1613	Perth-shire	M	U	Com.	NK.	R.P.C. V10 p.180	
919	Irwing	-.12. 1613	Perth-shire	M	U	Com.	NK.	R.P.C. V10 p.180	
920	Watty Bryis	17. 5. 1615	Dunblane	M	U	Com.	NK.	R.P.C. V10 p.329	

PRIVY COUNCIL CASES									
No.	Name	Date	Place	Sex	Mar. Stat	Trial Stat	Fate	Source	New Case
921	Jonnet Murriache	17. 5. 1615	Dunblane	F	U	Com.	NK.	R.P.C. V70 p.329	
922	Katherine Hill	9. 6. 1615	Queens-ferry	F	U	Com.	NK.	R.P.C. V10 p.335	
923	Jonet Johnstoun	23. 8. 1615	Queens-ferry	F	U	Com.	NK.	R.P.C. V10 p.388	
924	Jonet Hammyltoun	19. 3. 1616	Hamilton	F	W	Com.	NK.	R.P.C. V10 pp.418 -419	
925	Bessie Stewinstone	19. 3. 1616	Hamilton	F	M	Com.	NK.	R.P.C. V10 pp.418 -419	
926	Jonet Andirsone	21. 2. 1617	Stirling	F	U	Men.	NK.	R.P.C. 2nd S., V8 p.345 -346	
927	Margaret Rid	6. 3. 1617	Bathgate	F	U	Com.	NK.	R.P.C. V11 p.59	
928	Agnes Knox	6. 3. 1617	Bathgate	F	M	Com.	NK.	R.P.C. V11 p.59	
929	Patrick Rid	6. 3. 1617	Bathgate	M	M	Com.	NK.	R.P.C. V11 p.59	
930	Andro Turnbull	16. 4. 1617	Hill-house	M	U	Com.	NK.	R.P.C. V11 p.104	
931	John Stewart	2. 1. 1618	Irvine	M	U	Com.	Misc	R.P.C. V11 pp. CXXXIX;3 6;401	
932	Margaret Barclay	2. 1. 1618	Irvine	F	M	Com.	Ex.	R.P.C. V77 pp. CXXXIX;3 6;401	

PRIVY COUNCIL CASES									
No.	Name	Date	Place	Sex	Mar. Stat	Trial Stat	Fate	Source	New Case
933	William Nicoll	16. 1. 1618	Ayr	M	U	Com.	NK.	R.P.C. V11 p.412	
934	Malie Wilson	16. 1. 1618	Ayr	U	U	Com.	NK.	R.P.C. V11 p.412	
935	Jonnett Gardiner	24. 2. 1618	Angus Aberlenno	F	U	Com.	NK.	R.P.C. V11 p.320	
936	Margaret Kennedy	2. 7. 1618	Linlith-gow	F	U	Com.	NK.	R.P.C. V11 p.367	
937	Issobell Scherar	2. 7. 1618	Irvine	F	U	Com.	Ex.	R.P.C. V11 pp. CXXIX; 367;401	
938	Janet Gardiner	- - 1618	Brechin	F	U	Com.	NK.	Ander-son	
939	Isobel Insh	- - 1618	Irvine	F	U	Men.	Misc	R.P.C. V11 p.CXI	
940	Margaret Wod	30. 1. 1621	Crail	F	U	Com.	NK.	R.P.C. V12 p.412	
941	Margaret Kent	13. 2. 1621	Inver-keithing	F	U	Com.	NK.	R.P.C. V12 p.423	
942	Christiane Hammyltoun	13. 2. 1621	Inver-keithing	F	U	Com.	NK.	R.P.C. V12 p.423	
943	Beatrice Mudie	13. 2. 1621	Inver-keithing	F	U	Com.	NK.	R.P.C. V12 p.423	
944	Bessie Chalmers	13. 2. 1621	Inver-keithing	F	U	Com.	NK.	R.P.C. V12 p.423	
945	Bessie Harlaw	13. 2. 1621	Inver-keithing	F	U	Com.	NK.	R.P.C. V12 p.423	

PRIVY COUNCIL CASES									
No.	Name	Date	Place	Sex	Mar. Stat	Trial Stat	Fate	Source	New Case
946	Marioun Chatto	31. 2. 1621	Inver-keithing	F	U	Com.	NK.	R.P.C. V12 p.423	
947	Cristiane Grahame	29. 3. 1621	Culross	F	U	Com.	NK.	R.P.C. V12 p.472	
948	Marioun Rutherford	31. 5. 1621	Kirkcaldy	F	U	Com.	NK.	R.P.C. V12 p.490	
949	John Ewart	31. 5. 1621	Selkirk	M	U	Com.	NK.	R.P.C. V12 p.490	
950	Christiane Graham	10. 8. 1621	Glasgow	F	U	Com.	NK.	R.P.C. V12 p.580	
951	Catherene Blair	3. 5. 1622	Glasgow	F	U	Com.	NK.	R.P.C. V12 p.711	
952	Thomas Stark	15. 5. 1622	Wigton-shire Drongan	M	U	Com.	NK.	R.P.C. V12 p.720	
953	Jonet Maglene	6. 6. 1622	Tranent	F	M	Com.	NK.	R.P.C. V12 p.734	
954	Helene Nwere	6. 6. 1622	Tranent	F	U	Com.	NK.	R.P.C. V12 p.734	
955	Janet McIllwhichill	13. 6. 1622	Ardroch	F	U	Com.	NK.	R.P.C. V12 p.738	
956	Barbara Home Alias Winzit	25. 6. 1622	Kilpont	F	U	Com.	NK.	R.P.C. V12 p.750	
957	Katherene Rannald	25. 6. 1622	Kilpont	F	M	Com.	NK.	R.P.C. V12 p.750	
958	Agnes Robertsone	28. 8. 1622	Aberdour	F	U	Men.	NK.	R.P.C. V13 pp. 49-50	

PRIVY COUNCIL CASES									
No.	Name	Date	Place	Sex	Mar. Stat	Trial Stat	Fate	Source	New Case
959	Janet Robertsone	28. 8. 1622	Aberdour	F	M	Men.	NK.	R.P.C. V13 pp. 49 - 50	
960	Agnes Quarrier	28. 8. 1622	Aberdour	F	W	Men.	NK.	R.P.C. V13 pp. 49-50	
961	Helene Cummyng	28. 8. 1622	Aberdour	F	W	Men.	NK.	R.P.C. V13 pp. 49-50	
962	Alesoun Hutchesoune	28. 8. 1622	Aberdour	F	W	Men.	NK.	R.P.C. V13 pp. 49-50	
963	Janett Scott	18. 9. 1622	Ayr	F	U	Com.	NK.	R.P.C. V13 p.63	
964	Maig Knox	12.10. 1622	Largs	F	U	Com.	NK.	R.P.C. V13 p.69	
965	Marjorie Aitkyne	27. 2. 1623	Inver-keithing	F	U	Com.	NK.	R.P.C. V13 p.181	
966	Johne Young	27. 2. 1623	Inver-keithing	M	U	Com.	NK.	R.P.C. V13 p.181	
967	Jonnet Robesoun	27. 2. 1623	Inver-keithing	F	U	Com.	NK.	R.P.C. V13 p.181	
968	Margaret Merschell	27. 2. 1623	Inver-keithing	F	U	Com.	NK.	R.P.C. V13 p.181	
969	Bessie Logie	27. 2. 1623	Inver-keithing	F	U	Com.	NK.	R.P.C. V13 p.181	
970	Margaret Bull	27. 2. 1623	Inver-keithing	F	U	Com.	NK.	R.P.C. V13 p.181	
971	Christiane Balfour	27. 2. 1623	Inver-keithing	F	U	Com.	NK.	R.P.C. V13 p.181	

PRIVY COUNCIL CASES									
No.	Name	Date	Place	Sex	Mar. Stat	Trial Stat	Fate	Source	N C
972	Bessie Andersone	27. 2. 1623	Inver-keithing	F	U	Com.	NK.	R.P.C. V13 p.181	
973	Marioun Hendersone	27. 2. 1623	Inver-keithing	F	U	Com.	NK.	R.P.C. V13 p.181	
974	Elizabeth Broun	27. 2. 1623	Inver-keithing	F	U	Com.	NK.	R.P.C. V13 p.181	
975	Christiane Harlaw	27. 2. 1623	Inver-keithing	F	U	Com.	NK.	R.P.C. V13 p.181	
976	Margaret Kynnell	27. 2. 1623	Inver-keithing	F	U	Com.	NK.	R.P.C. V13 p.181	
977	Marjory Gibsoun	-. 2. 1623	Inver-keithing	F	U	Com.	NK.	R.P.C. V13 p.181	
978	Christiane Balfour	18. 3. 1623	Inver-keithing	F	U	Com.	NK.	R.P.C. V13 pp. 192-193	
979	Margaret Bull	18. 3. 1623	Inver-keithing	F	U	Com.	NK.	R.P.C. V13 pp. 192-193	
980	Jonet Keirie	18. 3. 1623	Inver-keithing	F	U	Com.	NK.	R.P.C. V13 pp. 192-193	
981	Bessie Logie	18. 3. 1623	Inver-keithing	F	U	Com.	NK.	R.P.C. V13 pp. 192-193	
982	Margaret Mershell	18. 3. 1623	Inver-keithing	F	U	Com.	NK.	R.P.C. V13 pp. 192-193	
983	Jonnet Robertsone	18. 3. 1623	Inver-keithing	F	U	Com.	NK.	R.P.C. V13 pp. 192-193	
984	Beatrix Thomsone	18. 3. 1623	Inver-keithing	F	U	Com.	NK.	R.P.C. V13 pp. 192-193	

PRIVY COUNCIL CASES									
No.	Name	Date	Place	Sex	Mar. Stat	Trial Stat	Fate	Source	New Case
985	Margaret Kinnell	14. 5. 1623	Inver-keithing	F	U	Com.	NK.	R.P.C. V13 p.230	
986	Marjorie Gibsoune	14. 5. 1623	Inver-keithing	F	U	Com.	NK.	R.P.C. V13 p.230	
987	Issobell Haldane	15. 5. 1623	Perth	F	U	Men.	Misc	R.P.C. 2nd S. V8 pp. 352-354	
988	Margaret Hormscleugh	19. 6. 1623	Perth	F	U	Com.	NK.	R.P.C. V13 p.270	
989	Janet Traill	18. 7. 1623	Perth	F	U	Men.	Ex.	R.P.C. 2nd S. V8 pp. 352-354	
990	Margaret Hormscleuch	18. 7. 1623	Perth	F	U	Men.	Ex.	R.P.C. 2nd S. V8 pp. 352-354	
991	Isobell Haldane	18. 7. 1623	Perth	F	U	Com.	Ex.	R.P.C. V13 p.270	
992	Elspet Paris	5. 2. 1624	West Lothian	F	M	Com.	NK.	R.P.C. V13 p.422	
993	David Langiandis	5. 2. 1624	West Lothian	M	M	Com.	NK.	R.P.C. V13 p.422	
994	Jonet Umphra	19. 2. 1624	Culross	F	U	Com.	NK.	R.P.C. V13 p.451	
995	Marioun Stirk	19. 2. 1624	Culross	F	U	Com.	NK.	R.P.C. V13 pp. 439-440	
996	Jonnet Umphra	19. 2. 1624	Culross	F	U	Com.	NK.	R.P.C. V13 pp. 439-440	

PRIVY COUNCIL CASES									
No.	Name	Date	Place	Sex	Mar. Stat	Trial Stat	Fate	Source	New Case
997	Alexander Clerk	19. 2. 1624	Culross	M	U	Com.	NK.	R.P.C. V13 pp. 439–440	
998	Marjorie Rowand	19. 2. 1624	Culross	F	U	Com.	NK.	R.P.C. V13 pp. 439–440	
999	Anna Smyth	19. 2. 1624	Torry-burn	F	U	Com.	NK.	R.P.C. V13 pp. 439–440	
1000	Mayse Umphra	19. 2. 1624	Culross Torryburn	F	U	Com.	NK.	R.P.C. V13 pp. 439–440	
1001	Jonnet Watt	19. 2. 1624	Culross	F	U	Com.	NK.	R.P.C. V13 pp. 439–440	
1002	Margaret Newros	24. 2. 1624	Pinker-ton	F	U	Com.	NK.	R.P.C. V73 pp. 443;485	
1003	Jonet Achesoun	24. 2. 1624	Pinker-ton	F	U	Com.	NK.	R.P.C. V13 pp. 443;485	
1004	Archibald Liddell	16. 3. 1624	Eyemouth	M	M	Com.	NK.	R.P.C. V13 pp. 460–461	
1005	Barbara Flint	16. 3. 1624	Eymouth	F	M	Com.	NK.	R.P.C. V13 pp. 460–461	
1006	Isobell Falconner	16. 3. 1624	Eyemouth	F	M	Com.	NK.	R.P.C. V13 pp. 460–461	
1007	Elspett Jamesoun	18. 3. 1624	West Lothian	F	U	Com.	NK.	R.P.C. V13 p.464	
1008	William Falconner	18. 3. 1624	West Lothian	M	U	Com.	NK.	R.P.C. V13 p.464	
1009	Marioun Symsoun	18. 3. 1624	West Lothian	F	M	Com.	NK.	R.P.C. V13 p.464	

PRIVY COUNCIL CASES									
No.	Name	Date	Place	Sex	Mar. Stat	Trial Stat	Fate	Source	New Case
1010	Elspett Fergusson	18. 3. 1624	West Lothian	F	U	Com.	NK.	R.P.C. V13 p.464	
1011	Christiane Hay	18. 3. 1624	West Lothian	F	U	Com.	NK.	R.P.C. V13 p.464	
1012	Jeane Lylburne	18. 3. 1624	West Lothian	F	U	Com.	NK.	R.P.C. V13 p.464	
1013	Jonnett Tor	30. 3. 1624	Langside	F	M	Com.	NK.	R.P.C. V13 p.484	
1014	Helene Ezatt	30. 3. 1624	Culross	F	U	Com.	NK.	R.P.C. V13 p.484	
1015	Issobell Cootis	30. 3. 1624	Barrow-stouness	F	U	Com.	NK.	R.P.C. V13 p.485	
1016	Jonnet Dunbar	30. 3. 1624	Barrow-stouness	F	U	Com.	NK.	R.P.C. V13 p.485	
1017	Katherine Blair	30. 3. 1624	Barrow-stouness	F	U	Com.	NK.	R.P.C. V13 p.485	
1018	Elizabeth Jamesone	30. 3. 1624	Barrow-stouness	F	M	Com.	NK.	R.P.C. V13 pp. 485-489	
1019	Marioun Boyd	28. 4. 1624	Spott	F	M	Com.	NK.	R.P.C. V13 p.499	
1020	Marable Couper	7. 7. 1624	Orkney Birsay	F	M	Men.	Ex.	R.P.C. 2nd S. V8 pp. 355-360	
1021	Anie Tailzeour Alias Cwna Rowa	15. 7. 1624	Orkney	F	U	Men.	Ex.	R.P.C. 2nd S. V8 pp. 360-364	

PRIVY COUNCIL CASES

No.	Name	Date	Place	Sex	Mar. Stat	Trial Stat	Fate	Source	New Case
1022	Marjorie Patersone	29. 7. 1625	Crail	F	U	Com.	NK.	R.P.C. 2nd S. V1 p.108	
1023	Issobell Mawer	16. 3. 1626	Wemyss	F	U	Com.	NK.	R.P.C. 2nd S. V1 p.246	
1024	Jonnet Budge	28. 3. 1626	Caith-ness	F	U	Com.	NK.	R.P.C. 2nd S. V1 p.258	
1025	Jonnet Pedie	13. 4. 1626	Wemyss	F	U	Com.	NK.	R.P.C. 2nd S. V1 p.275	
1026	Patrik Landrok	13. 4. 1626	Wemyss	M	U	Com.	NK.	R.P.C. 2nd S. V1 p.275	
1027	Helene Darumpill	13. 4. 1626	Wemyss	F	U	Com.	NK.	R.P.C. 2nd S. V1 p.275	
1028	Helene Dryburghe	13. 4. 1626	Wemyss	F	U	Com.	NK.	R.P.C. 2nd S. V1 p.275	
1029	Elizabeth Ross	6. 6. 1626	Wemyss	F	U	Men.	Misc	R.P.C. 2nd S. V1 pp. 297-298	
1030	Jonnet Dampstar	20. 6. 1626	West Wemyss Fife	F	U	Com.	NK.	R.P.C. 2nd S. V1 p.309	
1031	Annas Munk	21. 9. 1626	Dysart	F	U	Com.	NK.	R.P.C. 2nd S. V1 p.425	

PRIVY COUNCIL CASES									
No.	Name	Date	Place	Sex	Mar. Stat	Trial Stat	Fate	Source	New Case
1032	Elspet Neilsoun	-. 9. 1626	Dysart	F	U	Com.	NK.	R.P.C. 2nd S. V1 p.258	
1033	Helene Wilsoun	21.11. 1626	Dysart	F	U	Com.	NK.	R.P.C. 2nd S. V1 pp. 447-448	
1034	Marie Lauchtie	28.11. 1626	Thurso Caith-ness	F	U	Com.	NK.	R.P.C. 2nd S. V1 p.453	
1035	Euphame Rid	28.11. 1626	Geise Mikle Caithn.	F	M	Com.	NK.	R.P.C. 2nd S. V1 p.453	
1036	Walter Baird	30.11. 1626	Aberdeen	M	U	Com.	Ex.	R.P.C. 2nd S. V5 p.566	
1037	Cummer Muttoun	14.12. 1626	Aberdeen	U	U	Com.	NK.	R.P.C. 2nd S. V1 p.469	
1038	Issobell Leslie	14.12. 1626	Aberdeen	F	U	Com.	NK.	R.P.C. 2nd S. V1 p.469	
1039	Agnes Cairll	14.12. 1626	Aberdeen	F	U	Com.	NK.	R.P.C. 2nd S. V1 p.469	
1040	Johne Davie	14.12. 1626	Aberdeen-shire	M	U	Com.	NK.	R.P.C. 2nd S. V1 p.469	
1041	Jonnet Robbie	14.12. 1626	Newmilne Aber.	F	U	Com.	NK.	R.P.C. 2nd S. V1 p.469	

PRIVY COUNCIL CASES									
No.	Name.	Date	Place	Sex	Mar. Stat	Trial Stat	Fate	Source	New Case
1042	Annabell Cattenhead	14.12. 1626	Aberdeen-shire	F	U	Com.	NK.	R.P.C. 2nd S. V1 p.469	
1043	Margaret Cceroch	14.12. 1626	Aberdeen-shire	F	U	Com.	NK.	R.P.C. 2nd S. V1 p.469	
1044	Margaret McConnochie	14.12. 1626	Aboyne Aber	F	M	Com.	NK.	R.P.C. 2nd S. V1 p.469	
1045	Johnne Findlaw	14.12. 1626	Aberdeen-shire	M	U	Com.	NK.	R.P.C. 2nd S. V1 p.469	
1046	Agnes Durie	14.12. 1626	Aberdeen-shire	F	U	Com.	NK.	R.P.C. 2nd S. V1 p.469	
1047	Agnes Forbes	14.12. 1626	White-strypis Aber	F	U	Com.	NK.	R.P.C. 2nd S. V1 p.469	
1048	William Young	14.12. 1626	Ellon Aberdn-shire	M	U	Com.	NK.	R.P.C. 2nd S. V1 p.469	
1049	Johnne Propter	14.12. 1626	Aberdeen-shire	M	U	Com.	NK.	R.P.C. 2nd S. V1 p.469	
1050	Agnes Carle	23. 1. 1627	Aberdeen	F	U	Com.	NK.	R.P.C. 2nd S. V1 p.500	
1051	Jonnet Dovertie	23. 1. 1627	Aberdeen	F	U	Com.	NK.	R.P.C. 2nd S. V1 p.500	

PRIVY COUNCIL CASES									
No.	Name	Date	Place	Sex	Mar. Stat	Trial Stat	Fate	Source	New Case
1052	Nanse Durie	23. 1. 1627	Futtie Aberdn-shire	F	U	Com.	NK.	R.P.C. 2nd S. V1 p.500	
1053	Annabell Cattenheid	23. 1. 1627	Futtie Aberdn-shire	F	U	Com.	NK.	R.P.C. 2nd S. V1 p.500	
1054	Margaret Durie	23. 1. 1627	Aberdeen	F	U	Com.	NK.	R.P.C. 2nd S. V1 p.500	
1055	John Davie	23. 1. 1627	Aberdeen	M	U	Com.	NK.	R.P.C. 2nd S. V1 p.500	
1056	Walter Baird	25. 4. 1627	Futtie Aberdn-shire	M	U	Com.	NK.	R.P.C. 2nd S. V1 p.586	
1057	Agnes Watt	25. 4. 1627	Futtie Aberdn-shire	F	U	Com.	NK.	R.P.C. 2nd S. V1 p.586	
1058	Issobell Smyth	25. 4. 1627	Futtie Aberdn-shire	F	U	Com.	NK.	R.P.C. 2nd S. V1 p.586	
1059	Margaret Udny	25. 4. 1627	Aberdeen	F	U	Com.	NK.	R.P.C. 2nd S. V1 p.586	
1060	Alexander Mowat	25. 4. 1627	Turriff	M	M	Men.	NK.	R.P.C. 2nd S. V1 p.586	
1061	Christiane Craig	25. 4. 1627	Turriff	F	M	Men.	NK.	R.P.C. 2nd S. V1 p.586	

PRIVY COUNCIL CASES									
No.	Name	Date	Place	Sex	Mar. Stat	Trial Stat	Fate	Source	New Case
1062	Margaret Ronaldson	25. 4. 1627	Futtie Aberdeen-shire	F	U	Com.	NK.	R.P.C. 2nd S. V1 p.586	
1063	Bessie Broun	3. 5. 1627	Philips-toun Dalk'th	F	U	Com.	NK.	R.P.C. 2nd S. V1 p.596	
1064	Margaret Hendersoune	17. 5. 1627	Wemyss	F	U	Com.	NK.	R.P.C. 2nd S. V1 p.607	
1065	Eupham Dauling	27. 9. 1627	Dysart	F	M	Men.	NK.	R.P.C. 2nd S. V2 p.83	
1066	Kathrene Crystie	17.11. 1627	Dysart	F	W	Com.	NK.	R.P.C. 2nd S. V2 p.122 pp.142-3	
1067	Jonnat Reany	23. 4. 1628	Dumferm-line	F	M	Com.	NK.	R.P.C. 2nd S. V2 p.317	
1068	Mawsie Stowane	5. 6. 1628	Dumfries	F	M	Com.	NK.	R.P.C. 2nd S. V2. pp. 328-329	
1069	Agnes Charters	5. 6. 1628	Dumfries	F	W	Com.	NK.	R.P.C. 2nd S. V2 pp. 328-329	
1070	Agnes Dungalson	5. 6. 1628	Dumfries	F	M	Com.	NK.	R.P.C. 2nd S. V2 pp. 328-329	
1071	Helen Blaik	5. 6. 1628	Dumfries	F	W	Com.	NK.	R.P.C. 2nd S. V2 pp. 328-329	
1072	Christian Aitkenhead	5. 6. 1628	Dumfries Rottinrow	F	M	Com.	NK.	R.P.C. 2nd S.V2 pp.328-329	

PRIVY COUNCIL CASES									
No.	Name	Date	Place	Sex	Mar. Stat	Trial Stat	Fate	Source	New Case
1073	Janet Ireland	5. 6. 1628	Dumfries Rottinrow	F	W	Com.	NK.	R.P.C. 2nd S. V2 pp. 328-329	
1074	Agnes Hendersoun	3. 7. 1628	Stirling-shire	F	U	Com.	NK.	R.P.C. 2nd S. V2 p.353	
1075	Margaret Young	3. 7. 1628	Preston-pans	F	U	Com.	NK.	R.P.C. 2nd S. V2 p.353	
1076	Margaret Ridpeth	3. 7. 1628	Preston-pans	F	U	Com.	NK.	R.P.C. 2nd S. V2 p.353	
1077	Janet Reid	3. 7. 1628	Preston-pans	F	U	Com.	NK.	R.P.C. 2nd S. V2 p.353	
1078	Agnes Rankein	3. 7. 1628	Preston-pans	F	U	Com.	NK.	R.P.C. 2nd S. V2 p.353	
1079	Marion Mitchell	10. 7. 1628	Leith	F	U	Com.	NK.	R.P.C. 2nd S. V2 p.362	
1080	Agnes Liddell	15. 7. 1628	Preston-pans	F	U	Com.	NK.	R.P.C. 2nd S. V2 p.379	
1081	Margaret Oliver	15. 7. 1628	Preston-pans	F	U	Com.	NK.	R.P.C. 2nd S. V2 p.379	
1082	Barbara Mathie	15. 7. 1628	Preston-pans	F	U	Com.	NK.	R.P.C. 2nd S. V2 p.379	

PRIVY COUNCIL CASES									
No.	Name	Date	Place	Sex	Mar. Stat	Trial Stat	Fate	Source	New Case
1083	Bessie Riddell	15. 7. 1628	Preston-pans	F	U	Com.	NK.	R.P.C. 2nd S.V2 p.379	
1084	Agnes Dempstar	15. 7. 1628	Preston-pans	F	U	Com.	NK.	R.P.C. 2nd S. V2 p.379	
1085	Janet Schitlingtoun	29. 7. 1628	New-bottle Dalkeith	F	U	Com.	NK.	R.P.C. 2nd S. V2 pp. 410,442, 468-9,624	
1086	Bessie Wright	30. 7. 1628	Perth	F	U	Men.	NK.	R.P.C. 2nd S. V2 pp. 623-624	
1087	Janet Strauchane	8. 8. 1628	Preston-pans	F	M	Com.	NK.	R.P.C. 2nd S. V2 p.439	
1088	William Davidson	8. 8. 1628	Saltoun	M	U	Com.	NK.	R.P.C. 2nd S. V2 p.517	
1089	Beatrix Cuthbertson	8. 8. 1628	Preston-pans	F	U	Com.	NK.	R.P.C. 2nd S. V2 p.439	
1090	Janet Wright	28. 8. 1628	Niddry	F	U	Com.	NK.	R.P.C. 2nd S. V2 p.444	
1091	Margaret Barrowman	28. 8. 1628	Mid-lothian Newbattle	F	U	Com.	NK.	R.P.C. 2nd S. V2 pp. 471;482	
1092	Elspitt Duncan	28. 8. 1628	Mid-lothian	F	U	Com.	NK.	R.P.C. 2nd S. V2 pp.471; 482	

PRIVY COUNCIL CASES									
No.	Name	Date	Place	Sex	Mar. Stat	Trial Stat	Fate	Source	New Case
1093	Marioun Sheirar	28. 8. 1628	Mid-lothian	F	U	Com.	NK.	R.P.C. 2nd S. V2 pp. 471;482	
1094	Janet Smiberd	28. 8. 1628	Mid-lothian	F	U	Com.	NK.	R.P.C. 2nd S. V2 pp. 471;482	
1095	Jane Unes	28. 8. 1628	Mid-lothian	F	U	Com.	NK.	R.P.C. 2nd S. V2 p.444	
1096	Alesoun Chapman	28. 8. 1628	Mid-lothian	F	U	Com.	NK.	R.P.C. 2nd S. V2 p.444	
1097	Christian Tailyour	28. 8. 1628	Mid-lothian	U	U	Com.	NK.	R.P.C. 2nd S. V2 p.444	
1098	Issobell Thomsoun	28. 8. 1628	Mid-lothian	F	U	Com.	NK.	R.P.C. 2nd S. V2 p.444	
1099	Elspitt Hislop	28. 8. 1628	Long-niddry	F	M	Com.	NK.	R.P.C. 2nd S. V2 p.471	
1100	Janet Darlig	-. 8. 1628	Preston-pans	F	U	Com.	NK.	R.P.C. 2nd S. V2 p.439	
1101	Margaret Unes	27. 9. 1628	Dalkeith	F	U	Com.	NK.	R.P.C. 2nd S. V2 pp.410; 442;468-469;624	
1102	Margaret Cowane	27. 9. 1628	Edinburgh Broughton	F	M	Com.	NK.	R.P.C. 2nd S.V2 p.470	

PRIVY COUNCIL CASES									
No.	Name	Date	Place	Sex	Mar. Stat	Trial Stat	Fate	Source	New Case
1103	Alesoun Dempstar	28. 9. 1628	Leith	F	M	Com.	NK.	R.P.C. 2nd S. V2 p.362	
1104	Issobell Miller	28. 9. 1628	Long-niddry	F	M	Com.	NK.	R.P.C. 2nd S. V2 p.471	
1105	Issobell Howatsoun	28. 9. 1628	Selkirk Riddell	F	U	Com.	NK.	R.P.C. 2nd S. V2 p.471	
1106	Steven Malcome	28. 9. 1628	Stirling-shire	M	U	Com.	NK.	R.P.C. 2nd S. V2 p.353	
1107	Katharine Leithame	28. 9. 1628	Selkirk	F	U	Com.	NK.	R.P.C. 2nd S. V2 p.517	
1108	Margaret Muirhead	11.11. 1628	Mid-lothian	F	U	Com.	NK.	R.P.C. 2nd S. V2 p.482	
1109	William Watt	11.11. 1628	Mid-lothian	M	U	Com.	NK.	R.P.C. 2nd S. V2 p.482	
1110	Malie Turnour	11.11. 1628	Mid-lothian Stobhill	F	U	Com.	NK.	R.P.C. 2nd S. V2 p.482	
1111	Elspeth Simsoun	18.11. 1628	Tain Badarrach	F	M	Com.	NK.	R.P.C. 2nd S. V2 p.489	
1112	Marion Nein Gillimichaell	18.11. 1628	Tain Edirtayne	F	U	Com.	NK.	R.P.C. 2nd S. V2 p.489	

PRIVY COUNCIL CASES									
No.	Name	Date	Place	Sex	Mar. Stat	Trial Stat	Fate	Source	New Case
1113	Agnes Nein Donald	18.11. 1628	Tain Logie	F	U	Com.	NK.	R.P.C. 2nd S. V2 p.489	
1114	Helen Gow	18.11. 1628	Tain	F	M	Com.	NK.	R.P.C. 2nd S. V2 p.489	
1115	Janet Boyd	20.11. 1628	Dumbarton	F	M	Com.	NK.	R.P.C. 2nd S. V2 pp. 476–477 V3 pp 3–4	
1116	William Dageris	25.11. 1628	Jedburgh	M	U	Com.	NK.	R.P.C. 2nd S. V2 p.494	
1117	Kathrene Stewart	25.11. 1628	Jedburgh	F	U	Com.	NK.	R.P.C. 2nd S. V2 p.494	
1118	Margaret Jo	25.11. 1628	Mussel-burgh	F	U	Com.	NK.	R.P.C. 2nd S. V2 p.487	
1119	Margaret Burges	25.11. 1628	Nether Cramond	F	U	Com.	NK.	R.P.C. 2nd S. V2 p.494	
1120	Elspeth Baird	-.11. 1628	Leith	F	W	Com.	NK.	R.P.C. 2nd S. V2 p.494	
1121	Bessie Littil	4.12. 1628	Long-niddry	F	U	Com.	NK.	R.P.C. 2nd S. V2 p.516	
1122	Margaret Baine	4.12. 1628	Long-niddry	F	U	Com.	NK.	R.P.C. 2nd S. V2 p.516	

PRIVY COUNCIL CASES									
No.	Name	Date	Place	Sex	Mar. Stat	Trial Stat	Fate	Source	New Case
1123	John McReadie	4.12. 1628	Ranultoun Berwick	M	U	Com.	NK.	R.P.C. 2nd S. V2 p.516	
1124	Katherine Mosse	4.12. 1628	Litgert-wode Berwick	F	M	Com.	NK.	R.P.C. 2nd S. V2 p.517	
1125	Katherine Browne	4. 12. 1628	Lawder Berwick-shire	F	U	Com.	NK.	R.P.C. 2nd S. V2 p.517	
1126	George Litgertwode	4.12. 1628	Lawder Berwick-shire	M	M	Com.	NK.	R.P.C. 2nd S. V2 p.517	
1127	Alesoun Tailyeour	9.12. 1628	Pentcait-land	F	U	Com.	NK.	R.P.C. 2nd S V2 p.518	
1128	Sara Keith	9. 12. 1628	Pentcait-land	F	U	Com.	NK.	R.P.C. 2nd S. V2 p.518	
1129	Alexander Hamiltoun	9.12. 1628	Pentcait-land	M	U	Com.	NK.	R.P.C. 2nd S. V2 p.518	
1130	Young Mother of James Smith	18.12. 1628		F	U	Men.	NK.	R.P.C. 2nd S. V2 p.540	
1131	Isobel Thomesone	19.12. 1628	Craigs-ford Berwick	F	U	Com.	NK.	R.P.C. 2nd S. V2 p.540	
1132	Marion Bathcat	19.12. 1628	Dunbar Eistbarns	F	U	Com.	NK.	R.P.C. 2nd S. V2 p.540	

PRIVY COUNCIL CASES									
No.	Name	Date	Place	Sex	Mar. Stat	Trial Stat	Fate	Source	New Case
1133	Margaret Baxter	19.12. 1628	Dunbar	F	U	Com.	NK.	R.P.C. 2nd S. V2 p.540	
1134	Bessie Carrilie	23.12. 1628	Dumfries	F	U	Com.	NK.	R.P.C. 2 Ser. V2 p.540	*
1135	Bessie Carrilie	23.12. 1628	Twynholme	F	U	Com.	NK.	R.P.C. 2nd S. V2 p.542	
1136	Katherine Oswald	2. 1. 1628	Niddry	F	M	Com.	Ex.	R.P.C. 2nd S. V3 pp. 206;278; 290;293	
1137	Marion Hardie	20. 1. 1629	Eyemouth	F	M	Com.	Misc	R.P.C. 2nd S. V3 pp. 15;41-42	
1138	Gradoch Neinchat	20. 1. 1629	Ross-shire	F	U	Com.	NK.	R.P.C. 2nd S. V3 pp. 15-16	
1139	Katherine Memphersoun	20. 1. 1629	Ross-shire	F	U	Com.	NK.	R.P.C. 2nd S. V3 pp. 15-16	
1140	Marie Nein Eane Eir	20. 1. 1629	Ross-shire	F	U	Com.	NK.	R.P.C. 2nd S. V3 pp. 15-16	
1141	Katherine Nein Rob Aunchtie	20. 1. 1629	Ross-shire	F	U	Com.	NK.	R.P.C. 2nd S. V3 pp. 15-16	
1142	Bessie Make	20. 1. 1629	East Lothian Saltoun	F	U	Com.	NK.	R.P.C. 2nd S. V3 p.16	

PRIVY COUNCIL CASES									
No.	Name	Date	Place	Sex	Mar. Stat	Trial Stat	Fate	Source	New Case
1143	Sara Keith	20. 1. 1629	East Lothian Wyntoun	F	M	Com.	NK.	R.P.C. 2nd S. V3 p.16	
1144	Agnes Wallace	20. 1. 1629	Ayton	F	U	Com.	NK.	R.P.C. 2nd S. V3 p.15	
1145	Kathrene Young	3. 2. 1629	Peebles	F	M	Com.	NK.	R.P.C. 2nd S. V3 p.32	
1146	Marion Grige	3. 2. 1629	Peebles Scotts-town	F	M	Com.	NK.	R.P.C. 2nd S. V3 p.32	
1147	Isobel Rutherfurde	3. 2. 1629	Peebles	F	U	Com.	NK.	R.P.C. 2nd S. V3 p.32	
1148	Isobel Young	4. 2. 1629	Eastbarns	F	U	Com.	Ex.	R.P.C. 2nd S. V3 p.4	
1149	Jonet Neill	19. 2. 1629	Dumbarton	F	M	Com.	NK.	R.P.C. 2nd S. V3 pp. 123-124; 59;97	
1150	Bessie Meyne	24. 2. 1629	Selkirk	F	U	Com.	NK.	R.P.C. 2nd S. V3 p.62	
1151	Janet Minto	24. 2. 1629	Selkirk	F	U	Com.	NK.	R.P.C. 2nd S. V3 p.62	
1152	Janet Hendersoun	24. 2. 1629	Selkirk Lillis-lief	F	U	Com.	NK.	R.P.C. 2nd S. V3 p.62	
1153	Bessie Cumroy	24. 2. 1629	Selkirk Bowdoun	F	U	Com.	NK.	R.P.C. 2nd S. V3 p.62	
1154	Isobel Wright	24. 2. 1629	Selkirk	F	U	Com.	NK.	R.P.C. 2nd S. V3 p.62	

PRIVY COUNCIL CASES									
No.	Name	Date	Place	Sex	Mar. Stat	Trial Stat	Fate	Source	New Case
1155	Margaret Hunter	17. 3. 1629	Dumbarton	F	M	Com.	NK.	R.P.C. 2nd S. V3 pp. 123-124; 59;97	
1156	Janet Donald	17. 3. 1629	Dumbarton	F	M	Com.	Ex.	R.P.C. 2nd S. V3 pp. 123-124; 59;97	
1157	Isobel Thomsoun	17. 3. 1629	Crail-ford	F	U	Com.	NK.	R.P.C. 2nd S. V3 p.98	
1158	Janet Melros	17. 3. 1629	Chattil	F	U	Com.	NK.	R.P.C. 2nd S. V3 p.98	
1159	Alexander Drummond	24. 3. 1629	Dunferm-line	M	U	Com.	NK.	R.P.C. 2nd S. V3 p.104	
1160	Isobel Gray	24. 3. 1629	Lanark	F	U	Com.	Ex.	R.P.C. 2nd S. V3 p.110	
1161	Alexander Hunter	24. 3. 1629	Hadding-ton	M	U	Com.	NK.	R.P.C. 2nd S. V3 pp. 110-111	
1162	Janet Widdrow	31. 3. 1629	Inverkip	F	U	Com.	NK.	R.P.C. 2nd S. V3 p.125	
1163	Isobel Thomesoun	31. 3. 1629	Berwick-shire Ryslaw	F	U	Com.	NK.	R.P.C. 2nd S. V3 p.125	
1164	Margaret Wallace	15. 4. 1629	Langton	F	U	Com.	NK.	R.P.C. 2nd S. V3 p.98	
1165	Jean Cleilland	15. 4. 1629	Lanark-shire	F	U	Com.	NK.	R.P.C. 2nd S. V3 p.145	

PRIVY COUNCIL CASES									
No.	Name	Date	Place	Sex	Mar. Stat	Trial Stat	Fate	Source	New Case
1166	Margaret Haistie	15. 4. 1629	Lanark-shire	F	U	Com.	NK.	R.P.C. 2nd S. V3 p.145	
1167	James Frame	15. 4. 1629	Lanark	M	U	Com.	NK.	R.P.C. 2nd S. V3 p.145	
1168	Margaret Wilson	15. 4. 1629	Lanark	F	M	Com.	NK.	R.P.C. 2nd S. V3 p.270	
1169	Margaret Hutchesoun	15. 4. 1629	Lanark Kirkbanke	F	M	Com.	NK.	R.P.C. 2nd S. V3 p.270	
1170	Janet Weir	15. 4. 1629	Lanark Baruck	F	M	Com.	NK.	R.P.C. 2nd S. V3 p.270	
1171	Marion Schailer	15. 4. 1629	Lanark Law	F	U	Com.	NK.	R.P.C. 2nd S. V3 p.145	
1172	Jonet Scot	15. 4. 1629	Lanark Wicket-shaw	F	U	Com.	NK.	R.P.C. 2nd S. V3 p.145	
1173	Margaret Semphill	15. 4. 1629	Lanark Strafranke	F	U	Com.	NK.	R.P.C. 2nd S. V3 p.270	
1174	Janet Clerksoun	15. 4. 1629	Lanark Cauldlaw	F	U	Com.	NK.	R.P.C. 2nd S. V3 p.270	
1175	John Greinscheills	15. 4. 1629	Lanark-shire	M	U	Com.	NK.	R.P.C. 2nd S. V3 p.270	

PRIVY COUNCIL CASES									
No.	Name	Date	Place	Sex	Mar. Stat	Trial Stat	Fate	Source	New Case
1176	Margrat Fischer	15. 4. 1629	Lanark-shire	F	U	Com.	NK.	R.P.C. 2nd S. V3 p.270	
1177	Beatrix Crichtoun	15. 4. 1629	Lanark	F	U	Com.	NK.	R.P.C. 2nd S. V3 p.270	
1178	Isobel Quhyte	15. 4. 1629	Lanark Auchquhren	F	M	Com.	NK.	R.P.C. 2nd S. V3 p.270	
1179	Agnes Adam	15. 4. 1629	Lanark Cleg-horne	F	U	Com.	NK.	R.P.C. 2nd S. V3 p.270	
1180	Helene Simsoun	15. 4. 1629	Lanark Craig-nuick	F	U	Com.	NK.	R.P.C. 2nd S. V3 p.270	
1181	Janet Pursell	2. 6. 1629	Edinburgh Preston	F	U	Com.	NK.	R.P.C. 2nd S. V3 p.156	
1182	Janet Scherar	2. 6. 1629	Edinburgh Preston	F	U	Com.	NK.	R.P.C. 2nd S. V3 p.156	
1183	Janet Hill	2. 6. 1629	Edinburgh Preston	F	U	Com.	Misc	R.P.C. 2nd S. V3 p.156	
1184	Alexander Hay	2. 6. 1629	Aberdeen-shire	M	U	Com.	NK.	R.P.C. 2nd S. V3 p.155	
1185	Helen Knight	2. 6. 1629	Aberdeen-shire Grange	F	M	Com.	NK.	R.P.C. 2nd S. V3 p.155	

PRIVY COUNCIL CASES									
No.	Name	Date	Place	Sex	Mar. Stat	Trial Stat	Fate	Source	New Case
1186	Margaret Strath	2. 6. 1629	Aberdeen-shire	F	U	Com.	NK.	R.P.C. 2nd S. V3 p.155	
1187	Margaret Hamiltoun	2. 6. 1629	Fala	F	U	Com.	Ex.	R.P.C. 2nd S. V3 p.155	
1188	Janet Bowmaker	2. 6. 1629	Berwick-shire Dunce	F	U	Com.	NK.	R.P.C. 2nd S. V3 p.155	
1189	Bessie Sleigh	2. 6. 1629	Berwick-shire Dunce	F	U	Com.	NK.	R.P.C. 2nd S. V3 p.155	
1190	Janet Brother-stanes	2. 6. 1629	Berwick-shire	F	U	Com.	NK.	R.P.C. 2nd S. V3 p.155	
1191	Janet Barclay	9. 6. 1629	Fisher-row	F	W	Men.	NK.	R.P.C. V3 pp. 162-163	
1192	Janet Hardie	9. 6. 1629	Fisher-row	F	M	Men.	NK.	R.P.C. V3 pp. 162-163	
1193	Samuel Fairlie	11. 6. 1629	Foulden	M	U	Com.	NK.	R.P.C. V3 p.169	
1194	Jean Watsoun	11. 6. 1629	Peebles Glen-quhome	F	U	Com.	NK.	R.P.C. 2nd S. V3 p.170	
1195	Margaret Dicksoun	11. 6. 1629	Peebles Kailyie	F	U	Com.	NK.	R.P.C. 2nd S. V3 p.170	
1196	Margaret Johnestoun	11. 6. 1629	Peebles Traquair	F	U	Com.	NK.	R.P.C. 2nd S. V3 p.170	

PRIVY COUNCIL CASES									
No.	Name	Date	Place	Sex	Mar. Stat	Trial Stat	Fate	Source	New Case
1197	Janet Achesoun	11. 6. 1629	Peebles Menner	F	U	Com.	NK.	R.P.C. 2nd S. V3 p.170	
1198	Bessie Ur	11. 6. 1629	Peebles Lintoun	F	U	Com.	NK.	R.P.C. 2nd S. V3 p.170	
1199	Katherene Alexander	11. 6. 1629	Peebles Lintoun	F	U	Com.	NK.	R.P.C. 2nd S. V3 p.170	
1200	Helen Beatie	11. 6. 1629	Peebles Menner	F	U	Com.	NK.	R.P.C. 2nd S. V3 p.170	
1201	Margaret Gowanlock	11. 6. 1629	Peebles Athelstoun	F	U	Com.	NK.	R.P.C. 2nd S. V3 p.170	
1202	Marion Boyd	11. 6. 1629	Peebles Athelstoun	F	U	Com.	NK.	R.P.C. 2nd S. V3 p.170	
1203	Katherine Mairschell	11. 6. 1629	Peebles Athelstoun	F	U	Com.	NK.	R.P.C. 2nd S. V3 p.170	
1204	John Graham Alias Joke the Graham	11. 6. 1629	Peebles-shire	M	U	Com.	NK.	R.P.C. 2nd S. V3 p.170	
1205	Patrick Lintoun	11. 6. 1629	Peebles Melvin Sland	M	U	Com.	NK.	R.P.C. 2nd S. V3 p.170	
1206	Gilbert Hog	11. 6. 1629	Peebles Winkstoun	M	U	Com.	NK.	R.P.C. 2nd S. V3 p.170	

PRIVY COUNCIL CASES									
No.	Name	Date	Place	Sex	Mar. Stat	Trial Stat	Fate	Source	New Case
1207	Issobel Haddock	11. 6. 1629	Peebles Lyntoun	F	U	Com.	NK.	R.P.C. 2nd S. V3 p.170	
1208	Marion Croser	11. 6. 1629	Peebles Slipper-field	F	U	Com.	NK.	R.P.C. 2nd S. V3 p.170	
1209	Katherine Wode	11. 6. 1629	Peebles Spitel-hauche	F	U	Com.	NK.	R.P.C. 2nd S. V3 p.170	
1210	Agnes Thomesoun	11. 6. 1629	Peebles Lyntoun	F	U	Com.	NK.	R.P.C. 2nd S. V3 p.170	
1211	Janet Hendersoun	11. 6. 1629	Peebles Blythe	F	U	Com.	NK.	R.P.C. 2nd S. V3 p.170	
1212	Marie Johnestoun	11. 6. 1629	Peebles Lyntoun	F	U	Com.	NK.	R.P.C. 2nd S. V3 p.170	
1213	Katherine Broun	11. 6. 1629	Peebles Inerlethane	F	U	Com.	NK.	R.P.C. 2nd S. V3 p.170	
1214	Agnes Robesoun	11. 6. 1629	Peebles-shire	F	U	Com.	NK.	R.P.C. 2nd S. V3 p.170	
1215	Thomas Stoddart	11. 6. 1629	Peebles Mylne-know	M	U	Com.	NK.	R.P.C. 2nd S. V3 p.170	
1216	William Mathesoun	11. 6. 1629	Peebles Kirnaughe	M	U	Com.	NK.	R.P.C. 2nd S. V3 p.170	
1217	William Thomesoun	11. 6. 1629	Peebles Purves-hill	M	U	Com.	NK.	R.P.C. 2nd S. V3 p.170	
1218	Margaret Yerkine	11. 6. 1629	Peebles	F	U	Com.	NK.	R.P.C. 2nd S. V3 p.170	
1219	Sussanna Elphinstoun	11. 6. 1629	Peebles	F	U	Com.	NK.	R.P.C. 2nd S. V3 p.170	

PRIVY COUNCIL CASES									
No.	Name	Date	Place	Sex	Mar. Stat	Trial Stat	Fate	Source	New Case
1220	Agnes Chalmers	11. 6. 1629	Peebles	F	U	Com.	NK.	R.P.C. 2nd S. V3 p.170	
1221	Elspet Dunbar	19. 6. 1629	Moray Mylneton	F	U	Com.	NK.	R.P.C. 2nd S. V3 p.181	
1222	Janet Baxter	19. 6. 1629	Moray Mylneton	F	U	Com.	NK.	R.P.C. 2nd S. V3 p.181	
1223	Janet Brodie	19. 6. 1629	Moray Craig-heid	F	M	Com.	NK.	R.P.C. 2nd S. V3 p.181	
1224	Bessie Fraser	19. 6. 1629	Moray Calseat	F	M	Com.	NK.	R.P.C. 2nd S. V3 p.181	
1225	John Hasben	19. 6. 1629	Moray Calseat	M	M	Com.	NK.	R.P.C. 2nd S. V3 p.181	
1226	Donald Thomassone	2. 7. 1629	Caithness Spittell	M	U	Com.	NK.	R.P.C. 2nd S. V3 p.206	
1227	Isobel Bayne	2. 7. 1629	Caithness	F	W	Com.	NK.	R.P.C. 2nd S. V3 p.206	
1228	Mansoun Hucheoun	2. 7. 1629	Caithness	U	U	Com.	NK.	R.P.C. 2nd S. V3 p.206	
1229	Ewfame Dundas	2. 7. 1629	Caithness	F	U	Com.	NK.	R.P.C. 2nd S. V3 p.206	
1230	George Sinclair	2. 7. 1629	Caithness	M	U	Com.	NK.	R.P.C. 2nd S. V3 p.206	
1231	Janet Henries dochter	2. 7. 1629	Caithness	F	W	Com.	NK.	R.P.C. 2nd S. V3 p.206	
1232	Janet Dow	7. 7. 1629	Preston	F	U	Com.	NK.	R.P.C. 2nd S. V3 p.209	

PRIVY COUNCIL CASES									
No.	Name	Date	Place	Sex	Mar. Stat	Trial Stat	Fate	Source	New Case
1233	Margaret Loche	16. 7. 1629	Eyemouth	F	U	Com.	NK.	R.P.C. 2nd S. V3 p.222	
1234	Margaret Wallace	30. 7. 1629	Ayr Mylne-holme	F	U	Com.	NK.	R.P.C. 2nd S. V3 p.264	
1235	Margaret Kennedie	30. 7. 1629	Ayr	F	M	Com.	NK.	R.P.C. 2nd S. V3 p.264	
1236	Janet Thomesoun	30. 7. 1629	Ayr	F	U	Com.	NK.	R.P.C. 2nd S. V3 p.264	
1237	Helen McFersane	30. 7. 1629	Ayr	F	U	Com.	NK.	R.P.C. 2nd S. V3 p.264	
1238	Helen Huldie	1. 8. 1629	Berwick Colding-hame	F	M	Com.	NK.	R.P.C. 2nd S. V3 p.270	
1239	Margaret Spreuill	1. 8. 1629	Glasgow	F	U	Com.	NK.	R.P.C. V3 p.270	
1240	Helen Luddes	1. 8. 1629	Craik-furde	F	U	Com.	NK.	R.P.C. 2nd S. V3 p.270	
1241	Duplicates	1238							
1242	Issobel Cuninghame	1. 8. 1629	Berwick Paxtane	F	U	Com.	NK.	R.P.C. 2nd S. V3 p.270	
1243	Easter Moreis	1. 8. 1629	Berwick Foulden	F	U	Com.	NK.	R.P.C. 2nd S. V3 p.270	
1244	Sara Meslet	1. 8. 1629	Berwick Foulden	F	U	Com.	NK.	R.P.C. 2nd S. V3 p.270	
1245	Thomas Richartsoun	1. 8. 1629	Roxburgh Maxtoun	M	U	Com.	NK.	R.P.C. 2nd S. V3 p.270	

PRIVY COUNCIL CASES									
No.	Name	Date	Place	Sex	Mar. Stat	Trial Stat	Fate	Source	New Case
1246	Helen Scott	1. 8. 1629	Roxburgh Maxtoun	F	U	Com.	NK.	R.P.C. 2nd S. V3 p.270	
1247	Helene Gastoun	1. 8. 1629	Roxburgh Lassuden	F	U	Com.	NK.	R.P.C. 2nd S. V3 p.270	
1248	Margaret Patersoun	1. 8. 1629	Roxburgh Lang-newtoun	F	U	Com.	NK.	R.P.C. 2nd S. V3 p.270	
1249	Helene Scot	1. 8. 1629	Roxburgh Melrose	F	U	Com.	NK.	R.P.C. 2nd S. V3 p.270	
1250	Margaret Studgeon	1. 8. 1629	Lanark	F	U	Com.	NK.	R.P.C. 2nd S. V3 p.270	
1251	John Grein-scheill	1. 8. 1629	Lanark Dun-draven	M	U	Com.	NK.	R.P.C. 2nd S. V3 p.270	
1252	Agnes Adam	1. 8. 1629	Lanark Cleghorne	F	U	Com.	NK.	R.P.C. 2nd S. V3 p.270	
1253	Margaret Fisher	1. 8. 1629	Lanark	F	M	Com.	NK.	R.P.C. 2nd S. V3 p.270	
1254	Isobel Quhyte	1. 8. 1629	Lanark Auchuren	F	M	Com.	NK.	R.P.C. 2nd S. V3 p.270	
1255	Margaret Hastie	1. 8. 1629	Lanark Laidlie	F	W	Com.	NK.	R.P.C. 2nd S. V3 p.270	
1256	Bessie Carfa	1. 8. 1629	Hadding-ton	F	U	Men.	Ex.	R.P.C. 2nd S. V3 p.269	
1257	Thomas Carfa	1. 8. 1629	Hadding-ton	M	U	Com.	NK.	R.P.C. 2nd S. V3 p.269	
1258	Alison Borthwick	1. 8. 1629	Hadding-ton	F	M	Com.	NK.	R.P.C. 2nd S. V3 p.269	

PRIVY COUNCIL CASES									
No.	Name	Date	Place	Sex	Mar. Stat	Trial Stat	Fate	Source	New Case
1259	John Carfa	1. 8. 1629	Hadding-ton	M	M	Com.	NK.	R.P.C. 2nd S. V3 p.269	
1260	Beigs Wallace	21. 8. 1629	Preston	F	U	Com.	NK.	R.P.C. 2nd S. V3 p.27	
1261	Margaret Mathesoun	21. 8. 1629	Preston-pans	F	U	Com.	Ex.	R.P.C. 2nd S. V3 p.271	
1262	Christian Thomesoun	5. 9. 1629	Penicuik	F	U	Com.	Ex.	R.P.C. 2nd S. V3 p.290	
1263	Margaret Small	5. 9. 1629	Penicuik	F	U	Com.	Ex.	R.P.C. 2nd S. V3 p.290	
1264	Isabel Dryburgh	5. 9. 1629	Penicuik	F	U	Com.	Ex.	R.P.C. 2nd S. V3 p.290	
1265	Bessie Aitkine	5. 9. 1629	Berwick-shire	F	M	Com.	NK.	R.P.C. 2nd S. V3 p.290	
1266	David Nisbett	5. 9. 1629	Berwick-shire	M	U	Com.	NK.	R.P.C. 2nd S. V3 p.290	
1267	Janet Liddel	5. 9. 1629	Berwich-shire	F	U	Com.	NK.	R.P.C. 2nd S. V3 p.290	
1268	Margaret Beleny	5. 9. 1629	Berwick-shire Aytoun	F	U	Com.	NK.	R.P.C. 2nd S. V3 p.290	
1269	Agnes Falconer	5. 9. 1629	Berwick-shire	F	U	Com.	NK.	R.P.C. 2nd S. V3 p.290	
1270	Margaret Alexander	3.11. 1629	East Lothian	F	U	Com.	NK.	R.P.C. 2nd S. V3 p.334	
1271	Agnes Sinclair	3.11. 1629	East Lothian	F	U	Com.	NK.	R.P.C. 2nd S. V3 p.334	

PRIVY COUNCIL CASES									
No.	Name	Date	Place	Sex	Mar. Stat	Trial Stat	Fate	Source	New Case
1272	Bessie Lawder	3.11. 1629	East Lothian	F	U	Com.	NK.	R.P.C. 2nd S. V3 p.334	
1273	Katherine Lawder	3.11. 1629	East Lothian	F	U	Com.	NK.	R.P.C. 2nd S. V3 p.334	
1274	Bessie Duncan	3.11. 1629	East Lothian	F	U	Com.	NK.	R.P.C. 2nd S. V3 p.334	
1275	Margaret Mitchell	3.11. 1629	East Lothian	F	U	Com.	NK.	R.P.C. 2nd S. V3 p.334	
1276	Alesoun Carrick	3.11. 1629	East Lothian	F	U	Com.	NK.	R.P.C. 2nd S. V3 p.334	
1277	Katherine Kirktoun	3.11. 1629	East Lothian	F	U	Com.	NK.	R.P.C. 2nd S. V3 p.334	
1278	Bessie Hepburne	3.11. 1629	East Lothian	F	U	Com.	NK.	R.P.C. 2nd S. V3 p.334	
1279	Barbara Wod	6.11. 1629	Berwich-shire Lauder	F	M	Com.	NK.	R.P.C. 2nd S. V3 p.340	
1280	Susanna Skaitsone	6.11. 1629	Clerking-ton	F	U	Com.	NK.	R.P.C. 2nd S. V3 p.339	
1281	Agnes Rannick	6.11. 1629	Clerking-ton	F	U	Com.	NK.	R.P.C. 2nd S. V3 p.339	
1282	Marioun Tailzeor	6.11. 1629	Berwick-shire	F	U	Com.	NK.	R.P.C. 2nd S. V3 p.340	
1283	Janet Allane	6.11. 1629	Berwick-shire Lauder	F	M	Com.	NK.	R.P.C. 2nd S. V3 p.340	
1284	Marion Porteous	6.11. 1629	Preston	F	U	Com.	NK.	R.P.C. 2nd S. V3 p.340	

PRIVY COUNCIL CASES									
No.	Name	Date	Place	Sex	Mar. Stat	Trial Stat	Fate	Source	New Case
1285	Annie Purdie	6.11. 1629	Newhall	F	U	Com.	NK.	R.P.C. 2nd S. V3 p.339	
1286	Margaret Nicolsone	12.11. 1629	Dunblane	F	M	Com.	Acqu	R.P.C. 2nd S. V3 pp. 345; 358-359	
1287	Johnne Hog	12.11. 1629	Dunblane	M	M	Com.	Acqu	R.P.C. 2nd S.V3 pp.345; 358-359	
1288	Jean Thomesone	12.11. 1629	Dumfries	F	W	Men.	NK.	R.P.C. 2nd S.V3 pp.345; 390-391; 450	
1289	Margaret Maxwell	12.11. 1629	Dumfries	F	M	Men.	NK.	R.P.C. 2nd S.V3 pp.345; 390-391; 450	
1290	Agnes Campbell	24.11. 1629	Ayr	F	M	Com.	NK.	R.P.C. 2nd S. V3 p.358	
1291	Marion Sandersoun	24.11. 1629	Colding-ham	F	U	Com.	NK.	R.P.C. 2nd S. V3 p.358	
1292	Janet Miller	3.12. 1629	Glasgow	F	U	Com.	NK.	R.P.C. 2nd S. V3 p.363	
1293	Grissell Boill	3. 12. 1629	Glasgow	F	U	Com.	NK.	R.P.C. 2nd S. V3 p.363	
1294	Janet Bishop	3.12. 1629	Penicuik	F	U	Com.	Ex.	R.P.C. 2nd S. V3 p.363	
1295	Margaret Cuthbertson	3.12. 1629	Penicuik	F	U	Com.	NK.	R.P.C. 2nd S. V3 p.363	

PRIVY COUNCIL CASES									
No.	Name	Date	Place	Sex	Mar. Stat	Trial Stat	Fate	Source	New Case
1296	Jean Miller	3.12. 1629	Glasgow	F	U	Com.	NK.	R.P.C. 2nd S. V3 p.363	
1297	Lady Manderstone	10.12. 1629	Duns	F	M	Men.	Acqu	R.P.C. 2nd S.V3 pp.361; 378;381-382;397-400	
1298	Michael Areskine	17.12. 1629	New-battle	M	U	Men.	NK.	R.P.C. 2nd S. V3 p.181	
1299	William Stevinsoun	18.12. 1629	Duns Hirsell	M	M	Com.	NK.	R.P.C. 2nd S.V3 pp.378; 385;386	
1300	Alisoun Pringill	18.12. 1629	Duns Hirsell	F	M	Com.	NK.	R.P.C. 2nd S.V3 pp.378; 385;386	
1301	Susanna Elphinstoun	22.12. 1629	Peebles	F	U	Com.	NK.	R.P.C. 2nd S. V3 p.391	
1302	Margaret Johnstone	22.12. 1629	Peebles	F	U	Com.	NK.	R.P.C. 2nd S. V3 p.391	
1303	John Graham	22.12. 1629	Peebles	M	U	Com.	NK.	R.P.C. 2nd S. V3 p.391	
1304	Gellie Robson	22.12. 1629	Dumfries	F	U	Com.	NK.	R.P.C. 2nd S. V3 pp. 340;390	
1305	Margaret Balliem	- - 1629	Eyemouth	F	U	Men.	NK.	R.P.C. 2nd S.V5 pp.176-177;572; 593;605	
1306	Alison Wilson	- - 1629	Eyemouth	F	U	Men.	Ex.	R.P.C.2nd S.V5 pp.176 -177;572; 593;605	

PRIVY COUNCIL CASES									
No.	Name	Date	Place	Sex	Mar. Stat	Trial Stat	Fate	Source	New Case
1307	Agnes Wilson	- - 1629	Eyemouth	F	U	Men.	Ex.	R.P.C. 2nd S.V5 pp.176-177;572;593;605	
1308	Janet Mitchell	1. 1. 1630	Cardross Carington	F	W	Com.	NK.	R.P.C. 2nd S. V3 p.400	
1309	Andrew Abel	12. 1. 1630	Hill of Tillie-carie	M	U	Com.	NK.	R.P.C. 2nd S.V3 pp.583-584;603	
1310	Margaret Callander	21. 1. 1630	St. Andrews	F	U	Com.	NK.	R.P.C. 2nd S. V3 p.426	
1311	Margaret Rid	21. 1. 1630	Crimond	F	U	Com.	NK.	R.P.C. 2nd S. V3 p.426	
1312	Janet Currie	21. 1. 1630	Crimond	F	U	Com.	NK.	R.P.C. 2nd S. V3 p.426	
1313	Alexander Hamilton	22. 1. 1630		M	U	Com.	Ex.	R.P.C. 2nd S.V3 pp.222;290;397;443;X1	
1314	Janet Smaillie	4. 2. 1630	Ayr	F	U	Com.	NK.	R.P.C. 2nd S. V3 p.446	
1315	Jonnet Reid	4. 2. 1630	Ayr Sand-mylne	F	U	Com.	NK.	R.P.C. 2nd S. V3 p.446	
1316	Marion Hannay	4. 2. 1630	Dum-frieshire	F	U	Com.	NK.	R.P.C. 2nd S. V3 p.446	
1317	Katherine McCheyne	4. 2. 1630	Dum-frieshire	F	U	Com.	NK.	R.P.C. 2nd S. V3 p.446	

PRIVY COUNCIL CASES									
No.	Name	Date	Place	Sex	Mar. Stat	Trial Stat	Fate	Source	New Case
1318	Marioun Johnstoun	4. 2. 1630	Dum-frieshire	F	U	Com.	NK.	R.P.C. 2nd S. V3 p.446	
1319	Marg Affleck	4. 2. 1630	Dum-frieshire	F	U	Com.	NK.	R.P.C. 2nd S. V3 p.446	
1320	Marion Martine	4. 2. 1630	Dum-frieshire Barfill	F	U	Com.	NK.	R.P.C. 2nd S. V3 p.446	
1321	Jonet Clerk	4. 2. 1630	Dum-frieshire	F	M	Com.	NK.	R.P.C. 2nd S. V3 p.446	
1322	Agnes Kirk-patrick	4. 2. 1630	Dum-frieshire	F	U	Com.	NK.	R.P.C. 2nd S. V3 p.446	
1323	Janet Robsoun	4. 2. 1630	Dumfries	F	M	Com.	NK.	R.P.C. 2nd S. V3 p.446	
1324	John Neill	5. 2. 1630	Tweed-mouth	M	U	Com.	NK.	R.P.C. 2nd S.V3 pp.400; 443;448; 513;541; 563	
1325	Jean Thomson	9. 2. 1630	Dumfries	F	W	Men.	Misc	R.P.C. 2nd S. V3 pp. 450–451	
1326	Nicol Thomson	9. 2. 1630	Dumfries	M	M	Men.	Misc	R.P.C. 2nd S. V3 pp. 450–451	
1327	Margaret Maxwell	9. 2. 1630	Dumfries	F	M	Men.	Misc	R.P.C. 2nd S. V3 pp. 450–451	
1328	Mawsie Aslowane	9. 2. 1630	Dumfries	F	U	Men.	Ex.	R.P.C. 2nd S. V3 p.450	

PRIVY COUNCIL CASES

No.	Name	Date	Place	Sex	Mar. Stat	Trial Stat	Fate	Source	New Case
1329	Elspet Bladder-stouns	11. 2. 1630	Torry-burn	F	U	Com.	NK.	R.P.C. 2nd S. V3 p.454	
1330	Margaret Andersoun	25. 2. 1630	Aberdeen-shire Ally	F	M	Com.	NK.	R.P.C. 2nd S. V3 p.471	
1331	Thomas Grig	25. 2. 1630	Aberdeen-shire	M	U	Com.	NK.	R.P.C. 2nd S. V3 p.471	
1332	Jonet Ker	11. 3. 1630	Berwick-shire Gordon	F	U	Com.	NK.	R.P.C. 2nd S. V3 p.488	
1333	Bessie Nisbitt	11. 3. 1630	Berwick-shire	F	U	Com.	NK.	R.P.C. 2nd S. V3 p.488	
1334	Janet Scot	11. 3. 1630	Dysart	F	U	Com.	NK.	R.P.C. 2nd S. V3 p.488	
1335	Janet Galbraith	11. 3. 1630	Dysart	F	U	Com.	NK.	R.P.C. 2nd S. V3 p.488	
1336	William Broun	11. 3. 1630	Dysart	M	U	Com.	NK.	R.P.C. 2nd S. V3 p.488	
1337	Helen Bissat	11. 3. 1630	Dysart	F	U	Com.	NK.	R.P.C. 2nd S. V3 p.488	
1338	Bessie Guiddale	11. 3. 1630	Dysart	F	U	Com.	NK.	R.P.C. 2nd S. V3 p.488	
1339	Katherine Chrystie	16. 3. 1630	Dysart	F	W	Men.	Ex.	R.P.C. 2nd S. V4 p.59	
1340	Katherine Chrystie	16. 3. 1630	Dysart	F	W	Men.	Ex.	R.P.C. 2nd S. V3 pp. 489–490	
1341	Janet Wilkie	20. 3. 1630	Wester Wemyss	F	M	Com.	NK.	R.P.C. 2nd S.V3 p.496	

PRIVY COUNCIL CASES									
No.	Name	Date	Place	Sex	Mar. Stat	Trial Stat	Fate	Source	New Case
1342	Katherine Kirktoun	26. 3. 1630	East Lothian	F	U	Com.	NK.	R.P.C. 2nd S. V3 p.544	
1343	Bessie Duncane	26. 3. 1630	East Lothian	F	U	Com.	NK.	R.P.C. 2nd S. V3 p.544	
1344	Alison Carrick	26. 3. 1630	East Lothian	F	U	Com.	NK.	R.P.C. 2nd S. V3 p.544	
1345	Katherine Lawder	26. 3. 1630	East Lothian	F	U	Com.	NK.	R.P.C. 2nd S. V3 p.544	
1346	Margaret Borthuick	1. 4. 1630	Dalkeith Cousland	F	U	Com.	NK.	R.P.C. 2nd S. V3 p.518	
1347	Elizabeth Selkirk	1. 4. 1630	Cousland	F	U	Com.	NK.	R.P.C. 2nd S. V3 p.518	
1348	Margaret Veitche	21. 4. 1630	Dalkeith Cousland	F	U	Com.	NK.	R.P.C. 2nd S. V3 p.534	
1349		21. 4. 1630	Dalkeith Cousland	F	U	Com.	NK.	R.P.C. 2nd S. V3 p.534	
1350	Janet Patersoun	21. 4. 1630	Dalkeith Cousland	F	U	Com.	NK.	R.P.C. 2nd S. V3 p.534	
1351	Patrick Murray	21. 4. 1630	Hadding-ton	M	U	Com.	NK.	R.P.C. 2nd S. V3 p.535	
1352	Margaret Heriot	21. 4. 1630	Carring-ton	F	U	Com.	NK.	R.P.C. 2nd S. V3 p.535	
1353	Janet Beverage	21. 4. 1630	Dysart	F	M	Men.	Misc	R.P.C. 2nd S. V3 p.532	
1354	Alison Neving	21. 4. 1630	Dysart	F	U	Com.	NK.	R.P.C. 2nd S. V3 p.535	

PRIVY COUNCIL CASES									
No.	Name	Date	Place	Sex	Mar. Stat	Trial Stat	Fate	Source	New Case
1355	Margaret Dasoun	21. 4. 1630	Dysart	F	U	Com.	NK.	R.P.C. 2nd S. V3 p.535	
1356	Lady Samuelston	10. 5. 1630		F	W	Men.	NK.	R.P.C. 2nd S. V3 pp. X11;541	
1357	Marion Bankes	26. 5. 1630	Dalkeith Cousland	F	M	Com.	NK.	R.P.C. 2nd S. V3 p.544	
1358	Marioun Andersoun	26. 5. 1630	Dalkeith Cousland	F	U	Com.	NK.	R.P.C. 2nd S. V3 p.534	
1359	John Phenick	26. 5. 1630	Dalkeith Cousland	M	M	Com.	NK.	R.P.C. 2nd S. V3 p.534	
1360	Giles Swintoun	26. 5. 1630	Dalkeith Cousland	M	S	Com.	NK.	R.P.C. 2nd S. V3 p.544	
1361	Christian Steill	26. 5. 1630	Dalkeith Cousland	F	U	Com.	NK.	R.P.C. 2nd S. V3 p.544	
1362	Janet Richardson	26. 5. 1630	Dalkeith Cousland	F	U	Com.	NK.	R.P.C. 2nd S.V3 p.544	
1363	Agnes Phenick	26. 5. 1630	Dalkeith Cousland	F	U	Com.	NK.	R.P.C. 2nd S. V3 p.544	
1364	Janet Sinclare	1. 6. 1630	Dumfries	F	U	Com.	NK.	R.P.C. 2nd S. V3 pp. 550-551	
1365	John Ray	1. 6. 1630	Dumfries	M	U	Com.	NK.	R.P.C. 2nd S. V3 pp. 550-551	
1366	Agnes Weir	1. 6. 1630	Dumfries	F	U	Com.	NK.	R.P.C. 2nd S.V3 pp.550-551	

PRIVY COUNCIL CASES									
No.	Name	Date	Place	Sex	Mar. Stat	Trial Stat	Fate	Source	New Case
1367	Janet Fergusson	1. 6. 1630	Dum-frieshire	F	U	Com.	NK.	R.P.C. 2nd S. V3 pp. 550-551	
1368	Isobel Moffat	1. 6. 1630	Dumfries	F	M	Com.	NK.	R.P.C. 2nd S. V3 pp. 550-551	
1369	Janet Herries	1. 6. 1630	Dum-frieshire	F	U	Com.	NK.	R.P.C. 2nd S. V3 pp. 550-551	
1370	Marion Ritchie	8. 6. 1630	Newton of Ayr	F	U	Com.	NK.	R.P.C. 2nd S. V3 p.561	
1371	Katherine Wilson	17. 6. 1630	Duns	F	U	Men.	NK.	R.P.C. 2nd S. V3 p.571	
1372	John Smith	17. 6. 1630	Duns	M	U	Men.	NK.	R.P.C. 2nd S. V3 p.571	
1373	Alison Colin	17. 6. 1630	Duns	F	U	Men.	NK.	R.P.C. 2nd S. V3 p.571	
1374	Janet Wilson	17. 6. 1630	Almernes	F	U	Com.	NK.	R.P.C. 2nd S. V3 p.570	
1375	Isobel McNaught	17. 6. 1630	Auchlayne	F	U	Com.	NK.	R.P.C. 2nd S. V3 p.570	
1376	Katharine Major	17. 6. 1630	Dun-drennan	F	U	Com.	NK.	R.P.C. 2nd S. V3 p.570	
1377	Margaret Haliday	17. 6. 1630	Craig-toun	F	U	Com.	NK.	R.P.C. 2nd S. V3 p.570	
1378	Bessie Mitchell	22. 6. 1630	Crichton	F	U	Com.	NK.	R.P.C. 2nd S. V3 p.573	

PRIVY COUNCIL CASES									
No.	Name	Date	Place	Sex	Mar. Stat	Trial Stat	Fate	Source	New Case
1379	Johne Smith	1. 7. 1630	North Berwick	M	U	Men.	Misc	R.P.C. 2nd S. V3 pp. 587;603	
1380	Marion Aroane	6. 7. 1630	Catloch	F	U	Com.	NK.	R.P.C. 2nd S. V3 p.593	
1381	Elspet Watsoun	8. 7. 1630	Dysart	F	U	Com.	NK.	R.P.C. 2nd S. V3 p.602	
1382	John Phenick	8. 7. 1630	Dalkeith Cousland	M	M	Com.	NK.	R.P.C. 2nd S. V3 p.602	
1383	Elie Nesbit	30. 7. 1630	Hilton	F	U	Com.	NK.	R.P.C. 2nd S. V3 pp. 583-584; 603	
1384	Dod Nine Siacke Moir	9. 8. 1630	Tain	U	U	Com.	NK.	R.P.C. 2nd S. V4 p.13	
1385	Janet Moir	9. 8. 1630	Tain	F	U	Com.	NK.	R.P.C. 2nd S. V4 p.13	
1386	Janet Wallace	9. 8. 1630	Ayr Ochiltree	F	U	Com.	NK.	R.P.C. 2nd S. V4 p.13	
1387	Janet McGillichoan	9. 8. 1630	Fortrose Chanory	F	U	Com.	NK.	R.P.C. 2nd S. V4 p.13	
1388	Marion Hurdie	9. 8. 1630	Aberdeen	F	U	Com.	Ex.	R.P.C. 2nd S.V4 pp.13;39	
1389	Mallie Cowper	8. 9. 1630	Aberdeen Futtie	F	U	Com.	NK.	R.P.C. 2nd S. V4 p.39	
1390	Marion Rodgie	8. 9. 1630	Aberdeen	F	U	Com.	NK.	R.P.C. 2nd S. V4 p.39	

PRIVY COUNCIL CASES									
No.	Name	Date	Place	Sex	Mar. Stat	Trial Stat	Fate	Source	New Case
1391	Margaret Lumsden	8. 9. 1630	Aberdeen Futtie	F	U	Com.	NK.		
1392	Wife of Mathow Will	8. 9. 1630	Aberdeen Peter-head	F	M	Men.	NK.	R.P.C. 2nd S. V4 p.39	*
1393	Cowie	8. 9. 1630	Aberdeen Bownes	M	U	Men.	NK.	R.P.C. 2nd S. V4 p.39	*
1394	Margaret Buchane	8. 9. 1630	Aberdeen Bownes	F	M	Men.	NK.	R.P.C. 2nd S. V4 p.39	*
1395	Margaret Gilchrist	8. 9. 1630	Aberdeen Bownes	F	U	Men.	NK.	R.P.C. 2nd S. V4 p.39	*
1396	Margaret Ritchie	8. 9. 1630	Aberdeen Boddome	F	U	Men.	NK.	R.P.C. 2nd S. V4 p.39	*
1397	Margaret Buchan	8. 9. 1630	Aberdeen Boddome	F	U	Men.	NK.	R.P.C. 2nd S. V4 p.39	*
1398	Margaret Small	8. 9. 1630	Aberdeen Boddome	F	U	Men.	NK.	R.P.C. 2nd S. V4 p.39	*
1399	Margaret Whyte	8. 9. 1630	Aberdeen Peter-head	F	U	Men.	NK.	R.P.C. 2nd S. V4 p.39	*
1400	Margaret Ritchie	8. 9. 1630	Aberdeen Peter-head	F	U	Men.	NK.	R.P.C. 2nd S. V4 p.39	*
1401	Margaret Fisher	8. 9. 1630	Aberdeen Peter-head	F	U	Men.	NK.	R.P.C. 2nd S. V4 p.39	*
1402	Patrick Tod	8. 9. 1630	Eccles-greig	M	U	Com.	NK.	R.P.C. 2nd S. V4 p.39	
1403	Elie Nesbitt	4.11. 1630	Berwick-shire Merse	F	U	Men.	NK.	R.P.C. 2nd S.V4 pp.56;98	

PRIVY COUNCIL CASES									
No.	Name	Date	Place	Sex	Mar. Stat	Trial Stat	Fate	Source	New Case
1404	John Neill	4.11. 1630	Berwick-shire Merse	M	U	Men.	NK.	R.P.C. 2nd S. V4 pp. 56;98	
1405	Agnes Boyd	14.12. 1630	Paisley	F	U	Men.	Misc	R.P.C. 2nd S. V4 pp. 50;92-93	
1406	George Semill	-.12. 1630	Paisley	M	U	Men.	NK.	R.P.C. 2nd S. V4 pp. 24;50; 92-93	
1407	Walter Baird	- - 1630	Banff-shire	M	U	Men.	Ex.	R.P.C. 2nd S. V5 p.566	
1408	Bessie Purcell	11. 1. 1631	Edinburgh	F	M	Men.	NK.	R.P.C. 2nd S. V4 p.111	*
1409	John Philip	22. 2. 1631	Banff	M	U	Com.	Ex.	R.P.C. 2nd S.V4 pp.39; 637-639; V5 p.565	
1410	John Neill	10. 3. 1631	Merse	M	U	Men.	Ex.	R.P.C. 2nd S. V4 pp. 164-165	
1411	John Smith	5. 7. 1631	Duns	M	U	Men.	Ex.	R.P.C. 2nd S. V4 pp. 265-267; 280	
1412	Katharin Wilson	5. 7. 1631	Duns	F	U	Men.	NK.	R.P.C. 2nd S. V4 pp. 265-277; 280	
1413	Christian Paterson	21.12. 1631	Hermiston	F	M	Men.	Ex.	R.P.C. 2nd S. V4 pp. 334-335	

PRIVY COUNCIL CASES									
No.	Name	Date	Place	Sex	Mar. Stat	Trial Stat	Fate	Source	New Case
1414	Patrick Chrystinsone	- - 1631	Aber-ledie	M	U	Men.	NK.	R.P.C. 2nd S. V8 p.194	*
1415	Marion Mure	10. 1. 1632	Leith	F	W	Com.	Ex.	R.P.C. 2nd S. V4 pp. 405;423; 426;427; 435	
1416	Marioun Lumsden	6. 3. 1632	Leith	F	U	Com.	NK.	R.P.C. 2nd S. V4 pp. 441;427; 437	
1417	Helene Hamiltoun	6. 3. 1632	Leith	F	U	Com.	NK.	R.P.C. 2nd S. V4 pp. 427;437; 447	
1418	Helen Widdrow	13. 4. 1632	Bar-phillan	F	W	Men.	Misc	R.P.C. 2nd S. V4 p.473	*
1419	Janet Love	13. 4. 1632	Greenock	F	M	Men.	Misc	R.P.C. 2nd S. V4 p.473	
1420	Alison Nisbet	23. 7. 1632	Hilton	F	U	Men.	Ex.	R.P.C. 2nd S. V4 pp. 152;166	
1421	Gardener's Wife	- - 1632	Tranent	F	M	Men.	NK.	R.P.C. 2nd S. V4 p.433	
1422	Marion Layland	17. 3. 1633	Orkney	F	U	Men.	Ex.	R.P.C. 2nd S.V5 pp.544-548;551-555	
1423	Katherene Grieve	29. 5. 1633	Orkney	F	U	Men.	NCP	R.P.C. 2nd S. V5 pp. 556-559	

PRIVY COUNCIL CASES									
No.	Name	Date	Place	Sex	Mar. Stat	Trial Stat	Fate	Source	New Case
1424	Elizabeth Bathgate	9. 1. 1634	Eyemouth	F	M	Men.	Misc	R.P.C. 2nd S. V5 pp. 176-177; 572;593; 605-606	
1425	Isabel Sinclair	28. 3. 1634	Eyemouth	F	M	Men.	Ex.	R.P.C. 2nd S. V5 p.246	
1426	Alison Wilson	4. 6. 1634	Eyemouth Aytoun	F	U	Men.	Ex.	Spott. Misc.V2 pp.64-66	
1427	Elizabeth Bathgate	4. 6. 1634	Eyemouth	F	M	Com.	Acqu	R.P.C. 2nd S. V5 pp. 176-177; 572;593; 605	
1428	Patrick Smith	4. 6. 1634	Eyemouth	M	U	Men.	NK.	Spott. Misc.V2 pp.64-66	
1429	Jannet Williamson	4. 6. 1634	Eyemouth	F	U	Men.	NK.	Spott. Misc.V2 pp.64-66	
1430	Margaret Bellamie	4. 6. 1634	Eyemouth Aytoun	F	U	Men.	NK.	Spott. Misc.V2 pp.64-66	
1431	William Mearns	4. 6. 1634	Eyemouth Aytoun	M	U	Men.	Misc	Spott. Misc.V2 pp.64-66	
1432	Elspeth Wilson	4. 6. 1634	Eyemouth Aytoun	F	U	Men.	NK.	Spott. Misc.V2 pp.64-66	
1433	Agnes Wilson	4. 6. 1634	Eyemouth Aytoun	F	U	Men.	Ex.	Spott. Misc.V2 pp.64-66	
1434	Giles Chalmer	- - 1634	Angus Oathlaw	M	M	Men.	NK.	R.P.C. 2nd S. V5 pp. 179-180; 565-566; 574-575	

PRIVY COUNCIL CASES									
No.	Name	Date	Place	Sex	Mar. Stat	Trial Stat	Fate	Source	New Case
1435	George Fraser	– – 1634	Angus Oathlaw	M	M	Men.	NK.	R.P.C. 2nd S. V5 pp. 179-180; 565-566; 574-575	
1436	Katherine Cragie	17. 6. 1640	Orkney	F	U	Men.	Acqu	R.P.C. 2nd S. V7 pp. 474-477	
1437	Margaret Huttoun	7.11. 1642	Culross	F	M	Com.	Ex.	R.P.C. 2nd S. V8 p.12	
1438	Isobel Adamsone	10.11. 1642	Dumfries	F	U	Com.	Ex.	R.P.C. 2nd S. V7 p.340	
1439	Jean Barbour	15.11. 1642	Tongland	F	U	Com.	Ex.	R.P.C. 2nd S. V7 p.342	
1440	Agnes Grant	9. 1. 1643	Elgin	F	U	Com.	Misc	R.P.C. 2nd S. V7 pp. 595-596	
1441	Katherine Burgess	13. 6. 1643	Moray Cromdale	F	U	Com.	Ex.	R.P.C. 2nd S. V7 p.446	
1442	Jonet Reid	12. 7. 1643	Orkney	F	U	Com.	Ex.	R.P.C. 2nd S. V8 pp. 71-75	
1443	Katherine Craigie	12. 7. 1643	Orkney	F	U	Com.	Ex.	R.P.C. 2nd S. V8 pp. 65-70	
1444	Husband of E.Ranie	–. 7. 1643	Orkney	M	M	Men.	NK.	R.P.C. 2nd S. V8 p.64	
1445	Elizabeth Ranie	–. 7. 1643	Orkney	F	M	Men.	NK.	R.P.C. 2nd S. V8 p.64	

PRIVY COUNCIL CASES									
No.	Name	Date	Place	Sex	Mar. Stat	Trial Stat	Fate	Source	New Case
1446	Margaret Ranie	-. 7. 1643	Orkney	F	U	Men.	NK.	R.P.C. 2nd S. V8 p.64	
1447	Cristane Poock	-. 7. 1643	Orkney	F	U	Men.	NK.	R.P.C. 2nd S. V8 p.64	
1448	Thomas Rob	30. 11. 1643	Perth	M	U	Com.	Ex.	R.P.C. 2nd S. V8 pp. 18-19	
1449	Agnes Stoddart	30.11. 1643	Perth	F	U	Com.	Ex.	R.P.C. 2nd S. V8 pp. 18-19	
1450	Jean Rob	30.11. 1643	Perth	F	U	Com.	Ex.	R.P.C. 2nd S. V8 pp. 18-19	
1451	Some Witches	19.12. 1643	Queens-ferry	U	U	Com.	NK.	R.P.C. 2nd S. V8 p.20	
1452	Jean Lachlane	- - 1643	Lanark	F	U	Men.	NK.	R.P.C. 2nd S. V8 pp. 148-149	
1453	Helen Stewart	- - 1643	Lanark-shire Cadder	F	U	Men.	Ex.	R.P.C. 2nd S. V8 pp. 148-149	
1454	Mary Cuningham	6. 8. 1644	Culross	F	M	Men.	NK.	R.P.C. 2nd S. V8 pp. 37-39;43; 101-103; 105;139	
1455	Jonet Erskine	6. 8. 1644	Culross	F	U	Men.	NK.	R.P.C. 2nd S. V8 p.101	
1456	Mary Cunninghame	6. 8. 1644	Culross	F	W	Men.	NK.	R.P.C. 2nd S. V8 p.101	

PRIVY COUNCIL CASES									
No.	Name	Date	Place	Sex	Mar. Stat	Trial Stat	Fate	Source	New Case
1457	Margaret Young	8. 8. 1644	Queens-ferry	F	U	Men.	NK.	R.P.C. 2nd S. V8 p.104	
1458	Christiane Melvill	20. 8. 1644	Abercorn	F	U	Men.	Ex.	R.P.C. 2nd S. V8 p.110	
1459	Margaret Young	2.10. 1644	Dysart	F	M	Men.	Acqu	R.P.C. 2nd S. V8 p.28	
1460	Jonnet McKennan	6.11. 1644	Wigtown Balmurie	F	M	Com.	NK.	R.P.C. 2nd S. V8 pp. 133-134	
1461	Marion Shenan	6.11. 1644	Wigtown Droch-dooll	F	M	Com.	NK.	R.P.C. 2nd S. V8 pp. 133-134	
1462	Marion Russell	6. 11. 1644	Wigtown Glenluce	F	U	Com.	NK.	R.P.C. 2nd S. V8 pp. 133-134	
1463	Isobell Bigham	6.11. 1644	Wigtown Stranraer	F	U	Com.	NK.	R.P.C. 2nd S. V8 pp. 133-134	
1464	Elam Africk	6.11. 1644	Wigtown Knockibae	F	M	Com.	NK.	R.P.C. 2nd S. V8 pp. 133-134	
1465	Margaret Thomsone	17.11. 1644	Mid Calder	F	M	Men.	Acqu	R.P.C. 2nd S. V8 pp. 37;108-109;117-119;138	
1466	Agnes Finnie	18.12. 1644	Edinburgh	F	U	Men.	Ex.	R.P.C. 2nd S. V8 pp. 134-135	
1467	Jean Lachlane	31.12. 1644	Carnwaith	F	U	Com.	Ex.	R.P.C. 2nd S.V8 pp.41;146-154	

PRIVY COUNCIL CASES									
No.	Name	Date	Place	Sex	Mar. Stat	Trial Stat	Fate	Source	New Case
1468	Jonet Lockie	31.12. 1644	Carnwath	F	U	Men.	NK.	R.P.C. 2nd S. V8 pp. 146-154	
1469	Mailie Pattersone	31.12. 1644	Carnwath	F	U	Men.	NK.	R.P.C. 2nd S. V8 pp. 146-154	
1470	Margaret Watsoun	31.12. 1644	Carnwath	F	U	Com.	Ex.	R.P.C. 2nd S. V8 pp. 146-154	
1471	Margaret Reid	- - 1644	Lanark-shire Carnwath	F	U	Men.	NK.	R.P.C. 2nd S. V8 pp. 155-157	
1472	Kathren Shaw	- - 1644	Lanark-shire Carnwath	F	U	Men.	Ex.	R.P.C. 2nd S. V8 pp. 155-157	
1473		- - 1648	Linlith-gow	U	U	Com.	NK.	G.145	*
1474		- - 1648	Linlith-gow	U	U	Com.	NK.	G.145	*
1475		- - 1648	Linlith-gow	U	U	Com.	NK.	G.145	*
1476		- - 1648	Linlith-gow	U	U	Com.	NK.	G.145	*
1477		- - 1648	Linlith-gow	U	U	Com.	NK.	G.145	*
1478		- - 1648	Linlith-gow	U	U	Com.	NK.	G.145	*
1479	The Pypers Mother	7. 6. 1649	Dirleton-Long-nidrie	F	U	Men.	Ex.	R.P.C. 2nd S. V8 p.189	*
1480	Agnes Clarkson	7. 6. 1649	Dirleton	F	W	Men.	Ex.	R.P.C. 2nd S. V8 pp. 189-190	

PRIVY COUNCIL CASES									
No.	Name	Date	Place	Sex	Mar. Stat	Trial Stat	Fate	Source	New Case
1481	John Weir	8. 6. 1649	Penston	M	M	Men.	NK.	R.P.C. 2nd S. V8 pp. 190–193	*
1482	Agnes Broun	8. 6. 1649	Penston	F	U	Men.	NK.	R.P.C. 2nd S. V8 pp. 190–193	*
1483	Helen Lauson	12. 6. 1649	Hadding-ton	F	U	Men.	NK.	R.P.C. 2nd S. V8 pp. 190–193	*
1484	Barbara Purdie	12. 6. 1649	Hadding-ton	F	U	Men.	NK.	R.P.C. 2nd S. V8 pp. 190–193	*
1485	Margaret Hog	12. 6. 1649	Hadding-ton	F	U	Men.	NK.	R.P.C. 2nd S. V8 pp. 190–193	*
1486	Margaret Bartilman	12. 6. 1649	Hadding-ton	F	M	Men.	NK.	R.P.C. 2nd S. V8 p.193	
1487	Margaret Russell	21. 6. 1649	Penston	F	U	Men.	NK.	R.P.C. 2nd S. V8 pp. 190–193	
1488	Marjorie Adamsone	21. 6. 1649	Penston	F	U	Men.	NK.	R.P.C. 2nd S. V8 pp. 190–193	
1489	Marione Richesone	21. 6. 1649	Penston	F	U	Men.	NK.	R.P.C. 2nd S. V8 pp. 190–193	
1490	Agnes Hunter	21. 6. 1649	Penston	F	U	Com.	NK.	R.P.C. 2nd S. V8 pp. 190–193	
1491	Margaret Dickson	21. 6. 1649	Penston	F	U	Com.	NK.	R.P.C. 2nd S.V8 pp.190–193	

PRIVY COUNCIL CASES									
No.	Name	Date	Place	Sex	Mar. Stat	Trial Stat	Fate	Source	New Case
1492	Issobell Murray	21. 6. 1649	Penston	F	U	Com.	NK.	R.P.C. 2nd S. V8 pp. 190–193	
1493	Margaret Staig	21. 6. 1649	Penston	F	U	Men.	NK.	R.P.C. 2nd S. V8 pp. 190–193	
1494	Duplicates	1479							
1495	Manie Halieburton	–. 6. 1649	Dirleton West Fenton	F	M	Men.	Ex.	R.P.C. 2nd S. V8 pp. 194–195	
1496	Besse Hogge	–. 6. 1649	Dirleton	F	U	Men.	Ex.	R.P.C. 2nd S. V8 pp. 189–190	
1497	Patrick Watson	–. 6. 1649	Dirleton	M	M	Men.	Ex.	R.P.C. 2nd S. V8 pp. 194–195	
1498	Issobell Broune	2. 7. 1649	Eyemouth	F	U	Men.	NK.	R.P.C. 2nd S. V8 p.195	
1499	Marion Robison	8. 7. 1649	Eyemouth	F	U	Men.	NK.	R.P.C. 2nd S. V8 p.197	
1500	Beatrix Young	8. 7. 1649	Eyemouth	F	U	Men.	NK.	R.P.C. 2nd S. V8 pp. 196–197	
1501	Alisone Cairnes	8. 7. 1649	Eyemouth	F	U	Men.	NK.	R.P.C. 2nd S. V8 p.196	
1502	Helene Tailzear	8. 7. 1649	Eyemouth	F	U	Men.	NK.	R.P.C. 2nd S. V8 pp. 196–197	

PRIVY COUNCIL CASES									
No.	Name	Date	Place	Sex	Mar. Stat	Trial Stat	Fate	Source	New Case
1503	Margaret Dobson	8. 7. 1649	Eyemouth	F	U	Men.	NK.	R.P.C. 2nd S. V8 p.196	
1504	Issobell Murray	12. 7. 1649	Hadding-ton	F	M	Men.	NK.	R.P.C. 2nd S. V8 p.193	
1505	Grissell Anderson	12. 7. 1649	Hadding-ton	F	M	Men.	NK.	R.P.C. 2nd S. V8 pp. 190-193	
1506	John Dickson	12. 7. 1649	Hadding-ton	M	U	Men.	NK.	R.P.C. 2nd S. V8 pp. 193-194	
1507	Margarit Robertson	13. 7. 1649	Hadding-ton	F	U	Men.	NK.	R.P.C. 2nd S. V8 pp. 197-198	
1508	Margrat Vaith	13. 7. 1649	Hadding-ton	F	U	Men.	NK.	R.P.C. 2nd S. V8 pp. 197-198	
1509	Mauld Gauld	14. 9. 1649	Kilbar-chan	F	M	Men.	NK.	R.P.C. 2nd S. V8 pp. 198-204	
1510	Agnes Watersoun	27. 9. 1649	Burnt-island	F	U	Com.	NK.	R.P.C. 2nd S. V8 p.200	
1511	Elspeth Ronaldsone	- - 1649	Burnt-island	F	U	Com.	NK.	R.P.C. 2nd S. V8 p.200	
1512	Jonet Murray	- - 1649	Burnt-island	F	U	Com.	NK.	R.P.C. 2nd S. V8 p.200	
1513	Elizabeth Lawson	- - 1649	East Lothian	F	U	Men.	NK.	R.P.C. 2nd S. V8 pp. 204-205	

PRIVY COUNCIL CASES

No.	Name	Date	Place	Sex	Mar. Stat	Trial Stat	Fate	Source	New Case
1514	Issobel Richardson	- - 1649	East Lothian Pilmore	F	U	Men.	NK.	R.P.C. 2nd S. V8 pp. 204-205	
1515	Patrick Meikkie	- - 1649	East Lothian	M	M	Men.	Acqu	R.P.C. 2nd S. V8 pp. 204-205	
1516	George Miltoun	- - 1649	East Lothian	M	U	Men.	NK.	R.P.C. 2nd S. V8 pp. 204-205	
1517	Christian Blek	- - 1649	East Lothian	F	M	Men.	Acqu	R.P.C. 2nd S. V8 pp. 204-205	
1518	Agnes Murray	- - 1649	East Lothian	F	U	Com.	NK.	R.P.C. 2nd S. V8 pp. 204-205	
1519	Jeane Deanes	- - 1649	East Lothian	F	U	Com.	NK.	R.P.C. 2nd S. V8 pp. 204-205	
1520	Begis Bathlat	- - 1649	East Lothian Baigbie	F	U	Com.	NK.	R.P.C. 2nd S. V8 pp. 204-205	
1521	Marion Wood	- - 1649	East Lothian	F	U	Com.	Ex.	R.P.C. 2nd S. V8 pp. 204-205	
1522	Euphame Haliburton	- - 1649	East Lothian	F	U	Com.	NK.	R.P.C. 2nd S. V8 pp. 204-205	
1523	Marion Hutson	- - 1649	East Lothian	F	U	Com.	NK.	R.P.C. 2nd S. V8 pp. 204-205	

PRIVY COUNCIL CASES									
No.	Name	Date	Place	Sex	Mar. Stat	Trial Stat	Fate	Source	New Case
1524	Issobell Hutson	- - 1649	East Lothian	F	U	Com.	NK.	R.P.C. 2nd S. V8 pp. 204-205	
1525	George Hutson	- - 1649	East Lothian	M	U	Com.	NK.	R.P.C. 2nd S. V8 pp. 204-205	
1526	Isobel Wilson	- - 1649	Carriden	F	U	Men.	NK.	R.P.C. 2nd S. V8 p.205	
1527	Elspeth Baillie	- - 1649	East Lothian Pilmore	F	U	Men.	NK.	R.P.C. 2nd S. V8 pp. 204-205	
1528	Issobell Stillie	- - 1649	East Lothian	F	M	Men.	Ex.	R.P.C. 2nd S. V8 pp. 204-205	
1529	Nicoll Stillie	- - 1649	East Lothian	M	M	Men.	Ex.	R.P.C. 2nd S. V8 pp. 204-205	
1530	Anna Pilmore	- - 1649	East Lothian	F	U	Men.	NK.	R.P.C. 2nd S. V8 pp. 204-205	
1531	Helen Deans	- - 1649	East Lothian	F	U	Men.	NK.	R.P.C. 2nd S. V8 pp. 204-205	
1532	Agnes Williamson	- - 1649	East Lothian	F	U	Men.	NK.	R.P.C. 2nd S. V8 pp. 204-205	
1533	Issobell Cairnes	- - 1649	East Lothian	F	U	Men.	Acqu	R.P.C. 2nd S. V8 pp. 204-205	
1534	Helen Sharpe	- - 1649	East Lothian	F	U	Men.	Acqu	R.P.C. 2nd S.V8 pp.204-205	

PRIVY COUNCIL CASES									
No.	Name	Date	Place	Sex	Mar. Stat	Trial Stat	Fate	Source	New Case
1535	Margaret Blak	- - 1649	East Lothian	F	M	Men.	Acqu	R.P.C. 2nd S. V8 pp. 204-205	
1536	John Home	- - 1649	East Lothian	M	M	Men.	Acqu	R.P.C. 2nd S. V8 pp. 204-205	
1537	Adam Harlaw	- - 1649	East Lothian	M	U	Men.	Acqu	R.P.C. 2nd S. V8 pp. 204-205	
1538	Susanna Bannatyne	- - 1649	East Lothian	F	U	Men.	Acqu	R.P.C. 2nd S. V8 pp. 204-205	
1539	Jonet Kempe	- - 1649	East Lothian	F	U	Men.	Acqu	R.P.C. 2nd S. V8 pp. 204-205	
1540	Issobel Cathie	- - 1649	East Lothian	F	U	Men.	Acqu	R.P.C. 2nd S. V8 pp. 204-205	
1541	Helen Wast	- - 1649	East Lothian	F	U	Men.	Acqu	R.P.C. 2nd S. V8 pp. 204-205	
1542	Helen Reid	- - 1649	East Lothian	F	M	Men.	Acqu	R.P.C. 2nd S. V8 pp. 204-205	
1543	Jeane Craufurd	26. 2. 1650	Renfrew	F	U	Men.	Ex.	R.P.C. 2 Ser. pp.211-235	
1544	Bargans	26. 2. 1650	Renfrew	M	U	Men.	Ex.	R.P.C. 2 Ser. V8 pp. 211-235	

PRIVY COUNCIL CASES									
No.	Name	Date	Place	Sex	Mar. Stat	Trial Stat	Fate	Source	New Case
1545	Jeanat Mountgomerie	26. 2. 1650	Renfrew	F	U	Men.	Ex.	R.P.C. 2nd S. V8 pp. 211-235	
1546	Thomas Lich or Leich	26. 2. 1650	Renfrew	M	U	Men.	Ex.	R.P.C. 2 Ser. V8 pp. 211-235	
1547	Margaret Finlasoun	26. 2. 1650	Renfrew	F	U	Men.	Ex.	R.P.C. 2nd S. V8 pp. 211-235	
1548	Margaret Keltie	- - 1660	Crook of Devon	F	U	Men.	NK.	Reid pp.230-232	*
1549	Three or Four Witches	24. 4. 1661	East Lothian	U	U	Men.	Ex.	R.P.C. 3rd S. V1 p.647	
1550		24. 4. 1661	East Lothian	U	U	Men.	Ex.	R.P.C. 3rd S. V1 p.647	
1551		24. 4. 1661	East Lothian	U	U	Men.	Ex.	R.P.C. 3rd S. V1 p.647	
1552		24. 4. 1661	East Lothian	U	U	Men.	Ex.	R.P.C. 3rd S. V1 p.647	
1553	Bessie Todrig	28. 5. 1661	East Lothian	F	U	Men.	NK.	R.P.C. 3rd S. V1 p.647	
1554	Bessie Dawsoun	29. 5. 1661	East Lothian	F	U	Men.	NK.	R.P.C. 3rd S. V1 pp. 647-648	
1555	Margaret Kee	29. 5. 1661	East Lothian	F	U	Men.	NK.	R.P.C. 3rd S. V1 pp. 647-648	*
1556	Margaret Bowar	29. 5. 1661	East Lothian	F	U	Men.	NK.	R.P.C.3rd S.V1 pp. 647-648	*

PRIVY COUNCIL CASES									
No.	Name	Date	Place	Sex	Mar. Stat	Trial Stat	Fate	Source	New Case
1557	Margaret Maislet	29. 5. 1661	East Lothian	F	U	Men.	NK.	R.P.C. 3rd S. V1 p.649	*
1558	Jonet Baigbie	29. 5. 1661	East Lothian	F	U	Men.	NK.	R.P.C. 3rd S. V1 p.649	
1559	Issobell Smith	7. 6. 1661	East Lothian Belton	F	U	Men.	NK.	R.P.C. 3rd S. V1 pp. 648-649	
1560	Anna Kemp	7. 6. 1661	East Lothian Belton	F	M	Com.	NK.	R.P.C. 3rd S. V1 pp. 650-651	
1561	Issobell Smythe	7. 6. 1661	East Lothian Pilmore	F	U	Com.	NK.	R.P.C. 3rd S. V1 p.650	
1562	Margaret Ker	7. 6. 1661	East Lothian Belton	F	U	Com.	NK.	R.P.C. 3rd S. V1 pp. 648-649	
1563	Margarett Nisbett	25. 7. 1661	Spott	F	U	Men.	NK.		
1564	Issobell Johnstoun	25. 7. 1661	Gullane	F	U	Com.	NK.	R.P.C. 3rd S. V1 p.11	
1565	Witches	1. 8. 1661	Dudding-ston Liberton	U	U	Com.	NK.	R.P.C. 3rd S. V1 pp. 16-17	
1566	Issobell Crockett	2. 8. 1661	Stirling	F	U	Com.	NK.	R.P.C. 3rd S. V1 pp. 26;75	
1567	Elizabeth Black	2. 8. 1661	Stirling	F	U	Com.	NK.	R.P.C. 3rd S. V1 pp. 26;75	
1568	Kathrin Black	2. 8. 1661	Stirling	F	U	Com.	NK.	R.P.C.3rd S V1 pp.26;75	

PRIVY COUNCIL CASES									
No.	Name	Date	Place	Sex	Mar. Stat	Trial Stat	Fate	Source	New Case
1569	Jean Getwood	6. 9. 1661	Ormiston	F	U	Com.	NK.	R.P.C. 3rd S. V1 p.34	
1570	Jean Hunter	6. 9. 1661	Ormiston	F	U	Com.	NK.	R.P.C. 3rd S. V1 p.34	
1571	Margret Nisbett	6. 9. 1661	Spott	F	U	Com.	NK.	R.P.C. 3rd S. V1 p.34	
1572	Elspeth Vester	6. 9. 1661	Spott	F	U	Com.	NK.	R.P.C. 3rd S. V1 p.34	
1573	James Jonstoun	6. 9. 1661	Spott	M	U	Com.	NK.	R.P.C. 3rd S. V1 p.34	
1574	George Watson	6. 9. 1661	Spott	M	U	Com.	NK.	R.P.C. 3rd S. V1 p.34	
1575	Margaret Elleot	6. 9. 1661	Spott	F	U	Com.	NK.	R.P.C. 3rd S. V1 p.34	
1576	Margaret Moffatt	6. 9. 1661	Spott	F	U	Men.	NK.	R.P.C. 3rd S. V1 p.34	
1577	Elspeth Grinlaw	6. 9. 1661	Queens-ferry	F	U	Com.	NK.	R.P.C. 3rd S. V1 p.91	
1578	Issobell Bathgate	6. 9. 1661	Queens-ferry	F	U	Com.	NK.	R.P.C. 3rd S. V1 p.34	
1579	Margaret Bartan	6. 9. 1661	Queens-ferry	F	U	Com.	NK.	R.P.C. 3rd S. V1 p.34	
1580	Elspeth Halliburton	6. 9. 1661	Ormiston	F	U	Com.	NK.	R.P.C. 3rd S. V1 p.34	
1581	Jean Howison	6. 9. 1661	Ormiston	F	U	Com.	NK.	R.P.C. 3rd S. V1 p.34	

PRIVY COUNCIL CASES									
No.	Name	Date	Place	Sex	Mar. Stat	Trial Stat	Fate	Source	New Case
1582	Mareon Grinlaw	6. 9. 1661	Ormiston	F	U	Com.	NK.	R.P.C. 3rd S. V1 p.34	
1583	William Hog	6. 9. 1661	Ormiston Neatoun	M	U	Com.	NK.	R.P.C. 3rd S. V1 p.34	
1584	Jon Harlaw	6. 9. 1661	Ormiston	M	U	Com.	NK.	R.P.C. 3rd S. V1 p.34	
1585	Katherin Johnstoun	6. 9. 1661	Ormiston	F	U	Com.	NK.	R.P.C. 3rd S. V1 p.34	
1586	Bessie Turnbull	6. 9. 1661	Ormiston	F	U	Com.	NK.	R.P.C. 3rd S. V1 p.34	
1587	Margaret Hawie	6. 9. 1661	Ormiston	F	U	Com.	NK.	R.P.C. 3rd S. V1 p.34	
1588	Jean Knox	6. 9. 1661	Ormiston	F	U	Com.	NK.	R.P.C. 3rd S. V1 p.34	
1589	Jonet Watsone	16. 9. 1661	Dalkeith	F	U	Com.	NK.	R.P.C. 3rd S. V1 p.46	
1590	Bessie Moffat	16. 9. 1661	Dalkeith	F	U	Com.	NK.	R.P.C. 3rd S. V1 p.46	
1591	Kathrin Hunter	16. 9. 1661	Dalkeith	F	U	Com.	NK.	R.P.C. 3rd S. V1 p.46	
1592	George Lumsdeall	2.10. 1661	Inner-leithen	M	U	Com.	NK.	R.P.C. 3rd S. V1 p.62	
1593	Jonnet Scot	2.10. 1661	Inner-leithen	F	U	Com.	NK.	R.P.C. 3rd S. V1 p.62	
1594	Agnes Williamson	7.11. 1661	Samuel-ston	F	U	Men.	NK.	R.P.C. 3rd S. V1 p.78	

PRIVY COUNCIL CASES									
No.	Name	Date	Place	Sex	Mar. Stat	Trial Stat	Fate	Source	New Case
1595	Jonet Curry	7.11. 1661	Pentland	F	S	Com.	NK.	R.P.C. 3rd S. V1 p.74	
1596	Margaret Walker	7.11. 1661	Pentland	F	M	Com.	NK.	R.P.C. 3rd S. V1 p.74	
1597	Issobell Syrie	7.11. 1661	Forfar	F	U	Com.	Ex.	R.P.C. 3rd S. V1 p.74	
1598	Helen Belshes	7.11. 1661	Eyemouth	F	U	Com.	NK.	R.P.C. 3rd S. V1 p.73	
1599	Barbara Hood	7.11. 1661	Eyemouth	F	U	Com.	NK.	R.P.C. 3rd S. V1 p.73	
1600	Adam Robertson	7.11. 1661	Eyemouth	M	U	Men.	Acqu	R.P.C. 3rd S. V1 p.75	
1601	Helen Brinkinrig	7.11. 1661	Crichton	F	U	Com.	NK.	R.P.C. 3rd S. V1 p.74	
1602	Eupham Adair	7.11. 1661	Crichton	F	U	Com.	NK.	R.P.C. 3rd S. V1 p.74	
1603	Kathrin Kay	19.11. 1661	Newburgh	F	U	Com.	NK.	R.P.C. 3rd S. V1 p.90	
1604	Margret Liddell	19.11. 1661	Newburgh	F	U	Com.	NK.	R.P.C. 3rd S. V1 p.90	
1605	Helen Cothall	17.12. 1661	Forfar	F	U	Com.	Ex.	R.P.C. 3rd S. V1 p.122	
1606	Helen Guthrie	17.12. 1661	Forfar	F	U	Com.	Ex.	R.P.C. 3rd S. V1 p.122	
1607	Issobell Smith	17.12. 1661	Forfar	F	U	Com.	Ex.	R.P.C. 3rd S. V1 p.122	

PRIVY COUNCIL CASES

No.	Name	Date	Place	Sex	Mar. Stat	Trial Stat	Fate	Source	New Case
1608	Elspeth Guthrie	17.12. 1661	Forfar	F	U	Com.	Ex.	R.P.C. 3rd S. V1 p.122	
1609	Margaret Dron	9. 1. 1662	Perth Rhynd	F	U	Com.	Ex.	R.P.C. 3rd S. V1 p.132	
1610	Jon Boig	13. 1. 1662	Inverkip	M	U	Com.	NK.	R.P.C. 3rd S. V1 p.162	
1611	Jonet Morison	13. 1. 1662	Inverkip Gourock	F	M	Com.	NK.	R.P.C. 3rd S. V1 p.72	
1612	Beatrix Lyon	13. 1. 1662	Inverkip Fynok	F	M	Com.	NK.	R.P.C. 3rd S. V1 p.162	
1613	Issobell Marshall	16. 1. 1662	Perth Rhynd	F	U	Com.	Ex.	R.P.C. 3rd S. V1 p.137	
1614	Issobell McKessock	16. 1. 1662	Perth Rhynd	F	U	Com.	Ex.	R.P.C. 3rd S. V1 p.137	
1615	Eupham Hougan	16. 1. 1662	Perth Rhynd	F	U	Com.	Ex.	R.P.C. 3rd S. V1 p.137	
1616	Margaret Lauson	23. 1. 1662	Selkirk	F	U	Com.	NK.	R.P.C. 3rd S. V1 p.141	
1617	William Cowan	23. 1. 1662	Inner-wick	M	U	Com.	NK.	R.P.C. 3rd S. V1 p.143	
1618	James Murray	23. 1. 1662	Inner-leithen	M	U	Com.	NK.	R.P.C. 3rd S. V1 p.143	
1619	Jonet Christie	23. 1. 1662	Abernethy	F	U	Com.	NK.	R.P.C. 3rd S. V1 p.141	
1620	Margaret Mathie	23. 1. 1662	Abernethy	F	U	Com.	NK.	R.P.C. 3rd S. V1 p.141	

PRIVY COUNCIL CASES									
No.	Name	Date	Place	Sex	Mar. Stat	Trial Stat	Fate	Source	New Case
1621	Jon Dougleish	23. 1. 1662	Fife Flisk	M	U	Com.	NK.	R.P.C. 3rd S. V1 p.141	
1622	Jonet Edward	23. 1. 1662	Fife Flisk	F	U	Com.	NK.	R.P.C. 3rd S. V1 p.141	
1623	Margaret Dryburgh	23. 1. 1662	Falkland	F	U	Com.	NK.	R.P.C. 3rd S. V1 pp. 142-143	
1624	Elspeth Young	23. 1. 1662	Abernethy	F	U	Com.	NK.	R.P.C. 3rd S. V1 p.141	
1625	Margret Bell	23. 1. 1662	Kinnaird Abdie	F	U	Com.	NK.	R.P.C. 3rd S. V1 p.141	
1626	Elspeth Bruce	23. 1. 1662	Old Lindores Abdie	F	U	Com.	NK.	R.P.C. 3rd S. V1 p.141	
1627	Elspeth Seatoun	23. 1. 1662	Old Lindores Abdie	F	U	Com.	NK.	R.P.C. 3rd S. V1 p.141	
1628	Christian Gray	23. 1. 1662	Kinross	F	M	Com.	NK.	R.P.C. 3rd S. V1 p.142	
1629	Agnes Brounes	23. 1. 1662	Kilmany	F	U	Com.	NK.	R.P.C. 3rd S. V1 p.142	
1630	Jon Brounes	23. 1. 1662	Kilmany	M	U	Com.	NK.	R.P.C. 3rd S. V1 p.142	
1631	Christian Simson	23. 1. 1662	Penicuik	F	U	Com.	NK.	R.P.C. 3rd S. V1 p.73	
1632	Holen Wentoun	23. 1. 1662	Newburgh	F	U	Com.	NK.	R.P.C. 3rd S. V1 p.142	
1633	Issobell Page	23. 1. 1662	Newburgh	F	U	Com.	NK.	R.P.C. 3rd S. V1 p.142	

PRIVY COUNCIL CASES									
No.	Name	Date	Place	Sex	Mar. Stat	Trial Stat	Fate	Source	New Case
1634	Margaret Philp	23. 1. 1662	Newburgh	F	U	Com.	NK.	R.P.C. 3rd S. V1 p.142	
1635	Cristian Anderson	23. 1. 1662	Newburgh	F	U	Com.	NK.	R.P.C. 3rd S. V1 p.142	
1636	Cristian Bonar	23. 1. 1662	Newburgh	F	U	Com.	NK.	R.P.C. 3rd S. V1 p.142	
1637	Bessie Duncan	23. 1. 1662	Luthrie Creich	F	U	Com.	NK.	R.P.C. 3rd S. V1 p.142	
1638	Helen Balfour	23. 1. 1662	Kinross	F	U	Com.	NK.	R.P.C. 3rd S. V1 p.142	
1639	Cristian Steidman	23. 1. 1662	Kinross	F	M	Com.	NK.	R.P.C. 3rd S. V1 p.142	
1640	Jonnet Burrell	23. 1. 1662	Kinross	F	M	Com.	NK.	R.P.C. 3rd S. V1 p.142	
1641	Christian Cuthbertson	-. 1. 1662	Queens-ferry	F	U	Com.	NK.	R.P.C. 3rd S. V1 p.141	
1642	Elizabeth Soutar	6. 2. 1662	Oathlaw	F	U	Com.	NK.	R.P.C. 3rd S. V1 p.153	
1643	Margaret Wishart	6. 2. 1662	Collessie	F	U	Com.	NK.	R.P.C. 3rd S. V1 p.154	
1644	Jonet Staig	6. 2. 1662	Collessie	F	U	Com.	NK.	R.P.C. 3rd S. V1 p.154	
1645	Alison Melvill	6. 2. 1662	Collessie	F	U	Com.	NK.	R.P.C. 3rd S. V1 p.154	
1646	Jonat Mar	6. 2. 1662	Collessie	F	U	Com.	NK.	R.P.C. 3rd S. V1 p.154	

PRIVY COUNCIL CASES									
No.	Name	Date	Place	Sex	Mar. Stat	Trial Stat	Fate	Source	New Case
1647	Elspeth Millar	6. 2. 1662	Collessie	F	U	Com.	NK.	R.P.C. 3rd S. V1 p.154	
1648	Margaret Wylie	13. 2. 1662	Montrose	F	U	Com.	NK.	R.P.C. 3rd S. V1 p.162	
1649	Cristian Wylie	13. 2. 1662	Montrose	F	U	Com.	NK.	R.P.C. 3rd S. V1 p.162	
1650	George Ellies	13. 2. 1662	Forfar	M	U	Com.	NK.	R.P.C. 3rd S. V1 p.162	
1651	Jonet Howat	13. 2. 1662	Forfar	F	U	Com.	NK.	R.P.C. 3rd S. V1 p.162	
1652	Jonet Stout	13. 2. 1662	Forfar	F	U	Com.	NK.	R.P.C. 3rd S. V1 p.162	
1653	Margret Kirktoun	14. 3. 1662	Langton	F	U	Com.	NK.	R.P.C. 3rd S. V1 p.174	
1654	Issobell Mather	14. 3. 1662	Langton	F	U	Com.	NK.	R.P.C. 3rd S. V1 p.174	
1655	Bessie Proffit	14. 3. 1662	Berwick-shire	F	U	Com.	NK.	R.P.C. 3rd S.V1 pp.174-175	
1656	Elspeth Blyth	14. 3. 1662	Berwick-shire	F	U	Com.	NK.	R.P.C. 3rd S.V1 pp.174-175	
1657	Margret Edingtoun	14. 3. 1662	Berwick-shire Foulden	F	U	Com.	NK.	R.P.C. 3rd S.V1 pp.174-175	
1658	Helen Wight	14. 3. 1662	Berwick-shire	F	U	Com.	NK.	R.P.C. 3rd S.V1 pp.174-175	
1659	Margaret Robison	14. 3. 1662	Berwick-shire	F	U	Com.	NK.	R.P.C. 3rd S.V1 pp.174-175	

PRIVY COUNCIL CASES									
No.	Name	Date	Place	Sex	Mar. Stat	Trial Stat	Fate	Source	New Case
1660	Mareon Burnett	14. 3. 1662	Berwick-shire	F	U	Com.	NK.	R.P.C. 3rd S.V1 pp.174-175	
1661	Elspeth Bell	14. 3. 1662	Berwick-shire	F	U	Com.	NK.	R.P.C. 3rd S. V1 pp. 174-175	
1662	Margaret Jonstoun	14. 3. 1662	Berwick-shire Aitoun	F	U	Com.	NK.	R.P.C. 3rd S.V1 pp.174-175	
1663	Elspeth Hay	14. 3. 1662	Berwick-shire	F	U	Com.	NK.	R.P.C. 3rd S.V1 pp.174-175	
1664	Jonet Lauson	14. 3. 1662	Berwick-shire Aitoun	F	U	Com.	NK.	R.P.C. 3rd S.V1 pp.174-175	
1665	Issobell Lauson	14. 3. 1662	Berwick-shire Aitoun	F	U	Com.	NK.	R.P.C.3rd S.V1 pp. 174-175	
1666	Gray	1. 4. 1662	Perth Rhynd	U	U	Men.	Misc	R.P.C.3rd S.V1 pp. 188-189	
1667	Jonet Scrogges	1. 4. 1662	Perth Rhynd	F	U	Men.	Misc	R.P.C.3rd S.V1 pp. 188-189	
1668	Janet Breadheid	1. 4. 1662	Auldearn Balma-keith	F	M	Com.	NK.	R.P.C. 3rd S.V1 p.243	
1669	Cristian Vallandge	1. 4. 1662	Perth Rhynd	F	U	Men.	Misc	R.P.C.3rd S.V1 pp. 188-189	
1670	Elspeth Tod	1. 4. 1662	Perth Rhynd	F	U	Men.	Misc	R.P.C.3rd S.V1 pp. 188-189	
1671	Kathrin Bowar	1. 4. 1662	Perth Rhynd	F	U	Men.	Misc	R.P.C.3rd S.V1 pp. 188-189	
1672	Bessie Simson	2. 4. 1662	Fife Flisk	F	U	Com.	NK.	R.P.C. 3rd S.V1 p.191	

PRIVY COUNCIL CASES									
No.	Name	Date	Place	Sex	Mar. Stat	Trial Stat	Fate	Source	New Case
1673	Kathrin Blak	2. 4. 1662	Fife Eister Flisk	F	U	Com.	NK.	R.P.C. 3rd S. V1 p.191	
1674	Elspeth Anderson	2. 4. 1662	Fife Dinbug	F	U	Com.	NK.	R.P.C. 3rd S. V1 p.191	
1675	Isabel Rutherford	3. 4. 1662	Crook of Devon	F	U	Com.	Ex.	Reid pp.209-252	
1676	Bessie Hendersone	3. 4. 1662	Crook of Devon	F	U	Com.	Ex.	Reid pp.209-252	
1677	Agnes Murie	3.4. 1662	Crook of Devon	F	U	Com.	Ex.	Reid pp.209-252	
1678	Janet Paton	23. 4. 1662	Crook of Devon	F	M	Com.	Ex.	Reid pp.209-252	
1679	Margaret Lister	23. 4. 1662	Crook of Devon	F	M	Com.	Ex.	Reid pp.209-252	
1680	Bessie Neil	23. 4. 1662	Crook of Devon	F	U	Com.	Ex.	Reid pp.209-252	
1681	Robert Wilson	23. 4. 1662	Crook of Devon	M	M	Com.	Ex.	Reid pp.209-252	
1682	Agnes Pitten-dreich	23. 4. 1662	Crook of Devon	F	U	Com.	Acqu	Reid pp.209-252	
1683	Agnes Brugh	23. 4. 1662	Crook of Devon	F	U	Com.	Ex.	Reid pp.209-252	
1684	Janet Paton	5. 5. 1662	Crook of Devon	F	W	Com.	Ex.	Reid pp.209-252	
1685	Margaret Huggon	5. 5. 1662	Crook of Devon	F	W	Com.	NK.	Reid pp.209-252	

PRIVY COUNCIL CASES									
No.	Name	Date	Place	Sex	Mar. Stat	Trial Stat	Fate	Source	New Case
1686	Issobell Anderson	7. 5. 1662	Crailing	F	U	Com.	NK.	R.P.C. 3rd S. V1 pp. 207;245	
1687	Helen Hopkirk	7. 5. 1662	Craillng	F	U	Com.	NK.	R.P.C. 3rd S. V1 pp. 207;245	
1688	Margaret Letch	7. 5. 1662	Inverkip	F	U	Com.	NK.	R.P.C. 3rd S. V1 p.207	
1689	Jonet Hyman	7. 5. 1662	Inverkip	F	U	Com.	NK.	R.P.C. 3rd S. V1 p.207	
1690	Kathrin Scott	7. 5. 1662	Inverkip	F	U	Com.	NK.	R.P.C. 3rd S. V1 p.207	
1691	Mary Lawmont	7. 5. 1662	Inverkip	F	U	Com.	NK.	R.P.C. 3rd S. V1 p.207	
1692	Jonnet Anand	7. 5. 1662	Forgan	F	U	Com.	NK.	R.P.C. 3rd S. V1 p.208	
1693	Elizabeth Clow	7. 5. 1662	Forgan	F	U	Com.	NK.	R.P.C. 3rd S. V1 p.208	
1694	Barbara Innes	7. 5. 1662	Elgin	F	U	Com.	Ex.	R.P.C. 3rd S. V1 p.207	
1695	Margaret Kellie	7. 5. 1662	Elgin	F	U	Com.	Ex.	R.P.C. 3rd S. V1 p.207	
1696	Issobell Simson	7. 5. 1662	Murray Dyke	F	U	Com.	Ex.	R.P.C. 3rd S. V1 p.206	
1697	Issobell Elder	7. 5. 1662	Murray Dyke	F	U	Com.	Ex.	R.P.C. 3rd S. V1 p.206	
1698	Mary Nein Jon Vic Gilchrist	7. 5. 1662	Scatwell	F	U	Com.	NK.	R.P.C.3rd S. V1 p.74	

PRIVY COUNCIL CASES									
No.	Name	Date	Place	Sex	Mar. Stat	Trial Stat	Fate	Source	New Case
1699	Jonet Neill Donald Vic William Vic More	7. 5. 1662	Scatwell	F	U	Com.	NK.	R.P.C. 3rd S. V1 p.207	
1700	Agnes Nein Donald Oig	7. 5. 1662	Scatwell	F	U	Com.	NK.	R.P.C. 3rd S. V1 p.207	
1701	Jonet Airth	7. 5. 1662	Perth-shire	F	U	Com.	NK.	R.P.C. 3rd S. V1 p.208	
1702	Margrat Cruse	7. 5. 1662	Perth-shire	F	U	Com.	NK.	R.P.C. 3rd S. V1 p.208	
1703	Helen Wilson	7. 5. 1662	Perth-shire	F	U	Com.	NK.	R.P.C. 3rd S. V1 p.208	
1704	Issobell Goold	7. 5. 1662	Perth-shire	F	U	Com.	NK.	R.P.C. 3rd S. V1 p.208	
1705	Jonet Toyes	7. 5. 1662	Perth-shire	F	U	Com.	NK.	R.P.C. 3rd S. V1 p.208	
1706	Anna Law	7. 5. 1662	Perth-shire	F	U	Com.	NK.	R.P.C. 3rd S. V1 p.208	
1707	Elspeth Reid	7. 5. 1662	Perth-shire	F	U	Com.	NK.	R.P.C. 3rd S. V1 p.208	
1708	Issobell McKendley	7. 5. 1662	Perth-shire	F	U	Com.	NK.	R.P.C. 3rd S. V1 p.208	
1709	Agnes Ramsay	7. 5. 1662	Perth-shire	F	U	Com.	NK.	R.P.C. 3rd S. V1 p.208	
1710	Jonet Bining	7. 5. 1662	Perth-shire	F	U	Com.	NK.	R.P.C. 3rd S. V1 p.208	
1711	Jonet Young	7. 5. 1662	Perth-shire	F	U	Com.	NK.	R.P.C.3rd S.V1 p.208	

PRIVY COUNCIL CASES									
No.	Name	Date	Place	Sex	Mar. Stat	Trial Stat	Fate	Source	New Case
1712	Jonet Allane	7. 5. 1662	Perth-shire	F	U	Com.	NK.	R.P.C. 3rd S. V1 p.208	
1713	Jonet Mertin	7. 5. 1662	Perth-shire	F	U	Com.	NK.	R.P.C. 3rd S. V1 p.208	
1714	Jonet Robe	7. 5. 1662	Perth-shire	F	U	Com.	NK.	R.P.C. 3rd S. V1 p.208	
1715	Jean Dumbar	7. 5. 1662	Largs	F	U	Com.	NK.	R.P.C. 3rd S. V1 p.208	
1716	Jonet Crauford	7. 5. 1662	Largs	F	U	Com.	NK.	R.P.C. 3rd S. V1 p.208	
1717	Margaret Duff	7. 5. 1662	Inverkip	F	U	Com.	NK.	R.P.C. 3rd S. V1 p.207	
1718	Jean King	7. 5. 1662	Inverkip	F	U	Com.	NK.	R.P.C. 3rd S. V1 p.207	
1719	Margret Rankin Secundus	7. 5. 1662	Inverkip	F	U	Com.	NK.	R.P.C. 3rd S. V1 p.207	
1720	Margret Rankin	7. 5. 1662	Inverkip	F	U	Com.	NK.	R.P.C. 3rd S. V1 p.207	
1721	Margaret McNickell	7. 5. 1662	Bute	F	U	Men.	NK.	Hghd Pps. V3 pp. 3-30	
1722	Jonet McNicoll	7. 5. 1662	Bute	F	U	Men.	NK.	Hghd Pps. V3 pp. 3-30	
1723	Issobell McNicol	7. 5. 1662	Bute	F	U	Men.	NK.	Hghd Pps. V3 pp. 3-30	
1724	Margret McWilliam	7. 5. 1662	Bute	F	U	Com.	NK.	R.P.C. 3rd S. V1 p.208	

PRIVY COUNCIL CASES									
No.	Name	Date	Place	Sex	Mar. Stat	Trial Stat	Fate	Source	New Case
1725	Margret McIllvein	7. 5. 1662	Bute	F	U	Com.	NK.	R.P.C. 3rd S. V1 p.208	
1726	Issobell McCan	7. 5. 1662	Bute	F	U	Com.	NK.	R.P.C. 3rd S. V1 p.208	
1727	Jonet McIlmartin	7. 5. 1622	Bute	F	U	Com.	NK.	R.P.C. 3rd S. V1 p.208	
1728	Margret Edison	7. 5. 1662	Clova	F	U	Com.	Ex.	R.P.C. 3rd S. V1 p.207	
1729	Margaret McLevin	7. 5. 1662	Bute	F	U	Men.	NK.	Hghd Pps. V3 pp. 3-30	
1730	Wife of Soirle McAllexander	7. 5. 1662	Bute	F	M	Men.	NK.	Hghd Pps. V3 pp. 3-30	
1731	Jonat McNeill	7. 5. 1662	Bute	F	U	Men.	NK.	Hghd Pps. V3 pp. 3-30	
1732	Stewart	7. 5. 1662	Bute	F	U	Men.	NK.	Hghd Pps. V3 pp. 3-30	
1733	Marie Stewart	7. 5. 1662	Bute	F	U	Men.	NK.	Hghd Pps. V3 pp. 3-30	
1734	Annie Heyman	7. 5. 1662	Bute	F	U	Men.	NK.	Hghd Pps. V3 pp. 3-30	
1735	Daughter of Allexander McIllmartin	7. 5. 1662	Bute	F	U	Men.	NK.	Hghd Pps. V3 pp. 3-30	
1736	Eldest Son Katherine Moore	7. 5. 1662	Bute	M	U	Men.	NK.	Hghd Pps. V3 pp. 3-30	
1737	Katharine Moore	7. 5. 1662	Bute	F	U	Men.	NK.	Hghd Pps. V3 pp. 3-30	

PRIVY COUNCIL CASES									
No.	Name	Date	Place	Sex	Mar. Stat	Trial Stat	Fate	Source	New Case
1738	Cristine Ballantine	7. 5. 1662	Bute	F	U	Men.	NK.	Hghd Pps V3 pp. 3-30	
1739	Kathrine Frissell	7. 5. 1662	Bute	F	U	Men.	NK.	Hghd Pps V3 pp. 3-30	
1740	McIllmartine	7. 5. 1662	Bute	F	M	Men.	NK.	Hghd Pps V3 pp. 3-30	
1741	Issobell McKaw	7. 5. 1662	Bute	F	M	Men.	NK.	Hghd Pps V3 pp. 3-30	
1742	Patrick McKaw	7. 5. 1662	Bute	M	M	Men.	NK.	Hghd Pps V3 pp. 3-30	
1743	Kathrine Cristell	7. 5. 1662	Bute	F	U	Men.	NK.	Hghd Pps V3 pp. 3-30	
1744	Jonat McConachie	7. 5. 1662	Bute	F	M	Men.	NK.	Hghd Pps V3 pp. 3-30	
1745	John Gely	7. 5. 1662	Bute Barmore	M	M	Men.	NK.	Hghd Pps V3 pp. 3-30	
1746	Kathrine Stewart	7. 5. 1662	Bute	F	U	Men.	NK.	Hghd Pps V3 pp. 3-30	
1747	Jonet Morisoune	7. 5. 1662	Bute	F	U	Men.	NK.	Hghd Pps V3 pp. 3-30	
1748	Margaret McWilliam	7. 5. 1662	Bute	F	U	Men.	NK.	Hghd Pps V3 pp. 3-30	
1749	Isobell Blyth	19. 5. 1662	Auchter-muchty	F	U	Men.	NK.	R.P.C. 3rd S. V1 pp. 209-210	
1750	Jon Grieve	19. 5. 1662	Lauder	M	U	Com.	NK.	R.P.C. 3rd S. V1 p.209	

PRIVY COUNCIL CASES									
No.	Name	Date	Place	Sex	Mar. Stat	Trial Stat	Fate	Source	New Case
1751	Kathrin Scoby	19. 5. 1662	Methven	F	U	Com.	NK.	R.P.C. 3rd S. V1 p.209	
1752	Jonet Gilvory	19. 5. 1662	Methven	F	U	Com.	NK.	R.P.C. 3rd S. V1 p.209	
1753	Maisie Robison	19. 5. 1662	Lauder	F	U	Com.	NK.	R.P.C. 3rd S. V1 p.209	
1754	Agnes Wauch	19. 5. 1662	Lauder	F	U	Com.	NK.	R.P.C. 3rd S. V1 p.209	
1755	John Hay	19. 5. 1662	Inverness	M	U	Men.	Misc	R.P.C. 3rd S. V1 p.210	
1756	Issobell Gowdie	-. 5. 1662	Auldearn Lochloy	F	M	Com.	NK.	R.P.C. 3rd S. V1 p.243	
1757	Margaret McKenzie	12. 6. 1662	Greenock	F	U	Com.	NK.	R.P.C. 3rd S. V1 p.221	
1758	Agnes McGillivor-ich	12. 6. 1662	Nairn	F	M	Com.	NK.	R.P.C. 3rd S. V1 p.221	
1759	Agnes Nic Ean Vane	12. 6. 1662	Nairn	F	U	Com.	NK.	R.P.C. 3rd S. V1 p.221	
1760	Elizabeth Guthrie	12. 6. 1662	Montrose	F	U	Men.	NK.	R.P.C. 3rd S. V1 p.222	
1761	Margaret Guthrie	12. 6. 1662	Montrose	F	U	Men.	NK.	R.P.C. 3rd S. V1 p.222	
1762	Malie Jonstoun	12. 6. 1662	Rox-burgh	F	U	Com.	NK.	R.P.C. 3rd S. V1 p.221	
1763	Bessie Thomson	12. 6. 1662	Rox-burgh	F	U	Com.	NK.	R.P.C. 3rd S. V1 p.221	

PRIVY COUNCIL CASES									
No.	Name	Date	Place	Sex	Mar. Stat	Trial Stat	Fate	Source	New Case
1764	Male Turnbull	12. 6. 1662	Rox-burgh	F	U	Com.	NK.	R.P.C. 3rd S. V1 p.221	
1765	Agnes Quarie	12. 6. 1662	Rox-burgh	F	U	Com.	NK.	R.P.C. 3rd S. V1 p.221	
1766	Issobell Duff	26. 6. 1662	Inver-ness	F	U	Com.	NK.	R.P.C. 3rd S. V1 p.234	
1767	Beak Nein Ean Duy Vic Finley	26. 6. 1662	Conventh Buntoit	M	U	Com.	NK.	R.P.C. 3rd S. V1 pp. 233-234	
1768	Donald Vic McPhaill	26. 6. 1662	Conventh Buntoit	M	U	Com.	NK.	R.P.C. 3rd S. V1 pp. 233-234	
1769	Jonet Nein Ean Cheill	26. 6. 1662	Coventh	F	U	Com.	NK.	R.P.C. 3rd S. V1 pp. 233-234	
1770	Muriall Duy Nein Giliphadrick	26. 6. 1662	Conventh Buntoit	F	U	Com.	NK.	R.P.C. 3rd S. V1 pp. 233-234	
1771	Mary Nein Gowin	26. 6. 1662	Conventh Buntoit	F	M	Com.	NK.	R.P.C. 3rd S. V1 pp. 233-234	
1772	Cristian Nein Phaill	26. 6. 1662	Conventh Buntoit	F	M	Com.	NK.	R.P.C. 3rd S. V1 pp. 233-234	
1773	Cristian Nein Ferquhar Vic	26. 6. 1662	Conventh	F	M	Com.	NK.	R.P.C. 3rd S. V1 pp. 233-234	
1774	Mary Nein Allaster Vic	26. 6. 1662	Conventh Buntoit	F	U	Com.	NK.	R.P.C. 3rd S. V1 pp. 233-234	

PRIVY COUNCIL CASES									
No.	Name	Date	Place	Sex	Mar. Stat	Trial Stat	Fate	Source	New Case
1775	Cormul Nean Ean Duy Vic Conchie Vic Goune	26. 6. 1662	Conventh Buntoit	F	M	Com.	NK.	R.P.C. 3rd S. V1 pp. 233-234	
1776	Jonet Nein Rory Buy	26. 6. 1662	Conventh Buntoit	F	U	Com.	NK.	R.P.C. 3rd S. V1 pp. 233-234	
1777	Kathrin Nein Ean Vic Connell	26. 6. 1662	Conventh Buntoit	F	U	Com.	NK.	R.P.C. 3rd S. V1 pp. 233-234	
1778	Inian Dowie Vic Finley	3. 7. 1662	Strath-glass	F	U	Men.	NK.	R.P.C. 3rd S. V1 p.237	
1779	Cristian Neil Ferquhar Vic Ean Baik McNish	3. 7. 1662	Strath-glass	F	U	Men.	NK.	R.P.C. 3rd S. V1 p.237	
1780	Kathrin Nyn Owan Vic Omnoch	3. 7. 1662	Strath-glass	F	U	Men.	NK.	R.P.C. 3rd S. V1 p.237	
1781	Mary McFinley Vic Come	3. 7. 1662	Strath-glass	F	U	Men.	NK.	R.P.C. 3rd S. V1 p.237	
1782	Jonet Ninian Rory Mie	3. 7. 1662	Strath-glass	F	U	Men.	NK.	R.P.C. 3rd S. V1 p.237	
1783	Kathrin Ninian Ear Vic Ean Culleam	3. 7. 1662	Strath-glass	F	U	Men.	NK.	R.P.C. 3rd S. V1 p.237	
1784	Ninian Coell	3. 7. 1662	Strath-glass	F	U	Men.	NK.	R.P.C. 3rd S. V1 p.237	
1785	Mary Nein Goune Baike	3. 7. 1662	Strath-glass	F	U	Men.	NK.	R.P.C. 3rd S. V1 p.237	
1786	Gormye Grant	3. 7. 1662	Strath-glass	U	U	Men.	NK.	R.P.C. V1 p.237	

PRIVY COUNCIL CASES									
No.	Name	Date	Place	Sex	Mar. Stat	Trial Stat	Fate	Source	New Case
1787	Kathrin Nein Ferquhar McEan	3. 7. 1662	Strath-glass	F	U	Men.	NK.	R.P.C. V1 p.237	
1788	Mary Dollour	3. 7. 1662	Strath-glass	F	U	Men.	NK.	R.P.C. V1 p.237	
1789	Margaret McClean	3. 7. 1662	Strath-glass	F	U	Men.	NK.	R.P.C. V1 p.237	
1790	Jonet McClean	3. 7. 1662	Strath-glass	F	M	Men.	NK.	R.P.C. V1 p.237	
1791	Donald McCleanes	3. 7. 1662	Strath-glass	M	U	Men.	NK.	R.P.C. 3rd S. V1 p.237	
1792	Hectour McCleanes	3. 7. 1662	Strath-glass	M	U	Men.	NK.	R.P.C. 3rd S. V1 p.237	
1793	Agnes Wauch	10. 7. 1662	Lauder	F	U	Com.	NK.	R.P.C. 3rd S. V1 p.73	
1794	Jon Greir	10. 7. 1662	Lauder	M	U	Com.	NK.	R.P.C. 3rd S. V1 p.73	
1795	Christian Greive	21. 7. 1662	Crook of Devon	F	M	Com.	Ex.	Reid pp.209-252	
1796	Janet Brugh	21. 7. 1662	Crook of Devon	F	M	Com.	Ex.	Reid pp.209-252	
1797	Marjory Ritchie	28. 7. 1662	Forfar Inver-arty	F	U	Com.	Ex.	R.P.C. 3rd S. V1 pp. 209;245	
1798	Jean Dumbar	28. 7. 1662	Largs	F	U	Com.	NK.	R.P.C. 3rd S. V1 p.245	
1799	Cristian Small	28. 7. 1662	Largs	F	U	Com.	NK.	R.P.C. 3rd S. V1 p.245	

PRIVY COUNCIL CASES									
No.	Name	Date	Place	Sex	Mar. Stat	Trial Stat	Fate	Source	New Case
1800	Elspeth Jonstoun	28. 7. 1662	Methven	F	U	Com.	NK.	R.P.C. 3rd S. V1 p.244	
1801	Marjory Scott	28. 7. 1662	Largs	F	U	Com.	NK.	R.P.C. 3rd S. V1 p.245	
1802	Agnes Clerk	28. 7. 1662	Largs	F	U	Com.	NK.	R.P.C. 3rd S. V1 p.245	
1803	Marjorie Richie	28. 7. 1662	Inver-arity	F	U	Com.	NK.	R.P.C. 3rd S. V1 pp. 209;245	
1804	Jonet Muir	1. 8. 1662	Inverkip	F	U	Com.	NK.	R.P.C. 3rd S. V1 p.247	
1805	Jonet Holm	1. 8. 1662	Inverkip	F	U	Com.	NK.	R.P.C. 3rd S. V1 p.247	
1806	Agnes Gibson	1. 8. 1662	Inverkip	F	U	Com.	NK.	R.P.C. 3rd S. V1 p.247	
1807	Jonet Alexander	1. 8. 1662	Inverkip	F	U	Com.	NK.	R.P.C. 3rd S. V1 p.247	
1808	Vylet Gray	1. 8. 1662	Inverkip	F	U	Com.	NK.	R.P.C. 3rd S. V1 p.247	
1809	James Bog	1. 8. 1662	Inverkip	M	U	Com.	NK.	R.P.C. 3rd S. V1 p.247	
1810	Margaret Simson	1. 8. 1662	Cromarty	F	U	Com.	NK.	R.P.C. 3rd S. V1 p.248	
1811	Bessie Watson	1. 8. 1662	Cromarty	F	U	Com.	NK.	R.P.C. 3rd S. V1 p.248	
1812	Elspeth Bruce	8. 8. 1662	Forfar Cortachy	F	U	Com.	NK.	R.P.C. 3rd S. V1 p.237	

PRIVY COUNCIL CASES									
No.	Name	Date	Place	Sex	Mar. Stat	Trial Stat	Fate	Source	New Case
1813	Grissell Murray	8. 8. 1662	Bowden	F	U	Com.	NK.	R.P.C. 3rd S. V1 p.250	
1814	Bessie Morison	8. 8. 1662	Bowden	F	U	Com.	NK.	R.P.C. 3rd S. V1 p.250	
1815	Helen Lauder	- - 1662	Dalcove	F	U	Com.	NK.	R.P.C. 3rd S. V1 p.175	*
1816	Margaret Fyfe	- - 1662	Crook of Devon	F	U	Men.	NK.	Reid pp.230-232	*
1817	Elizabeth Dempster	- - 1662	Crook of Devon	F	U	Men.	NK.	Reid pp.230-232	*
1818	Brand	- - 1662	Crook of Devon	U	U	Men.	NK.	Reid pp.230-232	*
1819	Agnes Drysdale	- - 1662	Crook of Devon	F	U	Men.	NK.	Reid pp.230-232	*
1820	Margaret Beveridge	- - 1662	Crook of Devon	F	U	Men.	NK.	Reid pp.230-232	*
1821	Agnes Beveridge	- - 1662	Crook of Devon	F	U	Men.	NK.	Reid pp.230-232	*
1822	Christian Young	- - 1662	Crook of Devon	F	U	Men.	NK.	Reid pp.230-232	*
1823	Margaret McNish	- - 1662	Crook of Devon	F	U	Men.	NK.	Reid p. 226	*
1824	Margaret Young	- - 1662	Crook of Devon	F	U	Men.	NK.	Reid p.226	*
1825	Christian Crieff	- - 1662	Crook of Devon	F	U	Men.	NK.	Reid p.226	*
1826	Isabel Condie	- - 1662	Crook of Devon	F	U	Men.	NK.	Reid p.226	*

PRIVY COUNCIL CASES									
No.	Name	Date	Place	Sex	Mar. Stat	Trial Stat	Fate	Source	New Case
1827	Janet Hird	- - 1662	Crook of Devon	F	U	Men.	NK.	Reid p.226	*
1828	Agnes Sharp	- - 1662	Crook of Devon	F	U	Men.	NK.	Reid pp.220-221	*
1829	Gilleis Hutton	- - 1662	Crook of Devon	F	U	Men.	NK.	Reid pp.220-221	*
1830	Elspet Alexander	- - 1662	Forfar	F	U	Com.	Ex.	Anderson	
1831	Agnes Allene	- - 1662	Crook of Devon	F	U	Men.	NK.	Reid pp.220-221	*
1832	Helen Alexander	13. 2. 1663	Forfar	F	U	Men.	Misc	R.P.C. 3rd S. V1 p.336	*
1833	Mary Rynd	13. 2. 1663	Forfar	F	U	Men.	Misc	R.P.C. 3rd S. V1 p.336	*
1834	Jonet Patoun	6.11. 1663	Eastwood	F	U	Com.	NK.	R.P.C. 3rd S. V1 p.319	
1835	Elizabeth Bruce	24. 3. 1664	Cortachy	F	U	Men.	NK.	R.P.C. 3rd S. V1 p.524	
1836	Margaret Guthrie	9. 5. 1664	Carnbee	F	U	Com.	NK.	R.P.C. 3rd S. V2 p.165	
1837	Barbara Drumond	15. 6. 1664	Kilbride	F	M	Men.	Acqu	R.P.C. 3rd S. V2 pp. 55;172	
1838	Barbara Drumond	18.12. 1664	Kilbride	F	M	Com.	Misc	R.P.C. 3rd S. V1 p.635	
1839	Jonet Howat	11. 1. 1666	Forfar	F	U	Men.	NK.	R.P.C. 3rd S. V2 p.129	

PRIVY COUNCIL CASES									
No.	Name	Date	Place	Sex	Mar. Stat	Trial Stat	Fate	Source	New Case
1840	Several Witches	1. 2. 1666	Shetland	U	U	Men.	NK.	R.P.C. 3rd S. V2 p.136	
1841	Elspeth Guild	8. 9. 1666	Torry- burn	F	U	Com.	NK.	R.P.C. 3rd S. V2 p.192	
1842	Issobell Key	8. 9. 1666	St. Andrews	F	U	Com.	NK.	R.P.C. 3rd S. V2 p.246	
1843	Margret Dobie	8. 9. 1666	Torry- burn	F	U	Com.	NK.	R.P.C. 3rd S. V2 p.192	
1844	Grissel Anderson	8. 9. 1666	Torry- burn	F	U	Com.	NK.	R.P.C. 3rd S. V2 p.192	
1845	Margaret Home	8. 9. 1666	Torry- burn	F	U	Com.	NK.	R.P.C. 3rd S. V2 p.136	
1846	Cristian May	8. 9. 1666	Torry- burn	F	U	Com.	NK.	R.P.C. 3rd S. V2 p.136	
1847	Agnes Broun	8. 9. 1666	Torry- burn	F	U	Com.	NK.	R.P.C. 3rd S. V2 p.192	
1848	Margaret Cowie	8. 9. 1666	Torry- burn	F	U	Com.	NK.	R.P.C. 3rd S. V2 p.192	
1849	Several Persons	25. 2. 1669	Aberdeen	U	U	Men.	NK.	R.P.C. 3rd S. V2 p.614	
1850	Hendry Wilson	8. 4. 1669	Duns	M	U	Com.	NK.	R.P.C. 3rd S. V3 pp.7-8	
1851	Margret Abernethy	15. 7. 1669	Aberdeen Futtie	F	W	Com.	NK.	R.P.C. 3rd S. V3 p.45	
1852	Robert Shevies	15. 7. 1669	Aberdeen	M	U	Com.	NK.	R.P.C. 3rd S. V3 p.45	

PRIVY COUNCIL CASES									
No.	Name	Date	Place	Sex	Mar. Stat	Trial Stat	Fate	Source	New Case
1853	Issobell Spens	15. 7. 1669	Aberdeen	F	W	Com.	NK.	R.P.C. 3rd S. V3 p.45	
1854	Margaret Dury	15. 7. 1669	Aberdeen	F	M	Com.	NK.	R.P.C. 3rd S. V3 p.45	
1855	Certain Persons	-. 8. 1669	Aberdeen	U	U	Men.	Ex.	R.P.C. 3rd S. V3 p.212	
1856	Roy More	30. 9. 1669	Inverness-shire	M	U	Com.	NK.	R.P.C. 3rd S. V3 p.78	
1857	Margaret Neill Vayne	30. 9. 1669	Inverness-shire	F	U	Com.	NK.	R.P.C. 3rd S. V3 p.78	
1858	More Nain Duy McIvers	30. 9. 1669	Inverness-shire	U	U	Com.	NK.	R.P.C. 3rd S. V3 p.78	
1859	Grissell Jaffray	11.11. 1669	Dundee	F	M	Com.	Ex.	R.P.C. 3rd S. V3 p.91	
1860	Mareon Caskie	-. 7. 1670	Lanark	F	U	Com.	NK.	R.P.C. 3rd S. V3 pp. 166;189	
1861	Marget Bigland	16. 1. 1673	Scalloway	F	U	Com.	NK.	R.P.C. 3rd S. V4 p.5	
1862	Molphrie Porteous's Daughter	16. 1. 1673	Scalloway	F	U	Com.	NK.	R.P.C. 3rd S. V4 p.5	
1863	Bessie	16. 1. 1673	Scalloway	F	U	Com.	NK.	R.P.C. 3rd S. V4 p.5	
1864	Suna Voe	16. 1. 1673	Scalloway	F	U	Com.	NK.	R.P.C. 3rd S. V4 p.5	
1865	Jonet Harlaw	7. 4. 1673	Dunbar Innerwick	F	U	Com.	NK.	R.P.C. V10p.28	

PRIVY COUNCIL CASES									
No.	Name	Date	Place	Sex	Mar. Stat	Trial Stat	Fate	Source	New Case
1866	Alesoun Angus	7. 4. 1673	Dunbar	F	U	Com.	NK.	R.P.C. V10 p.28	
1867	Margaret Nicolsoun	28.11. 1675	Birgham	F	U	Com.	NK.	R.P.C. V10 p.414	
1868	Marjory Craig	18. 1. 1677	Pollock-shaws	F	U	Com.	Ex.	R.P.C. 3rd S. V5 pp. 95;104-105	
1869	Bessie Weir	18. 1. 1677	Pollock-shaws	F	M	Com.	Ex.	R.P.C. 3rd S. V5 pp. 95;104-105	
1870	Margret Jackson	18. 1. 1677	Pollock-shaws	F	W	Com.	Ex.	R.P.C. 3rd S. V5 pp. 95;104-105	
1871	Annabell Stewart	18. 1. 1677	Pollock-shaws	F	U	Com.	Misc	R.P.C. 3rd S. V5 pp. 95;104-105	
1872	Jon Stewart	18. 1. 1677	Pollock-shaws	M	U	Com.	Ex.	R.P.C. 3rd S. V5 pp. 95;104-105	
1873	Jonet Mathie	18. 1. 1677	Pollock-shaws	F	U	Com.	NK.	R.P.C. 3rd S. V5 pp. 95;104-105	
1874	Lizzie Mudie	-. 4. 1677	Hadding-ton	F	W	Com.	Ex.	R.P.C. 3rd S. V5 p.161	
1875	Jonet Mun	21. 7. 1677	Dumbarton	F	U	Com.	NK.	R.P.C. 3rd S. V5 p.171	

PRIVY COUNCIL CASES									
No.	Name	Date	Place	Sex	Mar. Stat	Trial Stat	Fate	Source	New Case
1876	Margaret Paterson	21. 7. 1677	Dumbarton	F	U	Com.	NK.	R.P.C. 3rd S. V5 p.171	
1877	Issobell Laing	21. 7. 1677	Dumbarton	F	U	Com.	NK.	R.P.C. 3rd S. V5 p.171	
1878	Christian Donald	21. 7. 1677	Dumbarton	F	U	Com.	NK.	R.P.C. 3rd S. V5 p.171	
1879	Margaret Wright	21. 1. 1677	Dumbarton Balvie	F	U	Com.	NK.	R.P.C. 3rd S. V5 p.171	
1880	Mary Mitchell	-. 7. 1677	Barloch	F	U	Com.	NK.	R.P.C. 3rd S. V5 pp. 187;193	
1881	John Gray	-. 7. 1677	Barloch	M	U	Com.	NK.	R.P.C. 3rd S. V5 pp. 187;193	
1882	Janet McNair	-. 7. 1677	Barloch	F	U	Com.	NK.	R.P.C. 3rd S. V5 pp. 187;193	
1883	Thomas Mitchell	-. 7. 1677	Barloch	M	U	Com.	NK.	R.P.C. 3rd S. V5 pp. 187;193	
1884	Annabell Stewart	10. 8. 1677	Paisley	F	U	Men.	NK.	R.P.C. 3rd S. V5 p.148	
1885	Margaret Phin	10. 8. 1677	Hadding-ton	F	U	Com.	NK.	R.P.C. 3rd S. V5 pp. 231-232	
1886	Marjorie Anderson	2. 5. 1678	Preston-pans	F	U	Com.	NK.	R.P.C. 3rd S. V5 pp 449-450	

PRIVY COUNCIL CASES									
No.	Name	Date	Place	Sex	Mar. Stat	Trial Stat	Fate	Source	New Case
1887	Agnes Kelly	2. 5. 1678	Preston-pans	F	W	Com.	NK.	R.P.C. 3rd S. V5 pp. 449-450	
1888	Gideon Penman	14. 8. 1678	Edinburgh	M	U	Men.	NK.	R.P.C. 3rd S. V5 p.494	
1889	Katharine Liddell	15. 8. 1678	Preston-pans	F	U	Men.	Ex.	R.P.C. 3rd S. V5 p.501	
1890	Helen Laying	13. 9. 1678	Peaston	F	U	Com.	Ex.	R.P.C. 3rd S. V6 p.627	
1891	Marion Veitch	13. 9. 1678	Peaston	F	U	Com.	Ex.	R.P.C. 3rd S. V6 p.627	
1892	Margaret Dods	13. 9. 1678	Peaston	F	U	Com.	Ex.	R.P.C. 3rd S. V6 p.627	
1893	Bessie Eliot	13. 9. 1678	Peaston	F	U	Com.	Ex.	R.P.C. 3rd S. V6 p.627	
1894	Margaret Whyte	9.10. 1678	Lasswade	F	U	Com.	NK.	R.P.C. 3rd S. V6 p.31	
1895	Bessie Bell	9.10. 1678	Lasswade	F	U	Com.	NK.	R.P.C. 3rd S. V6 p.31	
1896	Margaret Liddell	9.10. 1678	Lasswade	F	U	Com.	NK.	R.P.C. 3rd S. V6 p.31	
1897	Margaret Laing	9.10. 1678	Lasswade	F	U	Com.	NK.	R.P.C. 3rd S. V6 p.31	
1898	Janet Douglas	30. 3. 1679	Edinburgh	F	U	Men.	NCP	R.P.C. 3rd S. V6 pp. 650-651	

PRIVY COUNCIL CASES									
No.	Name	Date	Place	Sex	Mar. Stat	Trial Stat	Fate	Source	New Case
1899	Margaret Douglas	2. 3. 1682	Ayr	F	U	Men.	NK.	R.P.C. 3rd S. V7 p.350	
1900	Catharin MacTargett	30. 5. 1688	Dunbar	F	M	Com.	NK.	R.P.C. 3rd S. V13 pp. 245-262	
1901	McQuicken	- - 1695	Inverness	F	M	Com.	Ex.	Ch.V3 p.136	
1902	McRorie	- - 1695	Inverness	F	M	Com.	Ex.	Ch.V3 p.136	
1903	Agnes Naismith	- - 1697	Paisley	F	U	Com.	Ex.	Boul. V2 pp. 51-165	
1904	Margaret Fulton	- - 1697	Paisley	F	U	Com.	Ex.	Boul. V2 pp. 51-165	
1905	Agnes Dess	- - 1697	Ross-shire Kilernan	F	U	Men.	NK.	Sc. Rem.	*
1906	Donald Moir	- - 1697	Ross-shire Kilernan	M	U	Men.	Misc	Sc. Rem.	
1907	Margaret Lang	- - 1697	Paisley	F	U	Com.	Ex.	Boul. V2 pp. 51-165	
1908	Catherine Campbell	- - 1697	Paisley	F	U	Com.	Ex.	Boul. V2 pp. 51-165	
1909	John Reid	- - 1697	Paisley	M	U	Com.	Misc	Boul. V2 pp. 51-165	
1910	James Lindsay	- - 1697	Paisley	M	U	Com.	Ex.	Boul. V2 pp. 51-165	
1911	John Lindsay	- - 1697	Paisley	M	U	Com.	Ex.	Boul. V2 pp. 51-165	

PRIVY COUNCIL CASES									
No.	Name	Date	Place	Sex	Mar. Stat	Trial Stat	Fate	Source	New Case
1912	Unnamed People	- - 1697	Ross-shire Kilernan	U	U	Men.	NK.	Sc. Rem.	*
1913	Agnes Chisolm	- - 1697	Ross-shire Kilernan	F	U	Men.	NK.	Sc. Rem.	*
1914	Agnes Urich	- - 1697	Ross-shire Kilernan	F	U	Men.	NK.	Sc. Rem.	*
1915	Mary Millar	1. 3. 1698	Kirk-cudbright	F	U	Com.	NK.	Ch.V3 p.143	
1916	Elspeth McEwen	1. 3. 1698	Kirk-cudbright	F	U	Com.	Ex.	Ch.V3 p.193	
1917	John Glass	18. 7. 1699	Ross-shire Spittal	M	M	Com.	NCP	Ch.V3 pp.216-217	
1918	Erick Shayme	18. 7. 1699	Ross-shire	M	U	Com.	NK.	Ch.V3 pp.216-217	
1919	Mary Glass	18. 7. 1699	Ross-shire Newtoun	F	U	Com.	NK.	Ch.V3 pp.216-217	
1920	Mary Keill	18. 7. 1699	Ross-shire Ferintosh	F	U	Com.	NK.	Ch.V3 pp.216-217	
1921	Barbara Rassa	18. 7. 1699	Ross-shire Milntown	F	U	Com.	NK.	Ch.V3 pp.216-217	
1922	Christian Gilash	18. 7. 1699	Ross-shire Gilkovie	U	U	Com.	NK.	Ch.V3 pp.216-217	
1923	Barbara Monro	18. 7. 1699	Ross-shire	F	M	Com.	NCP	Ch.V3 pp.216-217	
1924	Margaret Munro	18. 7. 1699	Ross-shire Milntown	F	U	Com.	NCP	Ch.V3 pp. 216-217	

PRIVY COUNCIL CASES									
No.	Name	Date	Place	Sex	Mar. Stat	Trial Stat	Fate	Source	New Case
1925	Agnes Wrath	18. 7. 1699	Ross-shire Kilraine	F	U	Com.	NCP	Ch.V3 pp.216-217	
1926	Agnes Desk	18. 7. 1699	Ross-shire Kilraine	F	U	Com.	NK.	Ch.V3 pp.216-217	
1927	Donald McKulkie	18. 7. 1699	Ross-shire Drumamerk	M	U	Com.	NK.	Ch.V3 pp.216-217	
1928	Lachlan Rattray	-. 7. 1706	Inverness	M	U	Com.	Ex.	Ch.V3 p.302	
1929	George Rattray	-. 7. 1706	Inverness	M	U	Com.	Ex.	Ch.V3 p.302	

PARLIAMENT

No.	Name	Date	Place	Sex	Mar. Stat	Trial Stat	Fate	Source	New Case
1930	Elizabeth Crauford	3. 5. 1601	Samuel-ston	F	U	Com.	NK.	APS V7 p.235	
1931	Certain Persons	30. 5. 1649		U	U	Com.	NK.	APS V6 P2 p.272	
1932	Certain Persons	19. 6. 1649	East Lothian	U	U	Men.	NK.	APS V6 P2 p.490	
1933	Certain Persons	21. 6. 1649	Hadding-ton	U	U	Com.	NK.	APS V6 P2 p.420	
1934	Certain Persons	27. 6. 1649	Dalgety	U	U	Com.	NK.	APS V6 P2 p.498	
1935	Some Witches	5. 7. 1649	Fife East Lothian	U	U	Com.	Ex.	APS V6 P2 p.463	
1936	Certain Witches	12. 7. 1649	Fife & Berwick	U	U	Com.	Ex.	APS V6 P2 p.479	
1937	Some Witches	17. 7. 1649	Corstor-phine	U	U	Com.	NK.	APS V6 P2 p.484	
1938	Certain Persons	21. 7. 1649	Stranraer	U	U	Com.	NK.	APS V6 P2 p.453	
1939	Certain Persons	26. 7. 1649	Humbie Keith-Marshal	U	U	Com.	Ex.	APS V6 P2 p.497	
1940	Certain Persons	30. 7. 1649	Tranent	U	U	Com.	Ex.	APS V6 P2 p.506	
1941	The Wives of Magistrates	31. 7. 1649	Inver-keithing	F	M	Com.	NK.	APS V6 P2 p.510	
1942	Certain Persons	1. 8. 1649	Eyemouth	U	U	Com.	Ex.	APS V6 P2 p.516	
1943	Certain Persons	2. 8. 1649	Hadding-ton Dirleton	U	U	Com.	Ex.	APS V6 P2 p.518	
1944	Certain People	7. 8. 1649	Fife East Lothian	U	U	Com.	NK.	APS V6 P2 p.538	

PARLIAMENT									
No.	Name	Date	Place	Sex	Mar. Stat	Trial Stat	Fate	Source	New Case
1945	Janet Bowis	-.12. 1649	Biggar	F	U	Com.	NK.	Hntr. pp.384 -385	
1946	Many Witches	-.12. 1649		U	U	Com.	Ex.	Balfr. V3 pp. 433-434	
1947	Certain Persons	18. 5. 1650	Ayr	U	U	Com.	NK.	APS V6 P2 p.564	
1948	John McWilliam	2.12. 1650	Dumbarton	M	U	Com.	Ex.	APS V6 P2 p.614	
1949	Margaret McMurich	2.12. 1650	Dumbarton	F	U	Com.	Ex.	APS V6 P2 p.614	
1950	Margaret McInlay	2.12. 1650	Dumbarton	F	U	Com.	Ex.	APS V6 P2 p.614	
1951		2.12. 1650	Dumbarton	U	U	Men.	Acqu	APS V6 P2 p.614	
1952	Isobell Alexander	- - 1650		F	U	Com.	NK.	APS V6 P2 pp. 563-569	
1953	Cristine Umpherstoun	13. 1. 1661	East Lothian	F	M	Com.	NK.	APS V7 p.268	
1954	Mareoun Quheitt	3. 4. 1661	Samuel-ston	F	U	Com.	NK.	APS V7 p.31	
1955	Margaret Hartilman	3. 4. 1661	Samuel-ston	F	U	Com.	NK.	APS V7 p.31	
1956	Elspet Tailzeor	3. 4. 1661	Samuel-ston	F	U	Com.	NK.	APS V7 p.31	
1957	George Milnetown	3. 4. 1661	Samuel-ston	M	U	Men.	NK.	APS V7 p.31	
1958	Helene Deanes	3. 4. 1661	Samuel-ston	F	U	Men.	NK.	APS V7 p.31	
1959	Agnes Williamson	3. 4. 1661	Samuel-ston	F	U	Com.	NK.	APS V7 p.31	
1960	Christian Deanes	3. 4. 1661	Samuel-ston	F	U	Com.	NK.	APS V7 p.31	

PARLIAMENT									
No.	Name	Date	Place	Sex	Mar. Stat	Trial Stat	Fate	Source	New Case
1961	Jonet Carfrae	3. 4. 1661	Samuel-ston	F	U	Com.	NK.	APS V7 p.31	
1962	Elizabeth Sinclair	-. 5. 1661	Samuel-ston	F	U	Com.	NK.	APS V7 p.31	
1963	Jonet Maisson	3. 5. 1661	Samuel-ston	F	U	Men.	NK.	APS V7 p.31	
1964	Anna Pilmure	3. 5. 1661	Samuel-ston	F	U	Men.	NK.	APS V7 p.31	
1965	Patrik Cathie	3. 5. 1661	Samuel-ston	M	M	Com.	NK.	APS V7 p.31	
1966	Elspeth Crauford	3. 5. 1661	Samuel-ston	F	U	Men.	NK.	APS V7 p.31	
1967	Margaret Argyll	3. 5. 1661	Samuel-ston	F	U	Men.	NK.	APS V7 p.31	
1968	Margaret Baptie	3. 5. 1661	Samuel-ston	F	U	Men.	NK.	APS V7 p.31	
1969	Margaret Hall	3. 5. 1661	Preston-pans	F	U	Com.	NK.	APS V7 p.196	
1970	Margaret Auchinmoutie	3. 5. 1661	Preston-pans	F	U	Com.	NK.	APS V7 p.196	
1971	Margaret Butter	3. 5. 1661	Preston-pans	F	U	Com.	NK.	APS V7 p.196	
1972	Christian Blaik	3. 5. 1661	Preston-pans	F	U	Com.	NK.	APS V7 p.196	
1973	Helen Gibson	3. 5. 1661	Preston-pans	F	U	Com.	NK.	APS V7 p.196	
1974	Bessie Doughtie	3. 5. 1661	Fisherow	F	U	Com.	NK.	APS V7 p.197	
1975	Helen Cass	3. 5. 1661	Fisherow	F	U	Com.	NK.	APS V7 p.197	
1976	Robert Crafford	3. 5. 1661	Fisherow	M	U	Com.	NK.	APS V7 p.197	
1977	Issobell Ker	3. 5. 1661	East Lothian	F	U	Com.	NK.	APS V7 pp.196 -197	

PARLIAMENT									
No.	Name	Date	Place	Sex	Mar. Stat	Trial Stat	Fate	Source	New Case
1978	Catherine Coupland	3. 5. 1661	East Lothian	F	U	Com.	NK.	APS V7 pp.196 -197	
1979	Jonnet Wilson	3. 5. 1661	East Lothian	F	U	Com.	NK.	APS V7 pp.196 -197	
1980	Cristine Waderstoun	3. 5. 1661	East Lothian	F	U	Com.	NK.	APS V7 pp.196 -197	
1981	Jonnet Home	3. 5. 1661	East Lothian	F	U	Com.	NK.	APS V7 pp.196 -197	
1982	Agnes Cuthbertsone	3. 5. 1661	East Lothian	F	U	Com.	NK.	APS V7 pp.196 -197	
1983	Elizabeth Crafford	3. 5. 1661	East Lothian	F	U	Com.	NK.	APS V7 pp.196 -197	
1984	Margaret Barclay	3. 5. 1661	East Lothian	F	U	Com.	NK.	APS V7 pp.196 -197	
1985	Jonnet Maisson	3. 5. 1661	East Lothian	F	U	Com.	NK.	APS V7 pp.196 -197	
1986	Issobell Cairnes	9. 5. 1661	Hadding-ton	F	U	Com.	NK.	APS V7 p.199	
1987	Elspeth Lawson	9. 5. 1661	Hadding-ton	F	U	Com.	NK.	APS V7 p.199	
1988	Issobell Ritchardsone	9. 5. 1661	Hadding-ton	F	U	Com.	NK.	APS V7 p.199	
1989	Elspeth Bailie	9. 5. 1661	Hadding-ton	F	U	Com.	NK.	APS V7 p.199	
1990	Issobel Steills	9. 5. 1661	Hadding-ton	F	M	Com.	NK.	APS V7 p.199	
1991	Nical Steills	9. 5. 1661	Hadding-ton	M	M	Com.	NK.	APS V7 p.199	
1992	Jonnet Douglas	22. 5. 1661	Fisherow	F	U	Com.	NK.	APS V7 p.233	

PARLIAMENT									
No.	Name	Date	Place	Sex	Mar. Stat	Trial Stat	Fate	Source	New Case
1993	Katherine Cruikshank	22. 5. 1661	Fisherow	F	U	Com.	NK.	APS V7 p.233	
1994	Agnes Patersone	22. 5. 1661	Fisherow	F	U	Com.	NK.	APS V7 p.233	
1995	Bessie Fouler	22. 5. 1661	Fisherow	F	U	Com.	Ex.	APS V7 p.233	
1996	Agnes Aird	22. 5. 1661	Preston-pans	F	U	Com.	NK.	APS V7 p.233	
1997	Jonnet Gray	22. 5. 1661	Preston-pans	F	U	Com.	NK.	APS V7 p.233	
1998	Katherine Coupland	28. 5. 1661	Samuel-ston	F	U	Com.	NK.	APS V7 p.235	
1999	Margaret Bannatyne	28. 5. 1661	Samuel-ston	F	U	Com.	NK.	APS V7 p.235	
2000	Jonnet Wilson	28. 5. 1661	Samuel-ston	F	U	Com.	NK.	APS V7 p.235	
2001	Cristine Watherston	28. 5. 1661	Samuel-ston	F	U	Com.	NK.	APS V7 p.235	
2002	Jonet Wast	6. 6. 1661	Samuel-ston	F	M	Com.	NK.	APS V7 p.248	
2003	Rot Scott	6. 6. 1661	Samuel-ston	M	U	Com.	NK.	APS V7 p.248	
2004	Susanna Bannatyne	6. 6. 1661	Samuel-ston	F	U	Com.	NK.	APS V7 p.248	
2005	Cristine Blak	6. 6. 1661	Samuel-ston	F	U	Com.	NK.	APS V7 p.248	
2006	Issobell Thomsone	6. 6. 1661	Samuel-ston	F	U	Com.	NK.	APS V7 p.248	
2007	Issobel Cathie	6. 6. 1661	Samuel-ston	F	U	Com.	NK.	APS V7 p.248	
2008	Barbara Scot	6. 6. 1661	Samuel-ston	F	U	Com.	NK.	APS V7 p.248	
2009	James Welsh	6. 6. 1661	Samuel-ston	M	U	Com.	NK.	APS V7 p.248	

PARLIAMENT									
No.	Name	Date	Place	Sex	Mar. Stat	Trial Stat	Fate	Source	New Case
2010	Issobell Johnstoun	7. 6. 1661	East Lothian	F	U	Com.	NK.	APS V7 p.247	
2011	Bessie Knox	7. 6. 1661	East Lothian	F	U	Com.	NK.	APS V7 p.247	
2012	Euphame Bartlenan	13. 6. 1661	East Lothian	F	U	Com.	NK.	APS V7 p.268	
2013	Marion Ingrame	13. 6. 1661	East Lothian Newtown	F	U	Com.	NK.	APS V7 p.268	
2014	Jonet Hog	13. 6. 1661	Linton	F	U	Com.	NK.	APS V7 p.268	
2015	Jonnet Gibesone	13. 6. 1661	Liberton	F	U	Com.	NK.	APS V7 p.268	
2016	Marion Craig	13. 6. 1661	Liberton	F	U	Com.	NK.	APS V7 p.268	
2017	Margaret Handesyd	13. 6. 1661	Liberton	F	U	Com.	NK.	APS V7 p.268	
2018	Christine Thomson	13. 6. 1661	Liberton	F	U	Com.	NK.	APS V7 p.268	
2019	Margaret Hill	13. 6. 1661	Liberton	F	U	Com.	NK.	APS V7 p.268	
2020	Susanna Baillie	13. 6. 1661	Liberton	F	U	Com.	NK.	APS V7 p.268	
2021	John Ramsay	28. 6. 1661	Niddry	M	U	Com.	NK.	APS V7 p.283	
2022	Jonet Gibson	28. 6. 1661	Niddry	F	U	Com.	NK.	APS V7 p.283	
2023	Jeane Gibson	28. 6. 1661	Niddry	F	U	Com.	NK.	APS V7 p.283	
2024	Katherine Purdie	28. 6. 1661	Niddry	F	U	Com.	NK.	APS V7 p.283	
2025	Agnes Hill	28. 6. 1661	Niddry	F	U	Com.	NK.	APS V7 p.283	
2026	Jonnet Cleghorne	28. 6. 1661	Niddry	F	U	Com.	NK.	APS V7 p.283	

PARLIAMENT									
No.	Name	Date	Place	Sex	Mar. Stat	Trial Stat	Fate	Source	New Case
2027	Grissel Young	28. 6. 1661	Niddry	F	U	Com.	NK.	APS V7 p.283	
2028	Jonnet Young	28. 6. 1661	Niddry	F	U	Com.	NK.	APS V7 p.283	
2029	Sarah Ramage	28. 6. 1661	Niddry	F	U	Com.	NK.	APS V7 p.283	
2030	Jonnet Nidrie	12. 7. 1661	Gilmerton	F	U	Com.	NK.	APS V7 p.336	
2031	Agnes Bowie	12. 7. 1661	Gilmerton	F	U	Com.	NK.	APS V7 p.336	
2032	Christine Bell	12. 7. 1661	Gilmerton	F	U	Com.	NK.	APS V7 p.336	
2033	Gilbert Wynd	12. 7. 1661	Gilmerton	F	U	Com.	NK.	APS V7 p.336	
2034	Margaret Watson	12. 7. 1661	Gilmerton	F	U	Com.	NK	APS V7 p.336	
2035	Bessie Wilson	12. 7. 1661	Gilmerton	F	U	Com.	NK.	APS V7 p.336	
2036	Margaret Rid	12. 7. 1661	Gilmerton	F	U	Com.	NK.	APS V7 p.336	
2037	Jonnet Matheson	12. 7. 1661	Gilmerton	F	U	Com.	NK.	APS V7 p.336	

COMMITTEE OF ESTATES									
No.	Name	Date	Place	Sex	Mar. Stat	Trial Stat	Fate	Source	New Case
2038	Jeane Craig	20. 4. 1649	Tranent	F	M	Com.	NK.	RCE PA11/8 p.49	*
2039	Robert Maxwell	2. 5. 1649	Little Fordell	M	U	Com.	NK.	RCE PA11/8 p.62	*
2040	Janet Fairlie	4. 5. 1649	Kelso	F	M	Com.	NK.	RCE PA11/8 p.68	*
2041	Libra Watt	11. 5. 1649	Grange-pans	F	U	Com.	NK.	RCE PA11/8 p.72	*
2042	Agnes Scobie	11. 5. 1649	Murrays	F	M	Com.	NK.	RCE PA11/8 p.72	*
2043	Margaret Somervell	11. 5. 1649	Murrays	F	U	Com.	NK.	RCE PA11/8 p.72	*
2044	Catherine Wilson	11. 5. 1649	Grange-pans	F	U	Com.	NK.	RCE PA11/8 p.72	*
2045	Agnes Asfleck	23. 5. 1649	Tranent	F	U	Com.	NK.	RCE PA11/8 p.90	*
2046	Margaret Allan	23. 5. 1649	Long-niddrie	F	U	Com.	NK.	RCE PA11/8 p.90	*
2047	Agnes Tailzeor	23. 5. 1649	Burrow-stouness	F	M	Com.	NK.	RCE PA11/8 p.90	*
2048	Margaret Gibson	23. 5. 1649	Tranent	F	U	Com.	NK.	RCE PA11/8 p.90	*
2049	Margaret Strachan	23. 5. 1649	Tranent	F	U	Com.	NK.	RCE PA11/8 p.90	*
2050	Catherine Craig	23. 5. 1649	Tranent	F	U	Com.	NK.	RCE PA11/8 p.90	*

COMMITTEE OF ESTATES									
No.	Name	Date	Place	Sex	Mar. Stat	Trial Stat	Fate	Source	New Case
2051	Andrew Johnstoun	16. 8. 1649	Humbrie	M	U	Com.	NK.	RCE PA11/8 p.115	*
2052	Bessie Johnston	16. 8. 1649	Humbie	F	U	Com.	NK.	RCE PA11/8 p.115	*
2053	Marion Lawrie	16. 8. 1649	Humbie	F	U	Com.	NK.	RCE PA11/8 p.115	*
2054	Janet Patersone	16. 8. 1649	Humbie	F	U	Com.	NK.	RCE PA11/8 p.115	*
2055	Janet Carnecroce	16. 8. 1649	Lystoun	F	U	Com.	NK.	RCE PA11/8 p.115	*
2056	Patrick Andersone	16. 8. 1649	Paistoun	M	U	Com.	NK.	RCE PA11/8 p.114	*
2057	Margaret Pringle	16. 8. 1649	Paistoun	F	U	Com.	NK.	RCE PA11/8 p.114	*
2058	Margaret Murray	16. 8. 1649	Humbrie	F	U	Com.	NK.	RCE PA11/8 p.115	*
2059	James Dalgleish	21. 8. 1649	Pencait-land	M	U	Com.	NK.	RCE PA11/8 p.137	*
2060	William Scots	21. 8. 1649	Corstor-phine	M	U	Com.	NK.	RCE PA11/8 p.123	*
2061	Bessie Scots	21. 8. 1649	Corstor-phine	F	U	Com.	NK.	RCE PA11/8 p.123	*
2062	Rachael Horseburgh	28. 8. 1649	Pencait-land	F	U	Com.	NK.	RCE PA11/8 p.137	*
2063	Marion Durie	28. 8. 1649	Inner-keithen	F	U	Com.	NK.	RCE PA11/8 p.135	*

COMMITTEE OF ESTATES									
No.	Name	Date	Place	Sex	Mar. Stat	Trial Stat	Fate	Source	New Case
2064	Marion Broune	28. 8. 1649	W Pencait-land	F	U	Com.	NK	RCE PA11/8 p.137	*
2065	Elizabeth Wilson	28. 8. 1649	W Pencait-land	F	U	Com.	NK.	RCE PA11/8 p.137	*
2066	Marion Broune	28. 8. 1649	Woodhall	F	U	Com.	NK.	RCE PA11/8 p.137	*
2067	Geilles Wood	28. 8. 1649	Pencait-land	F	U	Com.	NK.	RCE PA11/8 p.137	*
2068	Janet Thomesone	-. 8. 1649		F	U	Com.	NK.	RCE PA11/8 p.101	*
2069	Isobel Keith	7. 9. 1649	Keith-marshall	F	U	Com.	NK.	RCE PA11/8 p.143	*
2070	Rachael Forrester	7. 9. 1649	Hadding-ton	F	U	Com.	NK.	RCE PA11/8 p.143	*
2071	Janet Robertsone	7. 9. 1649	Caridne	F	U	Com.	NK.	RCE PA11/8 p.144	*
2072	Jeane Walker	7. 9. 1649	Caridne	F	U	Com.	NK.	RCE PA11/8 p.143	*
2073	Elspet Douglas	7. 9. 1649	Hadding-ton	F	U	Com.	NK.	RCE PA11/8 p.143	*
2074	John Forrester	7. 9. 1649	Larstoun	M	U	Com.	NK.	RCE PA11/8 p.143	*
2075	Janet Nicolsone	7. 9. 1649	Neither-hailes	F	U	Com.	NK.	RCE PA11/8 p.143	*
2076	Janet Small	7. 9. 1649	Caridne	F	U	Com.	NK.	RCE PA11/8 p.144	*

COMMITTEE OF ESTATES									
No.	Name	Date	Place	Sex	Mar. Stat	Trial Stat	Fate	Source	New Case
2077	Margaret Blair	7. 9. 1649	Caridne	F	U	Com.	NK.	RCE PA11/8 p.144	*
2078	Catherine Allan	7. 9. 1649	Caridne	F	U	Com.	NK.	RCE PA11/8 p.144	*
2079	Katherine Hendersoun	14. 9. 1649	Chirne-syde	F	U	Com.	NK.	RCE PA11/8 p.163	*
2080	Marioun Robertsoun	14. 9. 1649	Chirne-syde	F	U	Com.	NK.	RCE PA11/8 p.163	*
2081	Beatrix Young	14. 9. 1649	Chirne-syde	F	U	Com.	NK.	RCE PA11/8 p.163	*
2082	Janet Gray	14. 9. 1649	Chirne-syde	F	U	Com.	NK.	RCE PA11/8 p.163	*
2083	Margaret Lyis	14. 9. 1649	Gallow-sheiles	F	U	Com.	NK.	RCE PA11/8 p.163	*
2084	Jonet Speid	14. 9. 1649	Dalkeith	F	U	Com.	NK.	RCE PA11/8 p.163	*
2085	Marioun Lyis	14. 9. 1649	Gallow-sheiles	F	U	Com.	NK.	RCE PA11/8 p.163	*
2086	Thomas Wilson	14. 9. 1649	Gallow-sheills	M	U	Com.	NK.	RCE PA11/8 p.163	*
2087	Agnes Forsyth	14. 9. 1649	Borthwick	F	U	Com.	NK.	RCE PA11/8 p.163	*
2088	Margaret Adinstoun	27. 9. 1649	Borthwick	F	U	Com.	NK.	RCE PA11/8	*
2089	Margaret Dick	27. 9. 1649	Borthwick	F	U	Com.	NK.	RCE PA11/8	*

COMMITTEE OF ESTATES									
No.	Name	Date	Place	Sex	Mar. Stat	Trial Stat	Fate	Source	New Case
2090	Janet Gibb	27. 9. 1649	Borthwick	F	U	Com.	NK.	RCE PA11/8	*
2091	Agnes Lason	27. 9. 1649	Queens-ferry	F	U	Com.	NK.	RCE PA11/8	*
2092	Christian Symead	27. 9. 1649	Queens-ferry	F	U	Com.	NK.	RCE PA11/8	*
2093	Agnes Waterson	27. 9. 1649	Brunt-island	F	U	Com.	NK.	RCE PA11/8	*
2094	Elspet Ronaldson	27. 9. 1649	Brunt-island	F	U	Com.	NK.	RCE PA11/8	*
2095	Janet Murray	27. 9. 1649	Brunt-island	F	U	Com.	NK.	RCE PA11/8	*
2096	Agnes Johnston	27. 9. 1649	Pencait-land	F	U	Com.	NK.	RCE PA11/8	*
2097	Janet Cockburn	27. 9. 1649	Pencait-land	F	U	Com.	NK.	RCE PA11/8	*
2098	Marjorie Hoy	27. 9. 1649	Pencait-land	F	U	Com.	NK.	RCE PA11/8	*
2099	Marjorie Temple	27. 9. 1649	Pencait-land	F	U	Com.	NK.	RCE PA11/8	*
2100	Margaret Hamilton	27. 9. 1649	Pencait-land	F	U	Com.	NK.	RCE PA11/8	*
2101	Cristian Forrest	27. 9. 1649	Pencait-land	F	U	Com.	NK.	RCE PA11/8	*
2102	Agnes Cairns	27. 9. 1649	Pencait-land	F	U	Com.	NK.	RCE PA11/8	*

COMMITTEE OF ESTATES									
No.	Name	Date	Place	Sex	Mar. Stat	Trial Stat	Fate	Source	New Case
2103	James Gourlay	27. 9. 1649	Pencait-land	M	U	Com.	NK.	RCE PA11/8	*
2104	Margaret Johnston	27. 9. 1649	Borthwick	F	U	Com.	NK.	RCE PA11/8	*
2105	Margaret Dalgleish	4.10. 1649	Lauder	F	U	Com.	NK.	RCE PA11/8	*
2106	Issobel Raich	4.10. 1649	Lauder	F	U	Com.	NK.	RCE PA11/8	*
2107	Christian Smith	4.10. 1649	Lauder	F	U	Com.	NK.	RCE PA11/8	*
2108	Isobel Brotherstane	4.10. 1649	Birkin-syde	F	U	Com.	NK.	RCE PA11/8	*
2109	Janet Lyes	4.10. 1649	Wedderlie	F	U	Com.	NK.	RCE PA11/8	*
2110	John Bronne	4.10. 1649	Bourhous	M	U	Com.	NK.	RCE PA11/8	*
2111	Robert Grieve	4.10. 1649	Lauder	M	U	Com.	NK.	RCE PA11/8	
2112	Janet Turnet	9.10. 1649	Sherrefs-hall	F	W	Com.	NK.	RCE PA11/8	*
2113	Margaret Barbour	16.10. 1649	Woolnut	F	W	Com.	NK.	RCE PA11/8	*
2114	Jonot Thomson	16.10. 1649	Edinstoun	F	M	Com.	NK.	RCE PA11/8	*
2115	Agnes Thomson	16.10. 1649	Crictoun	F	U	Com.	NK.	RCE PA11/8	*

COMMITTEE OF ESTATES									
No.	Name	Date	Place	Sex	Mar. Stat	Trial Stat	Fate	Source	New Case
2116	Issobell Brauckinrigg	16.10. 1649	Crictoun	F	U	Com.	NK.	RCE PA11/8	*
2117	Helen Atcheson	16.10. 1649	Crictoun	F	U	Com.	NK.	RCE PA11/8	*
2118	Katherine Fisher	16.10. 1649	Gallow-shiels	F	U	Com.	NK.	RCE PA11/8	*
2119	Marg Olvertheu	24.10. 1649	Paiston	F	U	Com.	NK.	RCE PA11/8	*
2120	John Steill	24.10. 1649	Paistoun?	M	U	Com.	NK.	RCE PA11/8	*
2121	Robert Acreskine	24.10. 1649	Borthwick	M	U	Com.	NK.	RCE PA11/8	*
2122	James Hugo	24.10. 1649	Borthwick	M	M	Com.	NK.	RCE PA11/8	*
2123	Christiane Steill	24.10. 1649	Borthwick	F	U	Com.	NK.	RCE PA11/8	*
2124	Agnes Gray	24.10. 1649	Ormies-toun	F	M	Com.	NK.	RCE PA11/8	*
2125	Janet Sympson	24.10. 1649	Ormies-toun	F	U	Com.	NK.	RCE PA11/8	*
2126	Marione Hulybuirton	24.10. 1649	Ormies-ton	F	U	Com.	NK.	RCE PA11/8	*
2127	Jonet Paton	24.10. 1649	Paiston	F	M	Com.	NK.	RCE PA11/8	*
2128	Christian Thomesone	6.11. 1649	Lyntoun	F	M	Com.	NK.	RCE PA11/8 p.187	*

COMMITTEE OF ESTATES									
No.	Name	Date	Place	Sex	Mar. Stat	Trial Stat	Fate	Source	New Case
2129	Katharine Govan	6.11. 1649	Wrae	F	U	Com.	NK.	RCE PA11/8 p.187	*
2130	Janet Hendersone	6.11. 1649	Wlyth	F	U	Com.	NK.	RCE PA11/8 p.187	*
2131	Janet Broune	6.11. 1649	Nether-vrile	F	M	Com.	NK.	RCE PA11/8 p.187	*
2132	Joan Greig	6.11. 1649	Grange	F	U	Com.	NK.	RCE PA11/8 p.187	*
2133	Jeaine Rennick	6.11. 1649	Grange	F	U	Com.	NK.	RCE PA11/8 p.187	*
2134	Joane Forrester	6.11. 1649	Kirk-urdie	F	U	Com.	NK.	RCE PA11/8 p.187	*
2135	John Simpsone	6.11. 1649	Kirk-urdie	M	U	Com.	NK.	RCE PA11/8 p.187	*
2136	Janet Andersone	6.11. 1649	Drumal-zeartoun	F	U	Com.	NK.	RCE PA11/8 p.187	*
2137	Marion Watsone	6.11. 1649	Cardone	F	U	Com.	NK.	RCE PA11/8 p.187	
2138	Isobell Dalmahoy	6.11. 1649	Deanes	F	U	Com.	NK.	RCE PA11/8 p.187	*
2139	Bessie Veitch	6.11. 1649	Milne of Stobo	F	U	Com.	NK.	RCE PA11/8 p.187	*
2140	Janet Markirdon	6.11. 1649	Nether-vrile	F	U	Com.	NK.	RCE PA11/8 p.187	*
2141	John Sibbald	6.11. 1649	Ladievrde	M	U	Com.	NK.	RCE PA11/8 p.187	*

COMMITTEE OF ESTATES									
No.	Name	Date	Place	Sex	Mar. Stat	Trial Stat	Fate	Source	New Case
2142	Jeane Abbot	6.11. 1649	Lyne	F	M	Com.	NK.	RCE PA11/8 p.187	*
2143	Marion Watson	6.11. 1649	Peebles	F	U	Com.	NK.	RCE PA11/8 p.187	
2144	Elspet Gray	6.11. 1649	Beigend	F	U	Com.	NK.	RCE PA11/8 p.187	*
2145	Marion Laidlaw	6.11. 1649	Stain-hope	F	U	Com.	NK.	RCE PA11/8 p.187	*
2146	Alexander Warrock	6.11. 1649	Bolden	M	U	Com.	NK.	RCE PA11/8 p.187	*
2147		6.11. 1649	Brugh-toun-sheilles	F	U	Com.	NK.	RCE PA11/8 p.187	*
2148	Bessie Gibson	6.11. 1649	Cardone	F	U	Com.	NK.	RCE PA11/8 p.187	*
2149	Helen Thomesone	6.11. 1649	Lyne	F	M	Com.	NK.	RCE PA11/8 p.187	*
2150	Robert Garner	6.11. 1649	Crichtoun	M	U	Com.	NK.	RCE PA11/8 p.188	*
2151	Nicoles Wichtman	6.11. 1649	Crichtoun	M	U	Com.	NK.	RCE PA11/8 p.163	*
2152	James Doddes	6.11. 1649	Lyntoun	M	M	Com.	NK.	RCE PA11/8 p.187	*
2153	Elspet Grahame	6.11. 1649	Nethr-vrile Stobo	F	U	Com.	NK.	RCE PA11/8 p.187	
2154	Marion Veitch	6.11. 1649	Nether-vrile	F	M	Com.	NK.	RCE PA11/8 p.187	

COMMITTEE OF ESTATES									
No.	Name	Date	Place	Sex	Mar. Stat	Trial Stat	Fate	Source	New Case
2155	Margaret Whyte	6.11. 1649	Over-hartstame	F	U	Com.	NK.	RCE PA11/8 p.187	*
2156	Isobel Greene	6.11. 1649	Over-hartstame	F	U	Com.	NK.	RCE PA11/8 p.187	*
2157	Bessie Eumond	6.11. 1649	Peebles	F	M	Com.	NK.	RCE PA11/8 p.187	*
2158	Margaret Wilsone	6.11. 1649	Peebles	F	W	Com.	NK.	RCE PA11/8 p.187	*
2159	Anna Hay	6.11. 1649	Romanno	F	U	Com.	NK.	RCE PA11/8 p.187	*
2160	Isobell Alexander	6.11. 1649	Scotstoun	F	U	Com.	NK.	RCE PA11/8 p.187	
2161	Christian Thomesone	6.11. 1649	Scotstoun	F	U	Com.	NK.	RCE PA11/8 p.187	*
2162	John Leishman	6.11. 1649	Strike-feild	M	U	Com.	NK.	RCE PA11/8 p.187	*
2163	Reidfoord	6.11. 1649	Stobo	U	U	Com.	NK.	RCE PA11/8 p.187	*
2164	Janet Laidlaw	6.11. 1649	Tueid-hopefoot	F	M	Com.	NK.	RCE PA11/8 p.187	*
2165	Janet Johnstone	6.11. 1649	New-bottle	F	U	Com.	NK.	RCE PA11/8 p.187	*
2166	Elizabeth Simpsone	6.11. 1649	Dysert	F	U	Com.	NK.	RCE PA11/8 p.187	*
2167	Katherine Hyislop	6.11. 1649	Stain-hope	F	U	Com.	NK.	RCE PA11/8 p.187	*

COMMITTEE OF ESTATES									
No.	Name	Date	Place	Sex	Mar. Stat	Trial Stat	Fate	Source	New Case
2168	Elspet Skongall	9.11. 1649	Whitting-hame	F	U	Com.	NK.	RCE PA11/8 p.189	*
2169	Beatrix Dolsoun	9.11. 1649	Whitting-hame	F	U	Com.	NK.	RCE PA11/8 p.189	*
2170	Marion Hongman	9.11. 1649	Whitting-hame	F	U	Com.	NK.	RCE PA11/8 p.189	*
2171	Euphane Dysdaill	9.11. 1649	Cairdie	F	U	Com.	NK.	RCE PA11/8 p.189	*
2172	Elizabeth Grahame	9.11. 1649	Kil-winning	F	U	Com.	NK.	RCE PA11/8 p.189	*
2173	Marion Twedie	13.11. 1649	Nether-bide	F	U	Com.	NK.	RCE PA11/8 p.190	
2174	Geilles Gilchrist	13.11. 1649	Leith	F	U	Com.	NK.	RCE PA11/8 p.190	*
2175	Bessie Wilsoun	20.11. 1649	Jedburgh	F	U	Com.	NK.	RCE PA11/8 p.195	*
2176	Katharine Frater	20.11. 1649	Melder-staines	F	U	Com.	NK.	RCE PA11/8 p.195	*
2177	Aliesone Clench	20.11. 1649	Clockpen	F	U	Com.	NK.	RCE PA11/8 p.195	*
2178	Issobel Word	20.11. 1649	Jedburgh	F	U	Com.	NK.	RCE PA11/8 p.195	*
2179	Jeane Olipher	20.11. 1649	Jedburgh	F	U	Com.	NK.	RCE PA11/8 p.195	*
2180	Jeane Binning	20.11. 1649	Caridyne	F	U	Com.	NK.	RCE PA11/8 p.195	*

COMMITTEE OF ESTATES									
No.	Name	Date	Place	Sex	Mar. Stat	Trial Stat	Fate	Source	New Case
2181	George Common	20.11. 1649	Obertoun	M	U	Com.	NK.	RCE PA11/8 p.195	*
2182	Marionn Turnbull	20.11. 1649	Jedburgh	F	U	Com.	NK.	RCE PA11/8 p.195	*
2183	Issobel Siatoun	20.11. 1649	Jedburghe	F	U	Com.	NK.	RCE PA11/8 p.195	*
2184	Jonet Young	20.11. 1649	Jedburghe	F	U	Com.	NK.	RCE PA11/8 p.195	*
2185	David/Doine Tullie	20.11. 1649	Jedburghe	M	U	Com.	NK.	RCE PA11/8 p.195	*
2186	Agnes Andersoun	20.11. 1649	Newtoun	F	U	Com.	NK.	RCE PA11/8 p.196	*
2187	Margaret Andersone	20.11. 1649	Crailling	F	S	Com.	NK.	RCE PA11/8 p.195	*
2188	Marionn Thyn	20.11. 1649	Litgert-woale	F	U	Com.	NK.	RCE PA11/8 p.195	*
2189	Agnes Davidsonne	20.11. 1649	Jedburghe	F	U	Com.	NK.	RCE PA11/8 p.195	*
2190	Issobell Allansone	20.11. 1649	Jedburghe	F	U	Com.	NK.	RCE PA11/8 p.195	*
2191	Adam Midleinst	20.11. 1649	Jedburghe	M	U	Com.	NK.	RCE PA11/8 p.195	*
2192	Johne Andersone	20.11. 1649	Cailling	M	U	Com.	NK.	RCE PA11/8 p.195	*
2193	Adam Kirktoun	20.11. 1649	Jedburghe	M	U	Com.	NK.	RCE PA11/8 p.195	*

COMMITTEE OF ESTATES									
No.	Name	Date	Place	Sex	Mar. Stat	Trial Stat	Fate	Source	New Case
2194	Anna Alexander	-.11. 1649	Ladievrde	F	M	Com.	NK.	RCE PA11/8 p.187	*
2195	Jeane Threipland	-.11. 1649	Bolden	F	M	Com.	NK.	RCE PA11/8 p.187	*
2196	Margaret Andersone	4.12. 1649	Heriot	F	U	Com.	NK.	RCE PA11/9 p.5	*
2197	Jonet Baird	4.12. 1649	Keith	F	U	Com.	NK.	RCE PA11/9 p.5	*
2198	Bigs Flayer	4.12. 1649	Karing-toun	F	U	Com.	NK.	RCE PA11/9 p.4	*
2199	Margaret Fothringhame	4.12. 1649	Keith	F	U	Com.	NK.	RCE PA11/9 p.5.	*
2200	Janet Contes	4.12. 1649	Peebles	F	U	Com.	NK.	RCE PA11/9 p.4	*
2201	Janet Wallace	4.12. 1649	Dalsngn-toun	F	U	Com.	NK.	RCE PA11/9 p.5	*
2202	Catharine Bonie	4.12. 1649	Qraviell-wood	F	U	Men.	NK.	RCE PA11/9 p.5	*
2203	Catharine Bonie	7.12. 1649	Qraviell-wood	F	U	Com.	NK.	RCE PA11/9 p.5	*
2204	Agnes Fleck	8.12. 1649	Unterstoun	F	U	Com.	NK.	RCE PA11/9 p.7	*
2205	Christian Rennick	8.12. 1649	Unterstoun	F	U	Com.	NK.	RCE PA11/9 p.7	*
2206	Barbara Patersone	8.12. 1649	Unterstoun	F	U	Com.	NK.	RCE PA11/9 p.7	*

COMMITTEE OF ESTATES									
No.	Name	Date	Place	Sex	Mar. Stat	Trial Stat	Fate	Source	New Case
2207	Catharine Veitch	8.12. 1649	Keith-Marshall	F	U	Com.	NK.	RCE PA11/7 p.7	*
2208	Marion Durie	- - 1649	Dunferme-ling	F	U	Com.	NK.	RCE PA11/8 p.157	*

OTHER CASES									
No.	Name	Date	Place	Sex	Mar. Stat	Trial Stat	Fate	Source	New Case
2209	Witches	- - 1560	Elgin	U	U	Men.	NK.	Mack. p.120	
2210	Jonet Lindsay	1. 9. 1562	Stirling	F	U	Men.	NCP	R.Brgh Stir. p.80	
2211	Isabell Keir	1. 9. 1562	Stirling	F	U	Men.	NCP	R.Brgh Stir. p.80	
2212	Two Witches	-. 7. 1563		U	U	T	Ex.	Laing V2 p.391	
2213		-. 7. 1563	East Lothian	U	U	T	Ex.	Laing V2 p.391	
2214		- - 1563	Fife & Galloway	F	U	Men.	NK.	Bk.Krk Sc.p.44	
2215		- - 1563	Fife & Galloway	F	U	Men.	NK.	Bk.Krk Sc.p.44	
2216	Four Women	- - 1563	Fife & Galloway	F	U	Men.	NK.	Bk.Krk Sc.p.44	
2217		- - 1563	Fife & Galloway	F	U	Men.	NK.	Bk.Krk Sc.p.44	
2218	Agnes Fergusson	- - 1568	Arbroath	F	U	Men.	Misc	Hay p.129	
2219	Nic Neville	- - 1569	St. Andrews	M	U	T	Ex.	Ch. V1 p.60	
2220	Witches	- - 1569	St. Andrews Dundee	U	U	Men.	Ex.	Duir. Rem.Occ. p.145	
2221	Lyon King of Arms	- - 1569	St. Andrews	M	U	T	Ex.	Pit.V1 p.510	
2222		28. 4. 1572	St. Andrews	U	U	Men.	Ex.	Bann. p.339	
2223	Mariorye Smytht	25. 1. 1575	St. Andrews	F	M	Men.	Misc	Reg.Krk Sess.St. And.p.414	

OTHER CASES									
No.	Name	Date	Place	Sex	Mar. Stat	Trial Stat	Fate	Source	New Case
2224	Anne Gib	- - 1580	Montrose	F	U	Men.	Acqu	Sp.Cl. Misc. V4 p.65	
2225	Bessy Robertsoune	26.10. 1581	St. Andrews	F	U	Men.	NK.	Reg.Krk Sess.St, And.p.455	
2226	James Findlaw	- - 1586		M	U	T	NK.	Dal. p.373	
2227	Unnamed Witches	- - 1586		U	U	T	NK.	Dal. p.373	
2228	Cruddal Watson	2.11. 1589	Perth	F	M	Men.	NK.	G.231	*
2229	Cuddal	2.11. 1589	Tirseppie	F	M	T	Acqu	Spott. Misc. V2 pp. 266-267	
2230	Sundry Witches	23. 7. 1590	Edinburgh	U	U	T	NK.	Calndr St.Pps V10 p.365	
2231	Barbara Keand or Card Alias Leslie	18. 9. 1590	Aberdeen	F	U	Men.	Ex.	Sp.Cl. Misc. V2 p.65	
2232	Several People	28. 2. 1592	Edinburgh	U	U	T	Ex.	Calndr St. Pps V10 p.649	
2233	Richard Graham	28. 2. 1592	Edinburgh	M	U	T	Ex.	Birrell	
2234	Patrick MacGueire	- - 1592	Calder	M	U	Men.	NK.	G.307	*
2235	Morven Witches	- - 1592	Calder	U	U	Men.	NK.	G.307	*
2236	Witches	23. 6. 1595	Edinburgh	U	U	T	Ex.	Calndr St.Pps V2 p.684	
2237	Agnes Meluill	10. 9. 1595	St. Andrews	F	U	T	Ex.	Reg.Krk Sess.St. And.p.800	

OTHER CASES

No.	Name	Date	Place	Sex	Mar. Stat	Trial Stat	Fate	Source	New Case
2238	Jonet Lochequoir	10. 9. 1595	St. Andrews	F	U	T	Ex.	Reg.Krk Sess.St. And.p.800	
2239	Elspot Gilchrist	10. 9. 1595	St. Andrews	F	U	T	Ex.	Reg.Krk Sess.St. And.p.800	
2240		15.10. 1595	Caithness	U	U	Men.	NCP	Calndr St.Pps V2 p.697	
2241		15.10. 1595	Caithness	U	U	Men.	NCP	Calndr St.Pps V2 p.697	
2242		15.10. 1595	Caithness	U	U	Men.	NCP	Calndr St.Pps V2 p.697	
2243	Isobel Cockie	19. 2. 1596	Aberdeen	F	U	Men.	Ex.	Sp.Cl. Misc. V1 pp. 110-116	
2244	Johnnet Wischert Wishart	-. 2. 1596	Aberdeen	F	M	Men.	Ex.	Sp.Cl. Misc.V1 pp.84-102	
2245	Thomas Leyis	-. 2. 1596	Aberdeen	M	U	Men.	Ex.	Sp.Cl. Misc. V1 pp. 84-102	
2246	Bessie Thom	9. 3. 1596	Aberdeen	F	U	Men.	Ex.	Sp.Cl. Misc.V1 pp.166-167,170	
2247	Issobel Barroun	9. 3. 1596	Aberdeen	F	U	Men.	Ex.	Sp.Cl. Misc. V1 pp. 168-170	
2248	John Leyis	22. 3. 1596	Aberdeen	M	M	Men.	Acqu	Sp.Cl. Misc.V1 pp.102-104	
2249	Jonet Leyis	22. 3. 1596	Aberdeen	F	U	Men.	NK.	Sp.Cl. Misc.V1 pp.102-104	

OTHER CASES

No.	Name	Date	Place	Sex	Mar. Stat	Trial Stat	Fate	Source	New Case
2250	Violat Leyis	22. 3. 1596	Aberdeen	F	U	Men.	NK.	Sp.Cl. Misc. V1 pp. 102-104	
2251	Elspet Leyis	22. 3. 1596	Aberdeen	F	U	Men.	NK.	Sp.Cl. Misc. V1 pp. 102-104	
2252	Isobell Manteith	- - 1596	Aberdeen	F	U	Men.	Misc	Sp.Cl. Misc. V1 p.52	
2253	Margaret Reid	- - 1596	Ayr	F	U	Men.	NCP	Ptson V1 p.101	
2254	Christen Michell	9. 3. 1597	Aberdeen	F	U	Men.	Ex.	Sp.Cl. Misc.V1 pp.164-165,170	
2255	Margrat Innes	9. 3. 1597	Aberdeen	F	U	Men.	NK.	Sp.Cl. Misc.V1 pp.164-165,170	
2256	Agnes Smelie	6. 4. 1597	Aberdeen	F	U	Men.	Ex.	Sp.Cl. Misc. Prf.p.53	
2257	Elspet Smithe	6. 4. 1597	Tillilair Aberdeen	F	U	Men.	NK.	Sp.Cl. Misc.V VI p.184-185	
2258	Jannet Guisett	6. 4. 1597	Aberdeen	F	U	Men.	NK.	Sp.Cl. Misc. V1 pp. 184-185	
2259	Jannet Smithe	6. 4. 1597	Cushtrie Aberdeen	F	U	Men.	NK.	Sp.Cl. Misc. V1 pp. 184-185	
2260	Margaret Sherare	6. 4. 1597	Kincardine Aberdeen	F	U	Men.	NK.	Sp.Cl. Misc. V1 pp. 184-185	

OTHER CASES									
No.	Name	Date	Place	Sex	Mar. Stat	Trial Stat	Fate	Source	New Case
2261	Agnes Forbes	6. 4. 1597	W.Kindar-dyne Aberdeen	F	U	Men.	NK.	Sp.Cl. Misc. V1 pp. 184-185	
2262	Katherine Fergus	6. 4. 1597	Aberdeen	F	U	Men.	Ex.	Sp.Cl. Misc. V1 Prf. p.53	
2263	Katherine Alshenour	6. 4. 1597	Aberdeen	F	U	Men.	Ex.	Sp.Cl. Misc. V1 Prf. p.53	
2264	Issobell Robie	6. 4. 1597	Aberdeen	F	U	Men.	NK.	Sp.Cl. Misc. V1 pp. 184-185	
2265	Duplicates	2258							
2266	Duplicates	2259							
2267	Marioun Grant	15. 4. 1597	Aberdeen	F	U	Men.	Ex.	Sp.Cl. Misc.V1 pp.170-172,177	
2268	Elspett Moiness	15. 4. 1597	Aberdeen	F	U	Men.	NK.	Sp.Cl. Misc.V1 pp.174-175,177	
2269	Christen Millar	15. 4. 1597	Aberdeen	F	U	Men.	NK.	Sp.Cl. Misc.V1 pp.174-175,177	
2270	Janet Degeddes	15. 4. 1597	Aberdeen	F	U	Men.	NK.	Sp.Cl. Misc.V1 pp.174-175,177	
2271	Marioun Wod Alias Erss	15. 4. 1597	Aberdeen	F	U	Men.	NK.	Sp.Cl. Misc. V1 p.176	

OTHER CASES									
No.	Name	Date	Place	Sex	Mar. Stat	Trial Stat	Fate	Source	New Case
2272	Margrat Smyth	15. 4. 1597	Aberdeen	F	U	Men.	NK.	Sp.Cl. Misc.V1 pp.174-175,177	
2273	Hellie Pennie	15. 4. 1597	Aberdeen	F	U	Men.	NK.	Sp.Cl. Misc.V1 pp.174-175,177	
2274	Christian Reid	15. 4. 1597	Aberdeen	F	U	Men.	NK.	Sp.Cl. Misc.V1 pp.172-174,177	
2275	Katherine Gerard	15. 4. 1597	Aberdeen	F	U	Men.	Ex.	Sp.Cl. Misc.V1 pp.174-175,177	
2276	Helene Frasser	21. 4. 1597	Aberdeen	F	U	Men.	NK.	Sp.Cl. Misc.V1 pp.105-110	
2277	Maly Skein	21. 4. 1597	Aberdeen	F	U	Men.	NK.	Sp.Cl. Misc.V1 pp.105-110	
2278	Malye Fynnie	21. 4. 1597	Aberdeen	F	U	Men.	NK.	Sp.Cl. Misc.V1 p.106	
2279	Jonat Davidsone	24. 4. 1597	Aberdeen	F	U	Men.	NK.	Sp.Cl. Misc.V1 pp.150-151,156	
2280	Margrat Og	24. 4. 1597	Aberdeen	F	U	Men.	NK.	Sp.Cl. Misc.V1 pp.142-145,154	
2281	Thomas Ego	25. 4. 1597	Aberdeen	M	U	Men.	NK.	Sp.Cl. Misc.V1 pp.182-184	
2282	Katherine Ferreis	25. 4. 1597	Aberdeen	F	U	Men.	NK.	Sp.Cl. Misc.V1 pp.182-184	

OTHER CASES									
No.	Name	Date	Place	Sex	Mar. Stat	Trial Stat	Fate	Source	New Case
2283	Bessie Paull	25. 4. 1597	Aberdeen	F	U	Men.	NK.	Sp.Cl. Misc.V1 pp.182-184	
2284	Issobel Forbes	25. 4. 1597	Aberdeen	F	U	Men.	NK.	Sp.Cl. Misc.V1 pp.182-184	
2285	Elspett Strathauchyn	25. 4. 1597	Aberdeen	F	U	Men.	NK.	Sp.Cl. Misc.V1 pp.182-184	
2286	Ellen Gray	27. 4. 1597	Aberdeen	F	U	Men.	NK.	Sp.Cl. Misc.V1 pp.125-128	
2287	Agnes Wobster	28. 4. 1597	Aberdeen	F	U	Men.	NK.	Sp.Cl. Misc.V1 pp.128-130	
2288	Jonat Lucas	-. 4. 1597	Aberdeen	F	U	Men.	NCP	Sp.Cl. Misc.V1 pp.147-149,156	
2289	Duplicates	2257							
2290	Issobell Oige	-. 4. 1597	Aberdeen	F	M	Men.	Ex.	Sp.Cl. V1 pp. 151-152, 155	
2291	Issobel Richie	-. 4. 1597	Aberdeen	F	U	Men.	NK.	Sp.Cl. Misc.V1 pp.140-142,154	
2292	Gilbert Bairnis	23. 5. 1597	Aberdeen	M	U	Men.	NK.	Sp.Cl. Misc.V5 p.69	
2293	A Great No. of People	-. 6. 1597	Thr'out Scotland	U	U	T	Ex.	Chron. Perth	

OTHER CASES									
No.	Name	Date	Place	Sex	Mar. Stat	Trial Stat	Fate	Source	New Case
2294	Many Witches	13. 7. 1597	St. Andrews	U	U	T	Ex.	Calndr St.Pps V2 p.739	
2295		19.10. 1597	Stirling	F	U	T	NK.	R.Brgh Stir. p.86	
2296	Maige Saythe	21.10. 1597	Aberdeen	F	U	Men.	NK.	Sp.Cl. Misc.V1 p.125	
2297	Meriorie Mutche	21.11. 1597	Aberdeen	F	U	Men.	NK.	Sp.Cl. Misc.V1 pp.131-133	
2298	Maige Saythe	- - 1597	Aberdeen	F	U	Men.	NK.	Sp.Cl. Misc.V1 pp.117-125	
2299	Elspet Graye	- - 1597	Aberdeen	F	U	Men.	NK.	Sp.Cl. Misc.V1 pp.117-125	
2300		- - 1597	Aberdeen	U	U	Men.	NK.	G.283	*
2301	Helene Makkie Alias Suppak	- - 1597	Aberdeen	F	U	Men.	NCP	Sp.Cl. Misc.V1 p.114 & Prf.p.52	
2302	Andro Man	- - 1597	Aberdeen	M	U	Men.	Ex.	Sp.Cl. Misc.V1 pp.117-125	
2303	Gilbert Fidlar	- - 1597	Aberdeen	M	U	Men.	Acqu	Sp.Cl. Misc.V1 pp.137-138	
2304	Jonat Leisk	- - 1597	Aberdeen	F	U	Men.	Acqu	Sp.Cl. Misc. V1 pp. 134-137	

OTHER CASES									
No.	Name	Date	Place	Sex	Mar. Stat	Trial Stat	Fate	Source	New Case
2305	Unnamed Persons	– – 1597	Aberdeen	U	U	Men.	NK.	Sp.Cl. Misc.V1 pp.117-125	
2306	Agnes Fren or Frem	– – 1597	Aberdeen	F	U	Men.	NK.	Sp.Cl. Misc.V1 pp.191-192	
2307	Janet Smyth	– – 1597	Burnt-island	F	U	T	Ex.	Ross p.343	
2308	Margaret Atkin	– – 1597	Balweary	F	U	T	Ex.	His.Ch. Sc. V3 pp.66-67	
2309	Many People	– – 1597	Perth-shire Atholl	U	U	T	NK.	Ch. V1 p.290	
2310	Janet Allane	– – 1598	Burnt-island	F	U	T	Ex.	Ross p.344	
2311	Unnamed Persons	– – 1598	Aberdeen	U	U	Men.	NK.	G.92	*
2312	Geillis Gray	22. 2. 1599	Crail	F	U	T	Misc	Reg.St. And. Pres.	
2313	William Murray	– – 1599	Leith	M	U	T	NCP	Bk Old Edin.Cl. V34 p.6	*
2314	Catherine McTeir	– – 1602	Dun-donald	F	U	Men.	Misc	Ptson V1 P2 p.425	
2315	Telis Trail	25. 9. 1603	Aberdeen	U	U	Men.	NK.	Sp.Cl. Misc. 151 p.29	*
2316	Donald Moir	2.12. 1603	Inverness	M	U	T	Ex.	R.Inv. V2 pp. 19-22	
2317	Nicole	– – 1603	Shetland	F	U	T	NK.	Dal. p.521	

OTHER CASES									
No.	Name	Date	Place	Sex	Mar. Stat	Trial Stat	Fate	Source	New Case
2318		- - 1603	Aberdeen	U	U	Men.	NK.	G.122	*
2319	Dorathie Oliphant	6. 6. 1604	Kirk-caldy	F	U	T	NCP	R.Brgh Kirk. pp. 154-155	
2320	Elspet Cant	-. 6. 1604	Elgin	F	U	Men.	NCP	R.Elgin V2 p.125	
2321	Gelis Gray	-. 6. 1604	Elgin	F	U	Men.	NCP	R.Elgin V2	
2322	Andrew Duncane	15. 7. 1604	Shetland	M	U	T	NK.	Dal. p.521	
2323	Helen Gib	- - 1604	Aberdeen	F	U	Men.	Acqu	G.233-234	*
2324	Katheren Flint	2. 3. 1606	Edinburgh	F	U	T	NK.	Dal. p.665	
2325	Elspet Adame	26. 5. 1606	Aberdeen	F	U	Men.	NK.	Abdn Sh. C.R. V2 p.86	*
2326	Margaret Scot	12. 5. 1607	Selkirk	F	U	Men.	NK.	Craig-Brown V1 p.180	
2327	Isabell Smith	23. 7. 1607	Banchory	F	U	T	Misc	Hndrson pp.216-217	
2328		15. 1. 1608	Aberdeen	U	U	Men.	NK.	Abdn Sh. C.R. V2 p.109	*
2329	Agnes Chapman	11.11. 1608	Aberdeen	F	U	Men.	NK.	Abdn Sh. C.R. V2 p.140	*
2330	Persons	- - 1609	Peeble-shire	U	U	Men.	NK.	G.92	*
2331	Persons	- - 1609	Glasgow	U	U	Men.	NK.	G.92	*
2332	Persons	- - 1609	Stirling-shire	U	U	Men.	NK.	G.92	*

OTHER CASES									
No.	Name	Date	Place	Sex	Mar. Stat	Trial Stat	Fate	Source	New Case
2333	Malcome Toir	-.12. 1610	Stirling	M	U	Men.	NCP	G.306	*
2334	John Faw	21. 8. 1612	Orkney	M	U	T	NK.	Dal. p.235	
2335	Elspet Cuming	19.12. 1613	Elgin	F	U	Men.	NK.	G.235	*
2336	George Semple	- - 1613	Killalan	M	U	Men.	Misc	G.309	*
2337	Grissal Gillaspie	21. 2. 1614	Stirling	F	U	Men.	NK.	Dal. p.264	
2338	Issobell Johnestowne	- - 1614	St. Andrews	F	U	T	NK.	Min.Syn. Fife 1611-1687 p.76	
2339	Agnes Anstruther	- - 1614	St. Andrews	F	U	T	NK.	Min.Syn. Fife 1611-1687 pp.61;76	
2340	Marion Murdoch	30. 5. 1615	Perth	F	U	Men.	NK.	Bk. Perth p.270	
2341	Katherine Bigland	7. 6. 1615	Orkney	F	U	T	Ex.	Mait.Cl. Misc.V2 pp.167-168	
2342	Catherine McNiven	- - 1615	Creiff	F	U	T	Ex.	Frgson No.112	
2343	Catherine Caray	3.1. 1616	Orkney	F	U	T	NK.	Dal. pp. 118;126; 536	
2344	Jonet Irving	5. 3. 1616	Orkney	F	U	T	NK.	Dal. pp. 243;554-555	
2345	Elspeth Reoch	12. 3. 1616	Orkney	F	U	T	Ex.	Mait.Cl. Misc.V2 pp.181-191	
2346	Oliver Leask	19. 3. 1616	Orkney	M	U	T	NK.	Dal. p.126	

OTHER CASES									
No.	Name	Date	Place	Sex	Mar. Stat	Trial Stat	Fate	Source	New Case
2347	Magnus Linday	-. 6. 1616	Orkney	M	M	T	NK.	Rog.V3 p.300	
2348	Agnes Scottie	-. 6. 1616	Orkney	F	U	T	NK.	Rog.V3 p.298	
2349	Geillis Sclaitter	-. 6. 1616	Orkney	F	M	T	NK.	Rog.V3 p.300	
2350	Patrick Petersone	12. 9. 1616	Shetland	M	U	T	NK.	Dal. p.378	
2351	Marjorie Ritchie	12. 9. 1616	Shetland	F	U	T	NK.	Dal. p.378	
2352	Barbara Thomas Dochter	2.10. 1616	Shetland Delting	F	U	T	NK.	Dal.pp. 118-119	
2353	Katherine Jones Dochter	2.10. 1616	Shetland	F	U	T	NK.	Dal.pp. 6;106; 532	
2354	Jonka Dyneis	2.10. 1616	Shetland	F	U	T	NK.	Dal.pp. 34;443; 474;630; 631	
2355	Geordie Archobald	- - 1616	Selkirk	M	U	T	NK.	Craig-Brown V1 p.181	
2356	Agnes Tulloch	- - 1616	Orkney	F	U	T	NK.	Rog.V3 pp.301-302	
2357	Helen Wallas	- - 1616	Orkney	F	U	T	NK.	Rog.V3 pp.302-303	
2358	William Gude	- - 1616	Orkney	M	U	T	NK.	Rog.V3 pp.299-300	
2359	Jonet Short	13. 5. 1617	Edinburgh Holyrood	F	U	Men.	NK.	Dal. p.522	
2360	Bessie Finlaysoune	16. 7. 1618	Logie	F	U	Men.	NK.	Frgson V1 p.87	

OTHER CASES									
No.	Name	Date	Place	Sex	Mar. Stat	Trial Stat	Fate	Source	New Case
2361		- - 1618	Ayr	U	U	Men.	NCP	G.247	*
2362		- - 1619	Aberdeen	U	U	Men.	NK.	G.247	*
2363	Marion Marnow	- - 1619		F	U	Men.	Ex.	His. Brechin p.73	
2364	James Stewart	18.12. 1620	Perth	M	U	Men.	NK.	Bk. Perth p.298	
2365	Witches	3. 1. 1623	Perth	U	U	Men.	NK.	Bk. Perth p.303	
2366	Bessie Smythe	10. 7. 1623	Lesh-mahagow	F	U	Men.	Acqu	Hntr p.379	
2367	Janet Barny	24. 7. 1623	Perth	F	U	Men.	NK.	G.212	*
2368	Witches	24. 7. 1623	Perth	F	U	Men.	NK.	G.213	*
2369	Katherine Grant	25.11. 1623	Orkney	F	U	T	Ex.	Dal.pp. 7-8;90; 107;124; 126-127; 388;390	
2370		- - 1623	Perth	U	U	Men.	NCP	G.247	*
2371	Margaret Hormscleuch	- - 1623	Perth	F	U	Men.	Misc	G.218-219	*
2372	Christian Gow	24. 4. 1624	Orkney	F	U	T	NK.	Dal. p.27	
2373	Janet	5. 5. 1626	Dysart	F	U	Men.	Misc	Dal. p.425	
2374	Bessie Wright	- - 1626	Scone	F	U	T	NK.	Bk. Perth p.207	
2375	Margaret Dalgleish	4. 1. 1627	Peebles	F	U	Men.	NCP	Ch. p.148	

OTHER CASES									
No.	Name	Date	Place	Sex	Mar. Stat	Trial Stat	Fate	Source	New Case
2376	Marioun George	21.10. 1628	Peebles	F	M	Men.	Misc	Buchan V2. p.177	
2377	Marioun McLintock	20.11. 1628	Dumbarton	F	U	Men.	NK.	Irv.V2 p.37	
2378	Katherine Young	- - 1628	Peeble- shire	F	U	Men.	NK.	Ch. p.155	
2379	Agnes Meldrum	- - 1628	Monifieth	F	U	T	NCP	Andrson	*
2380	Bessie Archer	- - 1628	Monifieth	F	U	T	NCP	Andrson	*
2381		- - 1628	Stirling	U	U	Men.	NCP	G.247	*
2382	Janett Weill	- - 1628	Dumbarton	F	M	Men.	NK.	G.323	*
2383	William Mathiesone	1. 3. 1629	Peebles Kirno	M	U	Men.	NK.	Doc. Pbles p.368	
2384	Elspeth Cursetter	29. 5. 1629	Orkney	F	U	T	NK.	Dal.pp 33-34; 150;564	
2385	Jonet Rendall	11.11. 1629	Orkney	F	U	T	Ex.	Ork. & Shet. Flklre pp.103-111	
2386	Jonet Forsyth	-.11. 1629	Orkney Westray	F	U	T	Ex.	Ork. & Shet. Flklre pp.75-80	
2387		- - 1629	Peebles	F	U	T	Ex.	Buchan V2 pp. 177-178	
2388		- - 1629	Peebles	F	U	T	Ex.	Buchan V2 pp. 177-178	
2389		- - 1629	Peebles	F	U	T	Ex.	Buchan V2 pp. 177-178	

OTHER CASES									
No.	Name	Date	Place	Sex	Mar. Stat	Trial Stat	Fate	Source	New Case
2390	Susanna Chancelar	-.10. 1630	Lanark	F	U	T	NK.	Reg. Pres. Lnrk p.7	
2391	Robert Simpson	- - 1630	Lasswade	M	U	Men.	NK.	Aitch. p.21	
2392	George Semple	- - 1630	Paisley	M	U	Men.	Misc	G.310	*
2393	Catie Wilson	- - 1630	Lauder	F	M	T	Misc	Thom. p.204	
2394	James Hall	- - 1630	Aberdeen	M	U	Men.	NK.	Abdn Krk Sess. R. p.111	
2395	Elspet Watsone	18. 9. 1631	Elgin	F	U	T	NCP	R.Elgin V2 p.220	
2396	Walker	5.10 1631	Inver-keithny	U	U	Men.	NK.	Pres.Bk Strath-bogie p.5	
2397	Thomas Murray	-.10. 1631	Inver-keithing	M	M	T	NK.	Pres.Bk Strath-bogie p.5	*
2398	Issobell Traye	-.10. 1631	Inver-keithing	F	M	T	NK.	Pres.Bk Strath-bogie p.5	*
2399	Several People	- - 1631	Bute	U	U	Men.	NK.	G.304	*
2400		12. 1. 1632	Dysart	F	U	Men.	NK.	Pres.Bk Kirk.p.35	
2401	Janet Love	-. 4. 1632	Renfrew	F	U	Men.	NK.	G.361	*
2402	Helen Hamilton	- - 1632	Leith	F	U	Men.	NK.	G.361	*
2403	John Sinclair	30. 1. 1633	Orkney Hoy	M	U	T	NK.	Dal. pp. 179-180	
2404	Thomas Carlips	-. 1. 1633		M	U	Men.	Misc	Spott. Misc.V2 p.63	

OTHER CASES									
No.	Name	Date	Place	Sex	Mar. Stat	Trial Stat	Fate	Source	New Case
2405	Sir John Colquoun of Luss	-. 1. 1633		M	U	Men.	Misc	Spott. Misc.V2 p.63	
2406	Issobell Sinclair	28. 2. 1633	Orkney	F	U	T	Ex.	Dal.pp. 193;470	
2407	James Knarstoun	28. 2. 1633	Orkney	M	U	T	NK.	Dal.pp. 153;377; 508-509; 511;565	
2408	Bessie Skebister	21. 3. 1633	Orkney	F	U	T	Ex.	Dal.pp. 451;470; 474;480; 491 512; 591	
2409	Margaret Chapman	30. 4. 1633	Stirling	F	U	Men.	NK.	Mait.Cl. Misc.V1 pp.472-473	
2410	William Coke	-.12. 1633	Kirk-caldy	M	S	T	Ex.	Webstr pp.113-124	
2411	Alison Dick	-.12. 1633	Kirk-caldy	F	M	T	Ex.	Webstr pp.113-124	
2412	Agnes Chrystie	22. 7. 1634	Stirling	F	U	T	NK.	Dal. p.213	
2413	Janet Taylor Witch of Monza	11.11. 1634	Stirling	F	U	Men.	NCP	Ronald p.354	
2414	Elizabeth Bathcat	- - 1634	Eyemouth	F	U	Men.	Misc	G.324 RPC 2 Ser. V5 pp. 176-177	
2415	Margaret Sandieson	13. 9. 1635	Orkney Sanday	F	U	T	NK.	Dal. p.388	
2416	Helene Isbuster	- - 1635	Orkney	F	U	T	NK.	Dal.pp. 270;307	
2417	Margaret Nicol	27. 8. 1636	Banff	F	U	T	NK.	Ann. Banff	

OTHER CASES									
No.	Name	Date	Place	Sex	Mar. Stat	Trial Stat	Fate	Source	New Case
2418	Margaret Fraser	14. 9. 1636	Aberdeen	F	U	Men.	NK.	Pres.Bk Strath-bogie p.7	
2419	John Patowne	6. 4. 1637	Dysart	M	U	Men.	NK.	Pres.Bk Kirk. p.113	
2420	Issobell Malcolme	12. 4. 1637	Botary	F	U	Men.	Acqu	Pres.Bk Strath-bogie p.15	
2421	Duplicates	2420							
2422	Marioun Grig	19. 7. 1638	Kirk-caldy	F	U	Men.	NK.	Pres.Bk Kirk. p.131	
2423	Christian Wilson	4.10. 1638	Kirk-caldy	F	U	Men.	NK.	Pres.Bk Kirk. p.135	
2424	Janet Durie	27.12. 1638	Kirk-caldy	F	U	T	NK.	Pres.Bk Kirk. pp. 135-136	
2425	Janet Lovie	- - 1639	Brechin	F	U	T	NK.	Andrson	*
2426	Graham	- - 1640	Peebles	U	U	Men.	Ex.	Ch. p.160	
2427	A Number of Witches	- - 1640	Peebles	U	U	Men.	NK.	Ch. p.160	
2428	Malie MacWatt	- - 1640	Culter	F	U	T	Acqu	Ch. pp. 160-161	
2429	Isabel Cuthbertson	- - 1640	Culter	F	U	T	NK.	Ch. pp. 160-161	
2430	Gilbert Robisone	- - 1640	Culter	M	U	T	NK.	Ch. pp. 160-161	
2431	Lillias Bertram	- - 1640	Culter	F	U	T	NK.	Ch. pp. 160-161	
2432	Agnes Muircone	-. 2. 1641	Elgin	F	U	Men.	NK.	G.219	*

OTHER CASES									
No.	Name	Date	Place	Sex	Mar. Stat	Trial Stat	Fate	Source	New Case
2433	Father of James Robesone	21. 4. 1641	Peebles	M	U	Men.	NK.	Buchan V2 p.178	
2434	Mali Lithgow	-. 9. 1641	Skirling	F	U	Men.	NK.	Hntr p.279	
2435	Katherine Mithell	- - 1641	Culross	F	U	T	Ex.	Dal. p.671	
2436	Marion Fisher	-. 2. 1643	Edinburgh	F	U	Men.	Misc	G.219-220	*
2437	Catherine Rowane	5. 3. 1643	Culross	F	U	Men.	NK.	Bev. p.203	*
2438	Thomas Cors	6. 4. 1643	Orkney	M	U	T	NK.	Dal.pp 492;493; 539	
2439	Cristian Marwick	6. 4. 1643	Orkney	F	U	T	NK.	Dal.pp. 5;52; 267	
2440	Cristane Leisk	21. 4. 1643	Orkney	F	U	T	NK.	Dal.pp 59;61; 255	
2441	Helen Hunter	-. 4. 1643	Orkney	F	U	T	NK.	Dal.pp. 109;256; 514	
2442	Elspeth Chalmers	-. 5. 1643	Orkney	F	U	T	NK.	Dal. p.372	
2443	Jonett Fentoun	20. 6. 1643	Dun-fermline	F	U	Men.	Misc	Hndrson p.309	
2444	Isobell Marr	17. 8. 1643	Dun-fermline	F	U	Men.	Misc	Hndrson p.310	
2445	Margaret Balfour	-. 9. 1643	St. Andrews	F	U	Men.	NK.	Lyon V2 p.18	
2446	Isobell Malcolme	4.10. 1643	Moray	F	U	Men.	NK.	Dunbar p.40	
2447	John Shand	4.10. 1643	Moray	M	U	Men.	NK.	Dunbar p.39	

OTHER CASES									
No.	Name	Date	Place	Sex	Mar. Stat	Trial Stat	Fate	Source	New Case
2448	Jonnet Smythe	31.10. 1643	Kinghorn	F	U	Men.	Misc	Min. Krk-Sess. Kinghn p.50	
2449	Katherine Wallace	31.10. 1643	Kinghorn	F	U	Men.	Misc	Min.Krk-Sess. Kinghn p.50	
2450	Wife of John Dawson	3.11. 1643	Pitten-weem	F	M	T	Ex.	Cook pp.49-50	
2451	John Dawson's Wife	3.11. 1643	Pitten-weem	F	M	Men.	Ex.	Cook p.49	
2452	Marion Fisher	16.11. 1643	Edinburgh	F	U	T	NCP	Dal.pp. 27;373; 665	
2453	Margaret Kingow	13.12. 1643	Pitten-weem	F	U	Men.	NK.	Cook p.49	
2454	Margaret Horsburgh	18.12. 1643	Pitten-weem	F	W	T	Ex.	Cook pp. 49-50	
2455	Wife of John Crombie	21.12. 1643	Pitten-weem	F	M	T	Ex.	Cook pp. 49-50	
2456	Janet Barker	28.12. 1643	Edinburgh	F	U	Men.	Ex.	Dal. p.252	
2457	Janet Brown	31.12. 1643	Markinch	F	U	T	NK.	Willis p.31	
2458	Grissel Morris	- - 1643	Dun-fermline	F	U	T	Ex.	Hndrson p.309	
2459	Margaret Brand	- - 1643	Dun-fermline	F	U	T	Ex.	Hndrson p.309	
2460	Katherine Elder	- - 1643	Dun-fermline	F	U	T	Ex.	Hndrson p.309	
2461	Jonet Thomesone	- - 1643	Orkney	F	U	T	NK.	Dal.pp. 32;58-59;73-74;260; 266;271; 593	

OTHER CASES									
No.	Name	Date	Place	Sex	Mar. Stat	Trial Stat	Fate	Source	New Case
2462	William Scottie	- - 1643	Orkney	M	U	T	NK.	Dal.pp. 109;125; 459	
2463	Agnes Kirk	- - 1643	Dun-fermline	F	U	T	Ex.	Hndrson p.309	
2464	Margaret Donaldson	- - 1643	Dun-fermline	F	U	Men.	Ex.	Hndrson p.309	
2465	Isobel Miller	- - 1643	Dun-fermline	F	U	Men.	Ex.	Hndrson p.309	
2466	Agnes Wallace	- - 1643	Crail	F	U	Men.	NK.	Lamont p.6	
2467	Mareon Cumlaquoy	- - 1643	Birsay	F	U	T	NK.	Dal.pp. 8;109; 390;459	
2468	Juenit or Janet Fraser	- - 1643	Shetland	F	U	Men.	Ex.	Hibbert pp.593-602	
2469	Janet Maconachie	- - 1643	Botary Aberdeen	F	U	Men.	NK.	Pres.Bk Strath-bogie p.38	
2470	Duplicates	2469							
2471	Agnes Muresone	3. 1. 1644	Elgin	F	U	Men.	NK.	R.Elgin V1 p.178	
2472	Wife of Archibald Wanderson	12. 1. 1644	Pitten-weem	F	M	T	Ex.	Cook p.50	
2473	Wife of Thomas Wanderson	12. 1. 1644	Pitten-weem	F	M	T	Ex.	Cook p.50	
2474	Agnes Bischope	11. 2. 1644	Mid Calder	F	U	T	Ex.	McCall p.226	
2475	Katherine Wallace	27. 2. 1644	Kinghorn	F	U	T	Ex.	Min.Krk Sess. Kinghn p.50	

OTHER CASES									
No.	Name	Date	Place	Sex	Mar. Stat	Trial Stat	Fate	Source	New Case
2476	Katherine Wallenge	27. 2. 1644	Kinghorn	F	U	Men.	NK.	G.266	*
2477	Patrick Malcolmie	-. 2. 1644	Botary Aberdeen	M	U	Men.	NK.	Pres.Bk Strath-bogie p.50,52	
2478	Duplicates	2477							
2479	Jean Mitchell	1. 3. 1644	Elgin	F	U	Men.	NK.	R.Elgin V2 p.248	
2480	Agnes Vassie	17.11. 1644	Mid Calder	F	U	Men.	Ex.	McCall p.32	
2481	Marioun Gibson	19.11. 1644	Mid Calder	F	U	Men.	Ex.	McCall p.32	
2482	Christian Roch	- - 1644	Pitten-weem	F	U	Men.	Ex.	Laing p.223	
2483	Janet Bruce	- - 1644	Nether William-ston	F	M	T	Ex.	McCall pp.32; 226	
2484	Margaret Ramsay	- - 1644	Leith	F	U	Men.	NK.	G.207	*
2485	Several Persons	- - 1644	Leith	U	U	Men.	NK.	G.207	*
2486	Marion Peebles	- - 1644	Shetland	F	U	T	Ex.	Hibbert pp.593-602	
2487	Bessie Mason	- - 1644	St. Andrews	F	U	Men.	NK.	Min.Syn. Fife p.139	
2488		- - 1644	Leith	U	U	T	Ex.	Ramsay p.71	
2489		- - 1644	Leith	U	U	T	Ex.	Ramsay p.71	
2490	Adam Donaldson	- - 1644	Culross	M	U	Men.	NK.	Bev. pp.208-209	

OTHER CASES									
No.	Name	Date	Place	Sex	Mar. Stat	Trial Stat	Fate	Source	New Case
2491		- - 1644	Leith	U	U	T	Ex.	Ramsay p.71	
2492		- - 1644	Leith	U	U	T	Ex.	Ramsay p.71	
2493		- - 1644	Leith	U	U	T	Ex.	Ramsay p.71	
2494		- - 1644	Leith	U	U	T	Ex.	Ramsay p.71	
2495		- - 1644	Leith	U	U	T	Ex.	Ramsay p.71	
2496		- - 1644	Leith	U	U	T	Ex.	Ramsay p.71	
2497		- - 1644	Leith	U	U	T	Ex.	Ramsay p.71	
2498	Marion Ramsay	- - 1644	Leith	F	U	Men.	NK.	McCall p.33	
2499	Rosina McCoskrie	- - 1644	Kirkcud-bright	F	U	Men.	NK.	Truckell No. 43	*
2500	Wife of John McNaught	- - 1644	Kirkcud-bright	F	M	Men.	Ex.	Truckell No. 43	*
2501	Margaret Sinclar	- - 1644	Kirkcud-bright	F	U	Men.	NK.	Truckell No.43	*
2502	Margaret Clerk	- - 1644	Kirkcud-bright	F	U	Men.	NK.	Truckell No. 43	*
2503	Janet McGowane	- - 1644	Kirkcud-bright	F	U	Men.	NK.	Truckell No. 43	*
2504	Elspeth Cant	- - 1644	Queens-ferry	F	U	T	Ex.	Fyfe pp. 84-101	
2505	Isobel Young	- - 1644	Queens-ferry	F	U	T	Ex.	Fyfe pp. 84-101	
2506	Helen Hill	- - 1644	Queens-ferry	F	M	T	Ex.	Fyfe pp. 84-101	
2507		- - 1644	Barrow-stounes	F	U	T	Ex.	Sinclar pp.208-209	

OTHER CASES									
No.	Name	Date	Place	Sex	Mar. Stat	Trial Stat	Fate	Source	New Case
2508		- - 1644	Barrow-stounes	F	U	T	Ex.	Sinclar pp.208-209	
2509	Helen Thomson	- - 1644	Queens-ferry	F	U	T	Ex.	Fyfe pp. 84-101	
2510	Janet Lowrie	- - 1644	Queens-ferry	F	M	T	Ex.	Fyfe pp. 84-101	
2511	Janet Mowbray	- - 1644	Queens-ferry	F	U	T	Acqu	Fyfe pp. 84-101	
2512	Margaret Brown	- - 1644	Queens-ferry	F	U	T	Acqu	Fyfe pp. 84-101	
2513	Catherin Thompson	- - 1644	Queens-ferry	F	U	T	Acqu	Fyfe pp. 84-101	
2514	Margaret Dauline	- - 1644	Queens-ferry	F	U	T	Acqu	Fyfe pp. 84-101	
2515	Marion Dauline	- - 1644	Queens-ferry	F	U	T	Acqu	Fyfe pp. 84-101	
2516	Catherine Logie	- 1644	Queens-ferry	F	U	T	Acqu	Fyfe pp. 84-101	
2517	Marioun Little	- - 1644	Queens-ferry	F	U	T	Ex.	Fyfe pp. 84-101	
2518	Marion Stein	- - 1644	Queens-ferry	F	U	T	Ex.	Fyfe pp. 84-101	
2519	Janet Kowie	9.10. 1645	Elgin	F	U	Men.	NK.	R.Elgin V2 p.254	
2520	Jeane Buchane	- - 1645	Fife Creich	F	U	Men.	NK.	Min.Syn. Fife p.142	
2521	Seweis	- - 1645	St. Andrews	F	U	T	NK.	Min.Syn. Fife p.76	
2522	Certain Witches	- - 1645	Mid Calder	U	U	Men.	NK.	McCall p.33	
2523	Marg Donald	- - 1645	Dun-fermline	F	U	Men.	NK.	Hndrson p.314	

OTHER CASES									
No.	Name	Date	Place	Sex	Mar. Stat	Trial Stat	Fate	Source	New Case
2524	Bessie Cuper	- - 1645	Fife Creich	F	U	Men.	NK.	Min.Syn. Fife p.142	
2525	Margaret McWilliam	- - 1645	Rothesay	F	U	Men.	NK.	G.194	*
2526	Marion Davidsone	- - 1646	Lesma-hagow	F	U	Men.	Misc	G.140	*
2527	Parker	- - 1646	Edinburgh	F	M	Men.	NK.	G.221	*
2528	Marie Mitchells	- - 1646	Kilmanie	F	U	Men.	Acqu	G.127	*
2529	Janet Mitchells	- - 1646	Kilmanie	F	U	Men.	Acqu	G.127	*
2530	Grissel Thomson	- - 1646	Cupar	U	U	Men.	Ex.	G.127	*
2531	Janet Cuj	- - 1646	Elgin	F	U	Men.	Misc	R.Elgin V2 pp. 356-357	
2532	Margaret Murray	- - 1646	Elgin	F	U	Men.	NK.	R.Elgin V2 pp. 356-357	
2533	Helen Young	- - 1648	Balmerino	F	U	Men.	Misc	Cam.pp. 380-381	
2534	Helen Small	- - 1648	Monimail	F	U	T	Acqu	Cam. p.381	
2535	William Chrichtoun	- - 1648	Dun-fermline	M	U	T	Ex.	Hndrson p.317	
2536	Several Persons	- - 1648	Carriden	U	U	Men.	NK.	G.145	*
2537	Beatrix Watsone	27. 3. 1649	Corstor-phine	F	U	Men.	Misc	Sc.Nts & Quer. V3 pp. 122-123	
2538	Marget McKirdy	27. 3. 1649	Bute	F	U	T	NK.	Hewison V2 p.267	
2539		-. 4. 1649	Dalgatie	M	U	Men.	NK.	G.208	*

OTHER CASES									
No.	Name	Date	Place	Sex	Mar. Stat	Trial Stat	Fate	Source	New Case
2540	John Murdoche	-. 4. 1649	Dun-fermline	M	U	Men.	NK.	G.208	*
2541	Isabell Peacock	-. 5. 1649	Dun-fermline	F	U	Men.	NK.	G.208	*
2542	Bessie Wilson	-. 5. 1649	Dun-fermline	F	U	Men.	NK.	G.208	*
2543	Issobell Kelloch	3. 6. 1649	Dalgety	F	U	Men.	NK.	Buckner pp.44-46	
2544	Very Many People	-. 7. 1649	Lothian Fife	U	U	T	Ex.	Lamont p.6	
2545	Margaret Bell	-. 7. 1649	Corstor-phine	F	U	T	Ex.	Sc.Nts & Quer. V4 pp. 27-29	
2546	Bessie Scott	19. 8. 1649	Corstor-phine	F	U	T	Ex.	Sc.Nts & Quer. V4 pp. 27-29	
2547	Marion Inglis	-. 8. 1649	Corstor-phine	F	U	T	NK.	Sc.Nts & Quer. V4 p.28	
2548		-. 8. 1649	Burnt-island	F	U	T	Ex.	Arnot pp. 401-402	
2549		-. 8. 1649	Burnt-island	F	U	T	Ex.	Arnot pp. 401-402	
2550	Janet Brown	-. 8. 1649	Burnt-island	F	U	T	Ex.	Arnot pp. 401-402	
2551		-. 8. 1649	Burnt-island	F	U	T	Ex.	Arnot pp. 401-402	
2552	Margaret Dunholme	2. 9. 1649	Stow	F	U	Men.	NK.	G.229	*
2553	William Scott	9. 9. 1649	Corstor-phine	M	U	Men.	NK.	Sc.Nts & Quer. V4 pp. 27-29	
2554	Janet Paterson	27. 9. 1649	Inverkip	F	U	Men.	NK.	Murray p.56	

OTHER CASES									
No.	Name	Date	Place	Sex	Mar. Stat	Trial Stat	Fate	Source	New Case
2555	Janet Galbraith	27. 9. 1649	Greenock	F	U	Men.	NK.	Murray pp.56-57	
2556	Jean Scott	27. 9. 1649	Inverkip	F	U	Men.	NK.	Murray p.56	
2557	Janet Loudon	27. 9. 1649	Inverkip	F	U	Men.	NK.	Murray p.56	
2558	James Henrison	-. 9. 1649	Selkirk-shire	M	M	T	NK.	Craig-Brown V1 p.451	
2559	Jonet Nicolsone	-. 9. 1649	Preston-kirk	F	U	T	Ex.	Waddell p.100	
2560	Marion Henrison	-. 9. 1649	Selkirk-shire	F	M	T	Ex.	Craig-Brown V1 p.451	
2561		-. 9. 1649	Dunbar	U	U	T	Ex.	Waddell p.101	
2562		-. 9. 1649	Dunbar	U	U	T	Ex.	Waddell p.101	
2563		-. 9. 1649	Dunbar	U	U	T	Ex.	Waddell p.101	
2564		-. 9. 1649	Dunbar	U	U	T	Ex.	Waddell p.101	
2565		-. 9. 1649	Dunbar	U	U	T	Ex.	Waddell p.101	
2566		-. 9. 1649	Dunbar	U	U	T	Ex.	Waddell p.101	
2567		-. 9. 1649	Dunbar	U	U	T	Ex.	Waddell p.101	
2568		-. 9. 1649	Dunbar	U	U	T	Ex.	Waddell p.101	
2569		-. 9. 1649	Dunbar	U	U	T	Ex.	Waddell p.101	
2570		-. 9. 1649	Dunbar	U	U	T	Ex.	Waddell p.101	

OTHER CASES									
No.	Name	Date	Place	Sex	Mar. Stat	Trial Stat	Fate	Source	New Case
2571	Bessie Graham	-.10. 1649	Kil-winning	F	U	T	Ex.	Sinclar pp.109-120	
2572	Isoble Kelman	21.11. 1649	Old Aberdeen	F	U	T	Acqu	R.Old Abdn p.371	
2573	Janet Coupere	25.11. 1649	Brechin	F	U	Men.	NK.	G.235	*
2574	Elspeth Graham	-.11. 1649	Peebles-shire	F	U	Men.	Ex.	Gunn pp. 50-51	
2575	Ishbel Alexander	-.11. 1649	Peebles	F	U	Men.	NK.	Gunn pp. 50-51	
2576		-.11. 1649	Whitting-ham	U	U	T	Ex.	Waddell p.101	
2577		-.11. 1649	Whitting-hame	U	U	T	Ex.	Waddell p.101	
2578		-.11. 1649	Whitting-hame	U	U	T	Ex.	Waddell p.101	
2579	Certain Persons	-.11. 1649	Renfrew-shire	U	U	T	NK.	Murray p.57	
2580	Eleven Old Women	6.12. 1649	Lanark	F	U	T	Acqu	R.Brgh Lnrk p.143	
2581	Certain People	-.12. 1649	Menmuir	U	U	T	NK.	His. Brechin p.75	
2582	Catharin Lyall	-.12. 1649	Montrose	F	U	Men.	NK.	G.384	*
2583	Elspeth Seith	- - 1649	Balmerino	F	U	T	Acqu	Min.Syn. Fife p.168	
2584		- - 1649	Burnt-island	F	U	T	Ex.	Arnot pp.402-403	
2585		- - 1649	Burnt-island	F	U	T	Ex.	Arnot pp.402-403	

OTHER CASES									
No.	Name	Date	Place	Sex	Mar. Stat	Trial Stat	Fate	Source	New Case
2586	Mauld Gott	- - 1649	Glasgow	F	U	Men.	NK.	G.203	*
2587	Geillis Frissell	- - 1649	Kingarth	F	U	Men.	NK.	G.213	*
2588	Isobel McKaw	- - 1649	Kingarth	F	U	Men.	NK.	G.213	*
2589	Isobel Thompson	- - 1649	Stow	F	U	Men.	Ex.	Craig-Brown V1 p.451	
2590	Jean Couts	- - 1649	Lanark	F	U	Men.	NK.	R.Brgh Lnrk p.143	
2591	John Donaldson	- - 1649	Brechin	M	U	T	NK.	Andrson	*
2592	Janet Bennet	- - 1649	Leith	F	U	Men.	NK.	G.144	*
2593	Marione McNab	- - 1649	Stirling	F	U	Men.	NK.	G.384	*
2594	Lachlan McKirdy	- - 1649	Kingarth	M	U	Men.	NK.	G.213	*
2595	Margaret Moore	- - 1649	Kingarth	F	U	Men.	NK.	G.213	*
2596	Issobel Bairdie	- - 1649	Burnt-island	F	U	T	Ex.	Arnot pp.402-403	
2597	Certain Persons	- - 1649	Tyning-hame	U	U	T	NK.	Waddell p.101	
2598	Margaret Dunham	- - 1649	Lauder	F	U	T	Ex.	Thom. p.210	
2599	Robert Grieve	- - 1649	Lauder	M	U	T	Ex.	Sinclar pp.45-55	
2600	Margaret Henderson, Lady Pittathrow	- - 1649	Inver-keithing	F	U	Men.	Misc	Lamont p.12	

OTHER CASES									
No.	Name	Date	Place	Sex	Mar. Stat	Trial Stat	Fate	Source	New Case
2601	Agnes Gourley	- - 1649	Humbie	F	U	T	NK.	Mait.Cl. Misc.V1 pp.438-439	
2602	Janet Castell	- - 1649	Fraser-burgh	F	U	T	NK.	Bucha Fld Cl. p.208	
2603	Alexander Scott	- - 1649	Corstor-phine	M	U	T	Ex.	Sc.Nts & Quer. V4 pp. 27-29	
2604	Kett Gibb	- - 1649	Corstor-phine	F	U	T	Ex.	Sc.Nts & Quer. V4 pp. 27-29	
2605	Certain Persons	6. 1. 1650	Auchter-house	U	U	Men.	NK.	Edr. Topogrph. Mag. V1 p.151	
2606	Some Witches	8. 1. 1650	Kelso Makerston	U	U	T	Ex.	R.Pres. Kelso	
2607		9. 1. 1650	Peebles	U	U	Men.	NK.	His. Pbles p.166	
2608		9. 1. 1650	Peebles	U	U	Men.	NK.	His. Pbles p.166	
2609		9. 1. 1650	Peebles	U	U	Men.	NK.	His. Pbles p.166	
2610		9. 1. 1650	Peebles	U	U	Men.	NK.	His. Pbles p.166	
2611		22. 1. 1659	Whitting-ham	M	U	Men.	Ex.	Waddell p.101	
2612		23. 1. 1650	Stenton	U	U	Men.	Ex.	Waddell p.101	
2613		23. 1. 1650	Stenton	U	U	Men.	Ex.	Waddell p.101	

OTHER CASES									
No.	Name	Date	Place	Sex	Mar. Stat	Trial Stat	Fate	Source	New Case
2614		23. 1. 1650	Stenton	U	U	Men.	Ex.	Waddell p.101	
2615		23. 1. 1650	Stenton	U	U	Men.	Ex.	Waddell p.101	
2616		23. 1. 1650	Stenton	U	U	Men.	Ex.	Waddell p.101	
2617		23. 1. 1650	Stenton	U	U	Men.	Ex.	Waddell p.101	
2618	Robert Bruce	-. 1. 1650	Angus Mearns	M	U	Men.	NK.	Andrson	*
2619	Jonet Coutts	-. 1. 1650	Peeble-shire	F	U	Men.	Ex.	His. Pbles	
2620	Marion Hunter	-. 1. 1650	Lanark-shire	F	U	Men.	NK.	Hntr p.386	
2621	Lillias Moffat	-. 1. 1650	Lanark-shire	F	U	Men.	NK.	Hntr p.386	
2622	Mali Laidlaw	-. 1. 1650	Lanark-shire	F	U	Men.	NK.	Hntr p.386	
2623	Marion Moffat	-. 1. 1650	Lanark-shire	F	U	Men.	NK.	Hntr p.386	
2624	Helen Aitchison	-. 1. 1650	Lanark-shire	F	U	Men.	NK.	Hntr p.386	
2625	Marion Watson	-. 1. 1650	Lanark-shire	F	U	Men.	NK.	Hntr p.386	
2626	Margaret Fraser	13. 2. 1650	Turriff	F	U	Men.	NK.	Pres.Bk Strath-bogie p.124	
2627	Elspet Gray	21. 2. 1659	Balwyllo	F	U	T	NK.	R.Pres. Brechin pp.25-28	
2628	Margaret Ogg	12. 3. 1650	Insch	F	U	Men.	Misc	Dvdson pp. 306-307	

OTHER CASES									
No.	Name	Date	Place	Sex	Mar. Stat	Trial Stat	Fate	Source	New Case
2629	Margaret Ogg	12. 3. 1650	Aberdeen	F	U	Men.	NK.	Dvdson	
2630	Archibald Watt	25. 3. 1650	Lanark-shire Douglas	M	U	Men.	NK.	Ch.V2 p.195	
2631		-. 3. 1650	Irvine	U	U	T	Ex.	Ptson V3 pp.263-264	
2632		-. 3. 1650	Irvine	U	U	T	Ex.	Ptson V3 pp. 263-264	
2633		-. 3. 1650	Irvine	U	U	T	Ex.	Ptson V3 pp. 263-264	
2634		-. 3. 1650	Irvine	U	U	T	Ex.	Ptson V3 pp. 263-264	
2635		-. 3. 1650	Irvine	U	U	T	Ex.	Ptson V3 pp. 263-264	
2636		-. 3. 1650	Irvine	U	U	T	Ex.	Ptson V3 pp. 263-264	
2637		-. 3. 1650	Irvine	U	U	T	Ex.	Ptson V3 pp. 263-264	
2638		-. 3. 1650	Irvine	U	U	T	Ex.	Ptson V3 pp. 263-264	
2639		-. 3. 1650	Irvine	U	U	T	Ex.	Ptson V3 pp. 263-264	
2640		-. 3. 1650	Irvine	U	U	T	Ex.	Ptson V3 pp. 263-264	

OTHER CASES									
No.	Name	Date	Place	Sex	Mar. Stat	Trial Stat	Fate	Source	New Case
2641		-. 3. 1650	Irvine	U	U	T	Ex.	Ptson V3 pp. 263-264	
2642		-. 3. 1650	Irvine	U	U	T	Ex.	Ptson V3 pp. 263-264	
2643	Agnes Kirkland	9. 4. 1650	Tyning-hame	F	U	Men.	Ex.	Waddell pp.55; 102	
2644	David Stewart	9. 4. 1650	Tyning-hame	M	U	Men.	Ex.	Waddell pp.55; 102	
2645		15. 4. 1650	Berwick-shire	F	U	T	Ex.	W'locke p.434	
2646		15. 4. 1650	Berwick-shire	F	U	T	Ex.		
2647		15. 4. 1650	Berwick-shire	F	U	T	Ex.	W'locke p.434	
2648		15. 4. 1650	Berwick-shire	M	U	T	Ex.	W'locke p.434	
2649		15. 4. 1650	Berwick-shire	M	U	T	Ex.	W'locke p.434	
2650	Jonet Robison	22. 4. 1650	Irvine	F	U	Men.	NK.	Stat.Acc. Ayrshire pp.632-633	
2651	Margaret Cooper	22. 4. 1650	Irvine	F	U	Men.	NK.	Stat.Acc. Ayrshire pp.632-633	
2652	Catherine Montgomerie	22. 4. 1650	Irvine	F	U	Men.	NK.	Stat.Acc. Ayrshire pp.632-633	
2653	Bessie Eumond	26. 4. 1650	Peebles	F	U	T	NCP	Ch.V2 p.178	
2654	Marioun Watsone	26. 4. 1650	Peebles	F	U	Men.	Misc	Doc. Pbles p.389	

OTHER CASES									
No.	Name	Date	Place	Sex	Mar. Stat	Trial Stat	Fate	Source	New Case
2655	Marion Watson	-. 4. 1650	Peebles	F	U	Men.	Acqu	G.223	*
2656		-. 4. 1650	Kilbuck-Drummond	M	U	Men.	NK.	G.204	*
2657	Robert Cousing	-. 4. 1650	Culross	M	U	Men.	NK.	G.204	*
2658	Margaret Turnbull	4. 5. 1650	Selkirk Lillies-leaf	F	U	Men.	NK.	Craig-Brown V1 p.201	
2659	Mary Chisholm	4. 5. 1650	Selkirk Lillies-leaf	F	U	Men.	NK.	Craig-Brown V1 p.201	
2660		7. 5. 1650	Irvine	U	U	T	Ex.	Ptson V3 p.264	
2661	Marion Cunnyngham	7. 5. 1650	Dun-fermline	F	U	Men.	NK.	Krk Sess. R.Dunferm-line pp. 33-34	
2662		7. 5. 1650	Irvine	U	U	T	Ex.	Ptson V3 p.264	
2663		7. 5. 1650	Irvine	U	U	T	Ex.	Ptson V3 p.264	
2664		7. 5. 1650	Irvine	U	U	T	Ex.	Ptson V3 p.264	
2665		7. 5. 1650	Irvine	U	U	T	Ex.	Ptson V3 p.264	
2666	Janet Smelie	14. 5. 1650	Ayr	F	U	Men.	Misc	Ptson V1 p.101	
2667	Certain Persons	6. 7. 1650	Glasgow	U	U	Men.	NK.	Wodrow V2 P2 p.72	
2668	Janet Hewison	26. 7. 1650	Kilallan	F	U	T	NK.	Pride p.151	
2669	William Grant	23.10. 1650	Bellie	M	U	Men.	NK.	Pres.Bk Strath-bogie p.161	

OTHER CASES									
No.	Name	Date	Place	Sex	Mar. Stat	Trial Stat	Fate	Source	New Case
2670	Jonet Couper	- - 1650	Brechin	F	U	T	Ex.	R.Pres. Brechin pp.31-35	
2671		- - 1650	Greenlaw	U	U	Men.	NK.	G.400	*
2672		- - 1650	Illies-leaf	U	U	Men.	NK.	G.229-230	*
2673	Janet Galloway	- - 1650	Angus Kirrie-muir	F	U	Men.	NK.	Andrson	*
2674	Finlayson	- - 1650	Angus Mearns	F	U	Men.	NK.	Andrson	*
2675	James Shanks	- - 1650	Brechin	M	U	T	NCP	Andrson	*
2676	Thomas Kyneir	- - 1650	Brechin	M	U	T	NCP	Andrson	*
2677	John Chrystison	- - 1650	Brechin	M	U	T	NCP	Andrson	*
2678	Isobel Reamy	- - 1650	Brechin	F	U	Men.	Misc	Andrson	*
2679	Thomas Humbell	- - 1650	Brechin	M	U	T	NCP	Andrson	*
2680	Issobel Fordell	- - 1650	Brechin	F	U	T	NK.	Andrson	*
2681	Marat Merchant	- - 1650	Brechin	F	U	T	Ex.	Andrson	
2682	Janet Couper	- - 1650	Brechin	F	U	T	Ex.	Andrson	*
2683	Several Persons	- - 1650	Dalry	U	U	Men.	NK.	G.139	*
2684	Marjorie Paterson	- - 1650	Dalkeith	F	U	Men.	NK.	G.380-381	*
2685	Several Persons	- - 1650	Dalkeith	U	U	Men.	NK.	G.380-381	*

OTHER CASES									
No.	Name	Date	Place	Sex	Mar. Stat	Trial Stat	Fate	Source	New Case
2686		- - 1650	Greenlaw	U	U	Men.	NK.	G.400	*
2687		- - 1650	Illies-leaf	U	U	Men.	NK.	G.229-230	*
2688	Agnes Gaston	- - 1650	Melrose	F	U	Men.	Misc	R.Mlrse V1 p.220	
2689	Jonet Birnie	- - 1650	Crawford	F	U	Men.	Misc	Hntr p.387	
2690	Finwell Hyndman	- - 1650	Bute	U	U	Men.	NK.	Hewison V2 p.262	
2691	Marat Merchant	- - 1650	Brechin	F	U	Men.	NK.	R.Pres. Brechin pp.18-23	
2692	Catharin Lyall	- - 1650	Brechin	F	U	Men.	NK.	R.Pres. Brechin pp.38-43	
2693	Catherin Walker	- - 1650	Brechin	F	U	Men.	NK.	R.Pres. Brechin pp.44-51	
2694	Catherine Skair	- - 1650	Brechin	F	U	T	Ex.	R.Pres. Brechin pp.35-38	
2695	Janet Anderson	- - 1650	Aberdour	F	U	Men.	Acqu	Ross pp. 325-328	
2696	Maggy Osborne	- - 1650	Ayr	F	U	T	Ex.	Ptson V1 pp. 59;101	
2697	Thomas Shanks	- - 1650	Peeble-shire	M	U	T	NK.	Gunn pp. 50-51	
2698	Marioun Robiesoune	- - 1650	Peeble-shire	F	U	T	NK.	Gunn pp. 50-51	
2699	Janet Coutts	- - 1650	Peeble-shire	F	U	T	NK.	Gunn pp. 50-51	
2700	Marioun Twedy	- - 1650	Peeble-shire	F	U	T	NK.	Gunn pp. 50-51	

OTHER CASES									
No.	Name	Date	Place	Sex	Mar. Stat	Trial Stat	Fate	Source	New Case
2701	Bessie Forrest	- - 1650	Peeble-shire	F	U	T	NK.	Gunn pp. 50-51	
2702	Witches	- - 1650	Eckford	U	U	Men.	Ex.	Berwick-shire Nat.Cl. His. V11 p.460	
2703		- - 1650	Wadington	U	U	Men.	Ex.	Ltrs & Pps p.136	
2704		- - 1650	Wadington	U	U	Men.	Ex.	Ltrs & Pps p.136	
2705		- - 1650	Wadington	U	U	Men.	Ex.	Ltrs & Pps p.136	
2706		- - 1650	Wadington	U	U	Men.	Ex.	Ltrs & Pps p.136	
2707		- - 1650	Wadington	U	U	Men.	Ex.	Ltrs & Pps p.136	
2708		- - 1650	Wadington	U	U	Men.	Ex.	Ltrs & Pps p.136	
2709		- - 1650	Wadington	U	U	Men.	Ex.	Ltrs & Pps p.136	
2710		- - 1650	Wadington	U	U	Men.	Ex.	Ltrs & Pps p.136	
2711		- - 1650	Wadington	U	U	Men.	Ex.	Ltrs & Pps p.136	
2712		- - 1650	Wadington	U	U	Men.	Ex.	Ltrs & Pps p.136	
2713		- - 1650	Wadington	U	U	Men.	Ex.	Ltrs & Pps p.136	

OTHER CASES									
No.	Name	Date	Place	Sex	Mar. Stat	Trial Stat	Fate	Source	New Case
2714		- - 1650	Wadington	U	U	Men.	Ex.	Ltrs & Pps p.136	
2715		- - 1650	Wadington	U	U	Men.	Ex.	Ltrs & Pps p.136	
2716		- - 1650	Wadington	U	U	Men.	Ex.	Ltrs & Pps p.136	
2717		- - 1650	Wadington	U	U	Men.	Ex.	Ltrs & Pps p.136	
2718		- - 1650	Wadington	U	U	Men.	Ex.	Ltrs & Pps p.136	
2719		- - 1650	Wadington	U	U	Men.	Ex.	Ltrs & Pps p.136	
2720		- - 1650	Wadington	U	U	Men.	Ex.	Ltrs & Pps p.136	
2721		- - 1650	Wadington	U	U	Men.	Ex.	Ltrs & Pps p.136	
2722		- - 1650	Wadington	U	U	Men.	Ex.	Ltrs & Pps p.136	
2723		- - 1650	Wadington	U	U	Men.	Ex.	Ltrs & Pps p.136	
2724		- - 1650	Wadington	U	U	Men.	Ex.	Ltrs & Pps p.136	
2725		- - 1650	Wadington	U	U	Men.	Ex.	Ltrs & Pps p.136	
2726		- - 1650	Wadington	U	U	Men.	Ex.	Ltrs & Pps p.136	

OTHER CASES									
No.	Name	Date	Place	Sex	Mar. Stat	Trial Stat	Fate	Source	New Case
2727		- - 1650	Wadington	U	U	Men.	Ex.	Ltrs & Pps p.136	
2728		- - 1650	Wadington	U	U	Men.	Ex.	Ltrs & Pps p.136	
2729		- - 1650	Wadington	U	U	Men.	Ex.	Ltrs & Pps p.136	
2730		- - 1650	Wadington	U	U	Men.	Ex.	Ltrs & Pps p.136	
2731		- - 1650	Wadington	U	U	Men.	Ex.	Ltrs & Pps p.136	
2732		- - 1650	Wadington	U	U	Men.	Ex.	Ltrs & Pps p.136	
2733	Marion Mackbeath	-. 7. 1652	Canisbay	F	U	Men.	NK.	G.203	*
2734	Several Witches	-. 9. 1652	Stirling	U	U	T	Acqu	Lamont p.47	
2735	Katharine Kay	-. 9. 1653	Newburgh	F	U	Men.	Acqu	Simpkins pp.98-99	
2736		- - 1653		M	U	Men.	Ex.	Nicoll p.106	
2737	Katherine Key	- - 1653	Newburgh	F	U	Men.	NK.	G.244	*
2738	Margaret Cant	- - 1654	Aberdour	F	U	T	NK.	Ross pp. 329-330	
2739	Susanna Alexander	- - 1654	Aberdour	F	U	T	Ex.	Ross pp. 329-330	
2740	Janet Bell	- - 1654	Aberdour	F	U	T	Ex.	Ross pp. 329-330	
2741	Catharine Robertson	- - 1654	Aberdour	F	U	T	Ex.	Ross pp. 329-330	

OTHER CASES									
No.	Name	Date	Place	Sex	Mar. Stat	Trial Stat	Fate	Source	New Case
2742	Margaret Currie	- - 1654	Aberdour	F	U	T	Ex.	Ross pp. 329-330	
2743	Janet Groat	23. 5. 1655	Caithness	F	U	Men.	NK.	Canisbay Krk Sess. R.	
2744	Wife of W. Barton	- - 1655	Kirklis-ton	F	M	T	Ex.	Sinclar pp.160-164	
2745	William Barton	- - 1655	Kirklis-ton	M	M	T	Ex.	Sinclar pp.160-164	
2746	John McWilliam	5. 2. 1656	Dumbarton	M	U	T	Ex.	Spott. Misc.V2 p.67	
2747		13. 2. 1656	Edinburgh	M	U	Men.	Ex.	Nicoll p.174	
2748		12. 3. 1656	Inver-keithing	F	U	Men.	Ex.	Nicoll p.175	
2749	Elspeth Craiche	-. 8. 1656	Culross	F	U	Men.	Misc	Bev. p.290	
2750	Janet Miller	- - 1656	Dun-drennan	F	M	Men.	NK.	McDwll p.375	
2751		- - 1656	Redgorton	M	U	Men.	NK.	G.263	*
2752		- - 1656	Redgorton	M	U	Men.	NK.	G.263	*
2753		- - 1656	Redgorton	M	U	Men.	NK.	G.263	*
2754		- - 1656	Redgorton	M	U	Men.	NK.	G.263	*
2755		27. 3. 1657	Dumfries	F	U	Men.	Ex.	McDwll p.377	
2756		14.10. 1657	Tranent	F	U	Men.	Ex.	Nicoll p.202	

OTHER CASES

No.	Name	Date	Place	Sex	Mar. Stat	Trial Stat	Fate	Source	New Case
2757	Margaret Anderson	2. 2. 1658	Haddington	F	U	T	Ex.	Spott. Misc.V2 pp.67-68	
2758		-. 2. 1658	Edinburgh	M	U	Men.	Ex.	Ch. V2 p.244	
2759		-. 2. 1658	Edinburgh	F	U	Men.	Misc	Ch. V2 p.244	
2760	Janet Scott	13. 5. 1658	Dumfries	F	U	T	NCP	Truckell	*
2761		12. 8. 1658	Edinburgh	F	U	T	Ex.	Nicoll p.276	
2762		12. 8. 1658	Edinburgh	F	U	T	Ex.	Nicoll p.276	
2763		12. 8. 1658	Edinburgh	F	U	T	Ex.	Nicoll p.276	
2764		12. 8. 1658	Edinburgh	F	U	T	Ex.	Nicoll p.276	
2765	James Hudson	-. 8. 1658	Alloa	M	U	Men.	NK.	Sc.Antiq. V9 pp. 49-52	
2766	James Kirk	-. 8. 1658	Alloa	M	U	Men.	NK.	Sc.Antiq. V9 pp. 49-52	
2767	Barbara Erskin	-. 8. 1658	Alloa	F	U	Men.	NK.	Sc.Antiq. V9 pp. 49-52	
2768	Jonet Miller	-. 8. 1658	Alloa	F	U	Men.	NK.	Sc.Antiq. V9 pp. 49-52	
2769	Kathren Blak	-. 8. 1658	Alloa	F	U	Men.	NK.	Sc.Antiq. V9 pp. 49-52	
2770	Margaret Dempherstoun	-. 8. 1658	Alloa	F	U	Men.	NK.	Sc.Antiq. V9 pp. 49-52	
2771	Elspet Blak	-. 8. 1658	Alloa	F	U	Men.	NK.	Sc.Antiq. V9 pp. 49-52	

OTHER CASES									
No.	Name	Date	Place	Sex	Mar. Stat	Trial Stat	Fate	Source	New Case
2772	Margaret Duchall	-. 8. 1658	Alloa	F	U	Men.	Misc	Sc.Antiq. V9 pp. 49-52	
2773	Samwell Blak	9. 9. 1658	Dumfries	M	U	Men.	NK.	Truckell No.43	*
2774	Janet Clark	9. 9. 1658	Dumfries	F	U	Men.	NK.	Truckell	*
2775	Kathren Penny	-. 9. 1658	Alloa	F	U	Men.	Ex.	Spott. Misc.V2 p.68	
2776	Jonet Blak	-. 9. 1658	Alloa	F	U	Men.	Ex.	Spott. Misc.V2 p.68	
2777	Besse Paton	-. 9. 1658	Alloa	F	U	Men.	Ex.	Spott. Misc.V2 p.68	
2778	Margaret Tailzeor	-. 9. 1658	Alloa	F	U	Men.	Ex.	Spott. Misc. V2 p.68	
2779	Jonet Saers	- - 1658	Ayr	F	U	T	Ex.	Firth p.382	
2780	Effie Rosie	- - 1658	Stroma	F	U	Men.	NK.	Canisbay Krk Sess. R.	
2781	John Wauch	-. 1. 1659.	Linlith-gow	M	U	Men.	NK.	Anal. Scot. V1 p.204	
2782	Jonet Anderson	-. 2. 1659	Edinburgh	F	U	T	Ex.	Nicoll pp.213-214	
2783	Bessie Stevenson	2. 3. 1659	Dumfries	F	U	T	Ex.	Spott. Misc.V2 p.68	
2784		9. 3. 1659	Dunbar	F	U	Men.	Ex.	Nicoll p.228	
2785		9. 3. 1659	Dunbar	F	U	Men.	Ex.	Nicoll p.228	

OTHER CASES									
No.	Name	Date	Place	Sex	Mar. Stat	Trial Stat	Fate	Source	New Case
2786		9. 3. 1659	Dunbar	F	U	Men.	Ex.	Nicoll p.228	
2787		9. 3. 1659	Dunbar	F	U	Men.	Ex.	Nicoll p.228	
2788		9. 3. 1659	Dunbar	F	U	Men.	Ex.	Nicoll p.228	
2789	Helen Tait	5. 4. 1659	Dumfries	F	U	T	NCP	McDwll p.376	
2790	Jean Tomson	5. 4. 1659	Dumfries	F	U	T	Ex.	McDwll p.376	
2791	Janet McGowane	5. 4. 1659	Dumfries	F	U	T	Ex.	McDwll p.376	
2792	Agnes Comenes	5. 4. 1659	Dumfries	F	U	T	Ex.	McDwll p.376	
2793	Margt Clerk	5. 4. 1659	Dumfries	F	U	T	Ex.	McDwll p.376	
2794	Janet McKendrig	5. 4. 1659	Dumfries	F	U	T	Ex.	McDwll p.376	
2795	Agnes Clerk	5. 4. 1659	Dumfries	F	U	T	Ex.	McDwll p.376	
2796	Janet Corsane	5. 4. 1659	Dumfries	F	U	T	Ex.	McDwll p.376	
2797	Helen Moorhead	5. 4. 1659	Dumfries	F	U	T	Ex.	McDwll p.376	
2798	Janet Callon	5. 4. 1659	Dumfries	F	U	T	Ex.	McDwll p.376	
2799	William Fleck	15. 5. 1659	Humbie	M	U	Men.	NK.	Dal. p.275	
2800	Margaret Watson	9. 7. 1659	Stroma	F	U	Men.	NK.	Canisbay Krk Sess. R.	
2801	Maly Purdie	-. 9. 1659	Skirling	F	U	Men.	NK.	Hay p.145	
2802	Murray	-. 9. 1659	Skirling	F	U	Men.	NK.	Hay p.145	

OTHER CASES									
No.	Name	Date	Place	Sex	Mar. Stat	Trial Stat	Fate	Source	New Case
2803	Marg Robisone	-. 9. 1659	Skirling	F	U	Men.	NK.	Hay p.145	
2804	Janet Burnes	14.11. 1659	Dumfries	F	U	Men.	NCP	Truckell No.43	*
2805	Marione Corsan	- - 1659	Dumfries	F	U	Men.	NK.	Truckell pp.7-17	*
2806	Janet Sym	- - 1659	Angus Brechin	F	U	Men.	NK.	Andrson	*
2807	Several Persons	- - 1660	Rothesay	U	U	Men.	NCP	G.255	*
2808	Jean Campbell	- - 1660	Bute	F	U	Men.	NK.	Reid p.93	
2809	Barbara Milne	-. 1. 1661	Edinburgh	F	U	Men.	NK.	Sharpe p.128	
2810	Bessie Fouler	-. 5. 1661	Mussel-burgh	F	U	T	Ex.	Sinclar p.213	
2811	Several Women	7. 7. 1661	Humbie	F	U	Men.	NK.	Dal. p.625	
2812	Jenet Millar	7. 8. 1661	Kirklis-ton	F	U	Men.	NK.	G.236-237	*
2813	Janet Millar	20. 8. 1661	Kirklis-ton	F	U	Men.	NK.	Dal. p.550	
2814	Elspet Bruice	-. 9. 1661	Cortachy	F	U	Men.	NK.	Proc. Antiq. V22 p.254	
2815		-.11. 1661	Newburgh	F	U	T	Ex.	Lamont p.142	
2816		-.11. 1661	Newburgh	F	U	T	Ex.	Lamont p.142	
2817	Isobel Smith	- - 1661	Forfar	F	U	Men.	NK.	Soc. Antiq. V22 pp. 257-258	
2818	Margaret Carvie	- - 1661	Falkland	F	U	Men.	NK.	Ch.V2 p.279	

OTHER CASES									
No.	Name	Date	Place	Sex	Mar. Stat	Trial Stat	Fate	Source	New Case
2819	Barbara Horniman	- - 1661	Falkland	F	U	Men.	NK.	Ch.V2 p.279	
2820		- - 1661	Elgin	U	U	Men.	NK.	G.141	*
2821	Several Persons	- - 1661	Salt-preston	U	U	Men.	NK.	G.382	*
2822	John Rind	- - 1661	Elgin	M	U	Men.	NK.	G.375	*
2823	Elspet Alexander	- - 1661	Forfar	F	U	Men.	NK.	Reliq. Antiq. Scot.pp. 113-145	
2824	Catherine Robertson	- - 1661	Aberdour	F	U	Men.	Ex.	Ross p.329	
2825	Margaret Currie	- - 1661	Aberdour	F	U	Men.	Ex.	Ross p.329	
2826	Marg Cant	- - 1661	Aberdour	F	U	Men.	Ex.	Ross pp. 329-330	
2827	Janet Stout	- - 1661	Forfar	F	U	Men.	NK.	Reliq. Antiq. Scot.pp. 113-114	
2828	Ketheren Portour	- - 1661	Forfar	F	U	Men.	NK.	Reliq. Antiq. Scot.pp. 113-145	
2829	Agnes Sparke	- - 1661	Forfar	F	U	Men.	NK.	Reliq. Antiq. Scot.pp. 113-145	
2830	Isobell Smith	- - 1661	Forfar	F	U	Men.	NK.	Reliq. Antiq. Scot.pp. 113-145	
2831	Isobell Shyrie	- - 1661	Forfar	F	U	Men.	NK.	Reliq. Antiq. Scot.pp. 113-145	

OTHER CASES									
No.	Name	Date	Place	Sex	Mar. Stat	Trial Stat	Fate	Source	New Case
2832	Janet Stoddart	- - 1661	Inveresk	F	U	Men.	NK.	Stir. p.142	
2833	Bessie Croket	- - 1661	Forfar	F	U	Men.	NK.	Soc. Antiq. V22 p.257	
2834		- - 1661	Elgin	U	U	Men.	NK.	G.141	*
2835		- - 1661	Elgin	U	U	Men.	NK.	G.141	*
2836		- - 1661	Elgin	U	U	Men.	NK.	G.141	*
2837		- - 1661	Paisley	F	U	T	Ex.	Brown V1 p.353	
2838	Marioun Tweedie	-. 1. 1662	Penicuik	F	U	Men.	Acqu	Wilson p.181	
2839	Agnes Elphinston	-. 1. 1662	Penicuik	F	U	Men.	Acqu	Wilson p.181	
2840	Christian Purdie	-. 1. 1662	Penicuik	F	U	Men.	Acqu	Wilson p.181	
2841	Elspethe Craiche	17. 3. 1662	Culross	F	U	Men.	NK.	Bev., Clrss & Tulli-allan V1 p.318	
2842	Marie Lamont	-. 3. 1662	Inverkip	F	U	Men.	NK.	Sharpe pp.130-134	
2843	Unnamed Persons	-. 3. 1662	Dyke	U	U	Men.	NK.	Brodie p.246; 307	
2844	George Patersone	-.10. 1662	Melrose	M	U	Men.	Misc	R.Regal. Mlrse V2 p.36	
2845	Agnes Beveridge	- - 1662	Angus Broughty	F	U	Men.	Acqu	Andrson	*

OTHER CASES									
No.	Name	Date	Place	Sex	Mar. Stat	Trial Stat	Fate	Source	New Case
2846	Janet Walker	- - 1662	Kirrie-muir	F	U	Men.	Ex.	Regal. Kirrie-muir p.83	
2847		- - 1662	Wardlaw	U	U	Men.	NK.	Chron. Fras. pp.446-447	
2848	Margaret McWilliam	- - 1662	Bute	F	U	T	NK.	G.304; 336	*
2849	John Tailzour	- - 1662	Forfar Oathlaw	M	U	Men.	NK.		
2850	Janet Huit	- - 1662	Oath	F	U	Men.	NK.	Reliq. Antiq. Scot.pp. 113-145	
2851		- - 1662	Wardlaw	U	U	Men.	NK.	Chron. Fras. pp.446-447	
2852		- - 1662	Forres	U	U	Men.	Ex.	Chron. Fras. pp.446-447	
2853		- - 1662	Elgin	U	U	Men.	Ex.	Chron. Fras. pp.446-447	
2854	Margaret Beveridge	- - 1662	Angus Broughty	F	U	Men.	Acqu	Andrson	*
2855		- - 1662	Wardlaw	M	U	Men.	NK.	Chron. Fras. pp.446-447	
2856	Unnamed Witches	- - 1662	Wardlaw	F	U	Men.	NK.	Chron. Fras. pp.446-447	

OTHER CASES									
No.	Name	Date	Place	Sex	Mar. Stat	Trial Stat	Fate	Source	New Case
2857		- - 1662	Elgin	U	U	Men.	Ex.	Chron. Fras. pp.446-447	
2858	Elspet Alexander	- - 1662	Forfar	F	U	Men.	Ex.	Reid p.83	
2859	Margaret Duff	- - 1662	Inverness	F	U	Men.	Ex.	Chron. Fras. pp.446-447	
2860		- - 1662	Wardlaw	U	U	Men.	NK.	Chron. Fras. pp.446-447	
2861		- - 1662	Wardlaw	U	U	Men.	NK.	Chron. Fras. pp.446-447	
2862		- - 1662	Forres	U	U	Men.	Ex.	Chron. Fras. pp.446-447	
2863	Several Persons	-. 1. 1663	Auchter-tool	U	U	Men.	NK.	Ross pp. 331-332	
2864	Isobel Elder	1. 5. 1663	Forres	F	U	Men.	Ex.	Brodie p.296	
2865	Isabel Simson	1. 5. 1663	Forres	F	U	Men.	Ex.	Brodie p.296	
2866	Gillies	16.10. 1663	North Berwick	F	M	Men.	NK.	Dal. p.100	
2867	Adam Gillies	16.10. 1663	North Berwick	M	M	Men.	NK.	Dal. p.100	
2868	Jonat Nein Giblie Gow	- - 1663	Tain	F	U	Men.	NK.	G.222	*
2869		-. 5. 1664	Inverkip	F	U	Men.	Misc	His. Renfrew	

OTHER CASES									
No.	Name	Date	Place	Sex	Mar. Stat	Trial Stat	Fate	Source	New Case
2870	Janet Burnes	14.11. 1664	Dumfries	F	U	Men.	NCP	His. Dumfrs p.375	
2871	Barbara Drummond	20.12. 1664		F	U	Men.	NK.	J.C. Edin. 1661-1678 V1 p.127	
2872	Margaret Tamsone	- - 1664	Elgin	F	U	Men.	NCP	G.255	*
2873		- - 1665	Culross	U	U	Men.	Ex.	Mcknzie Laws & Custms 1678 p.98	
2874	Janet Finnie	- - 1667	Paisley	F	U	Men.	Misc	His. Pais. V1 p.354	
2875	Witchcraft Cases	- - 1667	Dun-fermline	U	U	Men.	NK.	Hndrson Ann. Dun-fermline pp.338-339	
2876	James McPhee	-. 1. 1670	Kingarth	M	U	Men.	Acqu	G.233	*
2877	Janet Conochie	- - 1670	Borrow-stounness	F	M	Men.	Ex.	Br'ness & Dist. p.91	
2878	Meggie Cowie	- - 1670	Montrose	F	U	Men.	Ex.	Mcknlay p.216	
2879	Goodaile	- - 1670	Carron	F	M	Men.	Ex.	Sinclair p.211	
2880		- - 1670	Borrow-stounness	F	U	Men.	Ex.	Br'ness & Dist. p.91	
2881		-. 5. 1671	Dumfries	F	U	Men.	NK.	McDwll 2nd Ed. p.377	
2882		-. 5. 1671	Dumfries	F	U	Men.	NK.	McDwll 2nd Ed. p.377	

OTHER CASES									
No.	Name	Date	Place	Sex	Mar. Stat	Trial Stat	Fate	Source	New Case
2883		-. 5. 1671	Dumfries	F	U	Men.	NK.	McDwll 2nd Ed. p.377	
2884		-. 5. 1671	Dumfries	F	U	Men.	NK.	McDwll 2nd Ed. p.377	
2885		-. 5. 1671	Dumfries	F	U	Men.	NK.	McDwll 2nd Ed. p.377	
2886		-. 5. 1671	Dumfries	F	U	Men.	NK.	McDwll 2nd Ed. p.377	
2887		-. 5. 1671	Dumfries	F	U	Men.	NK.	McDwll 2nd Ed. p.377	
2888		-. 5. 1671	Dumfries	F	U	Men.	NK.	McDwll 2nd Ed. p.377	
2889	Bessie Pain	6. 6. 1671	Kirkcud-bright	F	U	Men.	NK.	Truckell	*
2890	Margaret Fleming	6. 6. 1671	Kirkcud-bright	F	U	Men.	NK.	Truckell	*
2891	Janet Lyon	2.11. 1671	Inverkip	F	U	Men.	NK.	Mtcalfe p.327	
2892		19. 6. 1672	Greenock	U	U	Men.	NK.	Mtcalfe p.327	
2893		19. 6. 1672	Greenock	U	U	Men.	NK.	Mtcalfe p.327	
2894	Elspet Smith	- - 1672	Hoy	F	U	Men.	NK.	Low p.575	
2895	Agnes Mor Nin Vick Ean-glaish	-. 5. 1675	Dingwall	F	U	Men.	NK.	G.302	*
2896	Jonet Drever	7. 6. 1675	Orkney	F	U	T	NCP	Mait.Cl. Misc. V2 pp. 167-168	

OTHER CASES									
No.	Name	Date	Place	Sex	Mar. Stat	Trial Stat	Fate	Source	New Case
2897	Kaitherin Sands	16. 7. 1675	Culross	F	U	Men.	Ex.	Smpkns pp.99-100	
2898	Issobell Inglis	16. 7. 1675	Culross	F	W	Men.	Ex.	Smpkns pp.99-100	
2899	Janet Hendries	16. 7. 1675	Culross	F	W	Men.	Ex.	Smpkns pp.99-100	
2900	Agnes Hendries	16. 7. 1675	Culross	F	W	Men.	Ex.	Smpkns pp.99-100	
2901		- - 1675	Shetland	F	U	Men.	Ex.	Sinclair p.231	
2902		- - 1675	Shetland	F	U	Men.	Ex.	Sinclair p.231	
2903	Grillies Robertson	- - 1675	Craill	F	U	Men.	NK.	G.138	*
2904	Isabel Davidson	-. 9. 1676	Belhelvie	F	U	Men.	Misc	Pres.Bk Strath-bogie p.XIV	
2905	John MacGregor	- - 1676	Greenock	M	U	Men.	Misc	G.207/378	*
2906	Andro Currie	25.12. 1677	Dun-fermline	M	M	Men.	Acqu	G.233	*
2907	Currie	25.12. 1677	Dun-fermline	F	M	Men.	Acqu	G.233	*
2908	Margaret Kirkwood	- - 1677	Hadding-ton	F	U	Men.	Misc	Reg. P.C.V5 p.171	
2909	Marion Campbell	-. 9. 1678	Peaston	F	U	Men.	NK.	Strang p.179	
2910		6.11. 1678	Fala	U	U	T	Ex.	Histrcl Notices V1 p.200	

OTHER CASES									
No.	Name	Date	Place	Sex	Mar. Stat	Trial Stat	Fate	Source	New Case
2911		6.11. 1678	Fala	U	U	T	Ex.	Histrcl Notices V1 p.205	
2912		6.11. 1678	Fala	U	U	T	NK.	Histrcl Notices V1 p.205	
2913		- - 1678	Edinburgh	U	U	Men.	Ex.	Histrcl Notices V1 p.200	
2914		- - 1678	Edinburgh	U	U	Men.	Ex.	Histrcl Notices V1 p.200	
2915		- - 1678	Edinburgh	U	U	Men.	Ex.	Histrcl Notices V1 p.200	
2916		- - 1678	Edinburgh	U	U	Men.	Ex.	Histrcl Notices V1 p.200	
2917		- - 1678	Edinburgh	U	U	Men.	Ex.	Histrcl Notices V1 p.200	
2918		- - 1678	Loanhead	F	U	Men.	Ex.	Dal. p.669	
2919		- - 1678	Loanhead	F	U	Men.	Ex.	Dal. p.669	
2920		- - 1678	Loanhead	F	U	Men.	Ex.	Dal. p.669	
2921		- - 1678	Loanhead	F	U	Men.	Ex.	Dal. p.669	
2922		- - 1678	Loanhead	F	U	Men.	Ex.	Dal. p.669	
2923		- - 1678	Loanhead	F	U	Men.	Ex.	Dal. p.669	
2924		- - 1678	Loanhead	F	U	Men.	Ex.	Dal. p.669	
2925		- - 1678	Loanhead	F	U	Men.	Ex.	Dal. p.669	

OTHER CASES									
No.	Name	Date	Place	Sex	Mar. Stat	Trial Stat	Fate	Source	New Case
2926		- - 1678	Loanhead	F	U	Men.	Ex.	Dal. p.669	
2927	Margaret Hamilton Secondus	-.12. 1679	Boness	F	U	Men.	Ex.	Webstr pp.95-103	
2928	Bessie Vicker	-.12. 1679	Boness	F	U	Men.	Ex.	Webstr pp.95-103	
2929	William Craw	-.12. 1679	Boness	M	U	Men.	Ex.	Webstr pp.95-103	
2930	Margaret Hamilton	-.12. 1679	Boness	F	U	Men.	Ex.	Webstr pp.95-103	
2931	Margaret Pringle	-.12. 1679	Boness	F	U	Men.	Ex.	Webstr pp.95-103	
2932	Annaple Thompson	-.12. 1679	Boness	F	U	Men.	Ex.	Webstr pp.95-103	
2933	Margaret Comb	13. 5. 1680	Edinburgh	F	U	Men.	Acqu	Bk Old Edin.Cl. V6 p.142	
2934	Ann Nin William	- - 1680		F	U	Men.	NK.	G.233	*
2935		- - 1680	Angus Arbroath	F	U	T	Acqu	Andrson	*
2936	Elspeth Kirkland	- - 1681	Aberdour	F	U	Men.	Acqu	Ross p.332	
2937	John MacQueen	2.12. 1684	Edinburgh	M	U	Men.	NCP	G.306-307	*
2938	Marion Purdie	- - 1684	Edinburgh	F	U	Men.	NCP	Foun. V2 p.561	
2939	Helen Eliot	- - 1684	Culross	F	U	Men.	Ex.	Sinclair pp.207-208	

OTHER CASES									
No.	Name	Date	Place	Sex	Mar. Stat	Trial Stat	Fate	Source	New Case
2940	William Easone	-.10. 1689	Auchter-gaven	M	M	Men.	NK.	G.306	*
2941	Janet Fraser	-. 7. 1691	Dumfries	F	U	Men.	NK.	Edin. Mag. & Lit. Misc.V2 pp.103-104	
2942	William Simpson	- - 1691	Broughton	M	U	Men.	NCP	G.305	*
2943	Marion Dickson	- - 1692	Dumfries	F	U	T	NK.	Ch. V3 p.66	
2944	Isobel Dickson	- - 1692	Dumfries	F	U	Men.	NK.	Ch.V3 p.66	
2945	Marion Herbertson	- - 1692	Dumfries	F	U	Men.	NK.	Ch.V3 p.66	
2946		- - 1694	Colding-ham	U	U	Men.	Ex.	Ch.V3 p.94	
2947		- - 1694	Colding-ham	U	U	Men.	Ex.	Ch.V3 p.94	
2948		- - 1694	Colding-	U	U	Men.	Ex.	Ch.V3 p.94	
2949		- - 1694	Colding-	U	U	Men.	Ex.	Ch.V3 p.94	
2950		- - 1694	Colding-	U	U	Men.	Ex.	Ch.V3 p.94	
2951		- - 1694	Colding-	U	U	Men.	Ex.	Ch.V3 p.94	
2952		- - 1694	Colding-	U	U	Men.	Ex.	Ch.V3 p.94	
2953	John Dougall	- - 1695	Inverkip	M	U	Men.	NK.	Murray, Kilmal-colm p.110	
2954		- - 1695	Old Kil-patrick	F	U	Men.	Ex.	Old Stat. Acc.Scot. 1791 V5 p.240	

OTHER CASES									
No.	Name	Date	Place	Sex	Mar. Stat	Trial Stat	Fate	Source	New Case
2955	Several Persons	5. 2. 1696	Kilmal-colm	U	U	Men.	NK.	Mtcalfe p.329	
2956	Janet Widdrow or Wodrow	- - 1696	Inchinan	F	U	Men.	NK.	Dal. p.664	
2957	Janet Wodrow	- - 1696	Paisley	F	U	Men.	Misc	G.389	*
2958	Several People	2. 5. 1697	Killearn	U	U	Men.	NK.	Smith, Strath. p.61	
2959	Several Witches	22. 5. 1697	Glasgow	U	U	Men.	NK.	Gl.Brgh R.1691-1777 p.254	
2960	Several Persons	- - 1697	Kirk-maiden	U	U	Men.	NK.	G.204 366	*
2961	Elizabeth Anderson	- - 1697	Bar-garran	F	U	Men.	NK.	G.303	*
2962	Several Warlocks	-. 3.	Glasgow	M	U	Men.	NK.	Gl.Brgh R.1691-1717 p.260	
2963	Several Witches	-. 3. 1698	Glasgow	F	U	Men.	NK.	Gl.Brgh R.1691-1717 p.260	
2964	Margaret Laird	-. 7. 1698	Kilma-colm	F	U	Men.	Acqu	Ch.V3	
2965	Marion Lillie	- - 1698	Spott	F	U	Men.	NK.	Old Stat. Acc.Scot. V5 p.454	
2966	Margaret Polwart	- - 1698	Colding-ham	F	U	Men.	NK.	Ch.V3 p.95	
2967	Alison Nisbet	- - 1698	Colding-ham	F	U	Men.	NK.	Ch.V3 p.95	
2968	Jean Hart	- - 1698	Colding-ham	F	U	Men.	NK.	Ch.V3 p.95	

OTHER CASES									
No.	Name	Date	Place	Sex	Mar. Stat	Trial Stat	Fate	Source	New Case
2969	Several Warlocks	12. 3. 1699	Glasgow	M	U	Men.	NK.	Clelnd p.100	
2970	Several Witches	12. 3. 1699	Glasgow	F	U	Men.	NK.	Clelnd p.100	
2971	Jonnet Buttar	- - 1700	Kinloch	F	U	Men.	NCP	G.256	*
2972	Ellen King	- - 1700	Shetland	F	U	Men.	Ex.	New Stat. Acc. Shet. p.60	
2973	Barbara Tulloch	- - 1700	Shetland	F	U	Men.	Ex.	New Stat. Acc. Shet. p.60	
2974	Meg Lawson	- - 1700	Selkirk	F	U	Men.	Ex.	Craig-Brown V2 p.100	
2975	Janet McRobert	-. 1. 1701	Kirkcud-bright	F	U	Men.	NCP	Wood pp. 82-87	
2976	Elizabeth Dick	-. 4. 1701	Anstru-ther-Easter	F	U	Men.	NK.	E.Fife R. Nov. 23 1894	
2977	Janet McRobert	- - 1701	Dumfries	F	U	T	NCP	Truckell No.43	*
2978	Margaret Myles	20.11. 1702	Edinburgh	F	U	Men.	Ex.	Ch.,Dom. Ann. V3 p.217	
2979	Molly Redmond	- - 1702	Minni-gaff	F	U	Men.	NCP	G.256	*
2980	Lady Tonderghee	- - 1702	Minni-gaff	F	U	Men.	NCP	G.256	*
2981	Grissel Anderson	- - 1703	Torry-burn	F	U	Men.	Ex.	Webstr p.138	
2982	Robert Bainzie	- - 1703	Oyne	M	U	Men.	NCP	Archae. Scot. V3 p.13	

OTHER CASES									
No.	Name	Date	Place	Sex	Mar. Stat	Trial Stat	Fate	Source	New Case
2983	Euphan Stirt	- - 1703	Torry-burn	F	U	Men.	Ex.	Webstr p.138	
2984	Janet McMurray	- - 1703	Dumfries	F	U	T	NCP	Truckell No.43	*
2985	Anna Wood	-. 1. 1704	Borrow-stounness	F	U	Men.	Misc	Salmon pp.119-121	
2986	Elspeth Williamson	-. 7. 1704	Torry-burn	F	U	Men.	NK.	Webstr pp.136-144	
2987	Lillias Adie	-. 7. 1704	Torry-burn	F	U	Men.	Misc	Webstr pp.129-144	
2988	Isobel Adam	- - 1704	Pitten-weem	F	U	Men.	NK.	Webstr pp.83; 90-91	
2989	Mrs. White	- - 1704	Pitten-weem	F	M	Men.	NK.	Webstr pp.83; 90-91	
2990	Janet Cornfoot	- - 1704	Fife	F	U	Men.	NK.	G.403	*
2991	Mary Wilson	- - 1704	Torry-burn	F	U	Men.	NK.	Webstr p.129	*
2992	Janet Whyte	- - 1704	Torry-burn	F	U	Men.	NK.	G.368-369	*
2993	Jean Bizet	- - 1704	Torry-burn	F	M	Men.	NK.	Webstr pp.129; 145	*
2994	Many Witches	-.10. 1705	Spott	U	U	Men.	Ex.	Old Stat. Acc.Scot. V5 p.454	
2995	Mary McNarin	-.11. 1705	Penning-hame	F	S	Men.	NCP	G.239 101-102	*
2996		- - 1705	Penning-hame	U	U	Men.	NK.	G.257	*
2997	Mary Stewart	- - 1705	Kilbride	F	U	Men.	NCP	G.257	*

OTHER CASES

No.	Name	Date	Place	Sex	Mar. Stat	Trial Stat	Fate	Source	New Case
2998	Beatrix Laing	- - 1705	Pitten-weem	F	U	Men.	NK.	Webstr pp.67-94	
2999	Thomas Brown	- - 1705	Pitten-weem	M	U	Men.	Misc	Webstr p.71	
3000	Nicolas Lawson	- - 1705	Pitten-weem	M	U	Men.	NK.	Webstr pp.67-94	
3001	Janet Corphat or Cornfoot	- - 1705	Pitten-weem	F	U	Men.	Misc	Webstr pp.67-94	
3002	Mary McNairn	- - 1705	Penning-hame	F	U	T	NK.	Truckell No.43	*
3003		- - 1706	Dumfries	F	U	Men.	NCP	Truckell No. 43	*
3004	Jean Brown	- - 1706	Penning-hame	F	U	T	Misc	Truckell No. 43	*
3005	John McNairn	- - 1706	Penning-hame	M	U	T	NK.	Truckell No. 43	*
3006	Jean Brown	- - 1706	Penning-hame	F	U	Men.	NK.	G.369	*
3007		- - 1706	Kilbride	U	U	Men.	NK.	G.302	*
3008	Janet McKeoner	9.11. 1707	Penning-hame	F	U	Men.	Ex.	Sess.Bk P'hame	*
3009	Alexander Deuart	- - 1707	Dumfries	M	U	Men.	NK.	Truckell No. 43.	*
3010	Kathrine Taylor	- - 1708	Strom-ness	F	U	Men.	NK.	Low pp. 201-203	
3011		- - 1709	Kilmorie	U	U	Men.	NK.	G.257	*
3012	Isobel Anderson	- - 1714	Dunnet	F	U	Men.	NCP	G.262	*
3013	Margaret Ogilvy	- - 1715	Perth	F	U	T	Ex.	Cowan V2 pp. 132-133	

OTHER CASES									
No.	Name	Date	Place	Sex	Mar. Stat	Trial Stat	Fate	Source	New Case
3014	Sarah Johnson	- - 1715	Perth	F	U	T	Ex.	Cowan V2 pp. 132-133	
3015	M'Huistan	- - 1718	Thurso	F	U	Men.	NK.	Sharpe pp.180-194	
3016	Margaret Callum	- - 1718	Thurso	F	U	Men.	NK.	Sharpe pp.180-194	
3017	Helen Andrew	- - 1718	Thurso	F	U	Men.	NK.	Sharpe pp.180-194	
3018	Jannet Pyper	- - 1718	Thurso	F	U	Men.	NK.	Sharpe pp.180-194	
3019	Margaret Oisone	- - 1718	Thurso	F	U	Men.	NK.	Sharpe pp.180-194	
3020	Margaret Nin Gilbert	- - 1718	Thurso	F	U	Men.	Misc	Sharpe pp.180-194	
3021	Unnamed Women	-. 1. 1720	Calder	F	U	Men.	Acqu	Sinclair pp.262-264	
3022	Several Persons	- - 1720	Linlith-gow	U	U	Men.	NK.	G.300-301	*
3023	Margaret Drummond	-. 6. 1723	Linton	F	U	Men.	NK.	G.203	*
3024		- - 1723	Linton	U	U	Men.	NCP	G.257	*
3025	Margaret Bain	18. 2. 1724	Canisbay	F	U	Men.	NK.	Cldr pp. 226-227	
3026	Several Witches	-. 5. 1726	Ross-shire	U	U	Men.	NK.	Wodrow V3 p.302	
3027	Horne	-. 6. 1727	Dornoch	F	U	T	Misc	Sharpe pp.199-200	

OTHER CASES									
No.	Name	Date	Place	Sex	Mar. Stat	Trial Stat	Fate	Source	New Case
3028	Janet Horne	-. 6. 1727	Dornoch	F	U	T	Ex.	Sharpe pp.199-200	
3029	Several Persons	- - 1750	Rosskeen	U	U	Men.	Misc	G.263	*
3030	John Mill	- - 1758	Shetland	M	M	Men.	NK.	G.307	*
3031	John Gordon	- - - -	Aberdeen	M	U	Men.	NCP	G.220	*
3032	Patrick Adamson	- - - -	St. Andrews	M	U	Men.	NK.	G.308	*
3033	Margaret Reid	- - - -	Kirk-caldy	F	U	Men.	Misc	G.146	*
3034	Curate of Anstruther	- - - -	Anstru-ther	M	U	Men.	NK.	G.305	*
3035	Archbishop Sharp	- - - -	St. Andrews	M	S	Men.	Misc	G.305	*
3036	Lillies Barrie	- - - -	South Leith	F	U	Men.	Acqu	G.222	*
3037	Isbell Dairsie	- - - -	St. Andrews	F	U	Men.	NK.	G.156	*
3038	Margaret Hay	- - - -	Elgin	F	U	Men.	NK.	G.27	*
3039	Margaret Balfour	- - - -	Elgin	F	U	Men.	NK.	G.27	*
3040	Isbell Dairsie	- - - -	St. Andrews	F	U	Men.	Misc	G.397	*
3041	Christine Dote	- - - -	St. Andrews	F	U	Men.	Misc	G.397	*
3042	Margaret Myrton	- - - -	St. Andrews	F	U	Men.	NK.	G.397	*
3043		- - - -	Lanark	F	U	Men.	Acqu	G.397	*
3044	Agnes Anstruther	- - - -	Kirk-caldy	F	U	Men.	Misc	G.119	*

OTHER CASES									
No.	Name	Date	Place	Sex	Mar. Stat	Trial Stat	Fate	Source	New Case
3045	Margaret Laird	- - - -	Kilma- colme	F	U	Men.	NK.	G.108	*
3046	Marion Maguate	- - - -	Coulter Nisbite	F	U	Men.	NK.	G.106	*
3047	Elspeth McEwan	- - - -	Dalry	F	U	Men.	NK.	G.219	*
3048		- - - -	Edinburgh	U	U	Men.	NK.	G.213	*
3049		- - - -	Elgin	U	U	Men.	NK.	G.213	*
3050	James Wodrow	- - - -	Erskine	M	U	Men.	NK.	G.106-119	*
3051		- - - -	Forfar	U	U	Men.	NK.	G.221	*
3052	John MacGregor	- - - -	Greenock	M	U	Men.	NK.	G.140	*
3053	Katherine Shaw	- - - -	Kirk- Caldy	F	U	Men.	Misc	G.146	*
3054		- - - -	Forfar	U	U	Men.	NK.	G.221	*
3055		- - - -	Lanark	F	U	Men.	Acqu	G.397	*
3056		- - - -	Lanark	F	U	Men.	Acqu	G.397	*
3057		- - - -	Lanark	F	U	Men.	Acqu	G.397	*
3058		- - - -	Lanark	F	U	Men.	Acqu	G.397	*
3059		- - - -	Lanark	F	U	Men.	Acqu	G.397	*
3060		- - - -	Lanark	F	U	Men.	Acqu	G.397	*
3061		- - - -	Lanark	F	U	Men.	Acqu	G.397	*

OTHER CASES									
No.	Name	Date	Place	Sex	Mar. Stat	Trial Stat	Fate	Source	New Case
3062		- - - -	Lanark	F	U	Men.	Acqu	G.397	*
3063		- - - -	Lanark	F	U	Men.	Acqu	G.397	*
3064	Margaret Provost	6.10. 1699	ffortross	F	U	Proc.	NK.	MS GUL	*
3065	Margaret Bezok	6.10. 1699	ffortross	F	M	Proc.	NK.	MS GUL	*
3066	Mary Nicinnarich	6.10. 1699	ffortross	F	U	Proc.	NK.	MS GUL	*
3067	Janet Drewer	7. 6. 1615	Orkney	F	U	T	Misc	Orkney Ct Bk pp.18-20	*
3068	Marioun Lewing	-. 6. 1615	Orkney	F	U	Men.	NK.	Orkney Ct Bk pp.18-20	*
3069	Marioun Tailzeour Mother of Katherine Bigland	-. 6. 1615	Orkney	F	U	Men.	NK.	Orkney Ct Bk pp.18-20	*

OTHER CASES									
No.	Name	Date	Place	Sex	Mar. Stat	Trial Stat	Fate	Source	New Case

OTHER CASES									
No.	Name	Date	Place	Sex	Mar. Stat	Trial Stat	Fate	Source	New Case

OTHER CASES									
No.	Name	Date	Place	Sex	Mar. Stat	Trial Stat	Fate	Source	New Case

SECTION II

TABLES

Note 1. The figures represent cases and not individuals, and at least 200 individuals appear in more than one source. While the figures for each court are likely to represent individuals, the totals should be treated with appropriate caution.

Note 2. The tables omit those who were merely mentioned as witches, except where otherwise stated.

TABLE 1

Trial status of all cases (including those merely mentioned in the papers) broken down by type of court.

COURT TYPE	TRIAL STATUS				TOTAL
	Mentioned	Processed	Commission	Tried	
High Court	306	191	0	211	708
Circuit Court	0	23	0	142	165
Privy Council	266	0	791	0	1057
Acts of Parliament	9	0	99	0	108
Committee of Estates	2	0	170	0	172
Other	595	0	0	264	859
TOTAL	1178	214	1060	617	3069

TABLE 2

Fate of accused broken down by type of court.

COURT TYPE	FATE					TOTAL
	Unknown	Miscellaneous	Acquitted etc.	Non-Capital Punishment	Executed	
High Court	125	80	84	5	108	402
Circuit Court	53	7	81	7	17	165
Privy Council	695	7	4	5	80	791
Acts of Parliament	88	0	0	0	11	99
Committee of Estates	170	0	0	0	0	170
Other	76	5	14	16	153	264
TOTAL	1207	99	183	33	369	1891

TABLE 3

Fate of accused broken down by type of court (including those only mentioned).

COURT TYPE	FATE					TOTAL
	Unknown	Miscellaneous	Acquitted etc.	Non-Capital Punishment	Executed	
High Court	392	84	84	5	143	708
Circuit Court	53	7	81	7	17	165
Privy Council	866	31	25	7	128	1057
Acts of Parliament	96	0	1	0	11	108
Committee of Estates	171	0	1	0	0	172
Other	405	55	49	50	300	859
TOTAL	1983	177	241	69	599	3069

TABLE 4

Cases broken down by decade and type of court.

COURT TYPE	PERIOD																	TOTAL
	Date Unknown	1560/1569	1570/1579	1580/1589	1590/1599	1600/1609	1610/1619	1620/1629	1630/1639	1640/1649	1650/1659	1660/1669	1670/1679	1680/1689	1690/1699	1700/1709	1710/1719	1720/1729	
High Court	4	5	4	6	29	7	7	5	9	9	129	67	63	25	2	31	0	0	402
Circuit Court	0	0	0	0	0	0	0	0	0	0	121	0	38	0	0	6	0	0	165
Privy Council	0	0	0	0	1	0	46	342	78	38	0	226	35	1	22	2	0	0	791
Acts of Parliament	0	0	0	0	0	1	0	0	0	15	5	78	0	0	0	0	0	0	99
Committee of Estates	0	0	0	0	0	0	0	0	0	170	0	0	0	0	0	0	0	0	170
Other	0	4	0	3	16	6	21	11	17	97	69	5	4	1	1	5	2	2	264
TOTAL	4	9	4	9	46	14	74	358	104	329	324	376	140	27	25	44	2	2	1891

TABLE 5

Cases broken down by decade and type of court (including those only mentioned).

COURT TYPE	PERIOD																		TOTAL
	Date Unknown	1560/1569	1570/1579	1580/1589	1590/1599	1600/1609	1610/1619	1620/1629	1630/1639	1640/1649	1650/1659	1660/1669	1670/1679	1680/1689	1690/1699	1700/1709	1710/1719	1720/1729	1750/1759	
High Court	4	6	4	6	101	12	8	10	9	33	161	226	69	25	3	31	0	0	0	708
Circuit Court	0	0	0	0	0	0	0	0	0	0	121	0	38	0	0	6	0	0	0	165
Privy Council	0	0	0	2	9	7	48	368	128	107	5	313	39	2	27	2	0	0	0	1057
Acts of Parliament	0	0	0	0	0	1	0	0	0	16	6	85	0	0	0	0	0	0	0	108
Committee of Estates	1	0	0	0	0	0	0	0	0	171	0	0	0	0	0	0	0	0	0	172
Other	33	13	2	6	85	19	31	26	37	180	203	69	57	8	30	41	9	8	2	859
TOTAL	38	19	6	14	195	39	87	404	174	507	496	693	203	35	60	80	9	8	2	3069

TABLE 6

Sex of accused broken down by type of court.

COURT TYPE	SEX			TOTAL
	Male	Female	Unknown	
High Court	60	339	3	402
Circuit Court	22	81	62	165
Privy Council	93	678	20	791
Acts of Parliament	6	79	14	99
Committee of Estates	26	143	1	170
Other	35	171	58	264
TOTAL	242	1491	158	1891

TABLE 7

Sex of accused broken down by type of court.
(including those only mentioned).

COURT TYPE	SEX			TOTAL
	Male	Female	Unknown	
High Court	117	583	8	708
Circuit Court	22	81	62	165
Privy Council	133	891	33	1057
Acts of Parliament	7	85	16	108
Committee of Estates	26	145	1	172
Other	104	567	188	859
TOTAL	409	2352	308	3069

TABLE 8

Marital status of accused broken down by type of court.

COURT TYPE	MARITAL STATUS				TOTAL
	Married	Single	Widowed	Unknown	
High Court	80	3	40	279	402
Circuit Court	12	0	3	150	165
Privy Council	111	2	20	658	791
Acts of Parliament	6	0	0	93	99
Committee of Estates	18	1	3	148	170
Other	18	1	1	244	264
TOTAL	245	7	67	1572	1891

TABLE 9

Marital status of accused broken down by type of court. (including those only mentioned).

COURT TYPE	MARITAL STATUS				TOTAL
	Married	Single	Widowed	Unknown	
High Court	152	4	42	510	708
Circuit Court	12	0	3	150	165
Privy Council	163	2	34	858	1057
Acts of Parliament	6	0	0	102	108
Committee of Estates	18	1	3	150	172
Other	39	3	4	813	859
TOTAL	390	10	86	2583	3069

TABLE 10

List of witches whose social or occupational status is recorded.

The status of a witch is rarely mentioned in the records, yet it is clear from internal evidence that the majority were the wives or widows of tenant farmers. It can be fairly safely assumed that those listed below had their status mentioned because it was unusual.

No.	Name	Status
18	Lady Fowlis	Nobility
19	Hector Munro	Nobility
33	Bessie Roy	Nurse/Servant to Laird of Boquane
38	John Fean	Schoolmaster
42	Agnes Sampsoune	"Of a rank and comprehension above the vulgar"
82	Barbara Napier	Husband a Burgess and brother a Laird
83	Ewfame Makcalzene	Daughter of Lord Cliftonhall. R.C.
85	Patrick Herring	Captain
105	Earl of Bothwell	Nobility
107	John Stewart	Master of Orkney
113	Christian Lewinstoun	A wise woman
117	Bessie Aiken	Midwife
118	James Reid	Servant
122	Issobel Griersoune	Spouse of workman
123	Bartie Petersoun	Tasker
131	Grissell Gairdner	Husband a Burgess of Newburgh
134	Robert Erskine	Nobility
135	Annas Erskine	Nobility
136	Issobell Erskine	Nobility
137	Helene Erskine	Nobility
138	Margaret Wallace	Husband a Merchant and Burgess of Glasgow
142	Isobell Young	Husband a Portioner in Eastbarns

No.	Name	Status
144	Katharine Oswald	Husband a Miller
148	Alexander Hamilton	Vagabond
149	Michaell Erskine	Miller
151	John Neil	Englishman
153	John Colquhoun	Laird of Luss
154	Thomas Carlips	Servant to J. Colquhoun. Burgess of Glasgow. 1629. German
156	Elizabeth Bathgate	Husband a Maltman
162	Margaret Lauder	Servant
163	Janet Barker	Servant
164	Jeane Craig	Husband a Collier
165	Agnes Finnie	Money-lender in Edinburgh
166	Helen Clerk	Husband a Fisher
190	Marione Sprott	Poor - she begged
192	Thomas Paton	He employed a servant
199	Elizabeth Maxwell	Aunt to Lady Midlebee. She employed a servant
208	John McWilliam	Slater
302	Bessie Stevenson	Husband a Gairner
304	Jonnet Man	Beggar - mother of three bastards
328	Elspeth Fouller	Poor
330	Jonet Thomson	Husband a Shoemaker
334	Marioun Lynn	Midwife
335	Marion Logan	Servant to John Auchinlock
336	Mareone Guild	Husband a Cordoner
346	Magdalen Blair	Poor - beggar.Mother of illegitimate child
362	Janet Daill	Husband a Collier
377	Beatrix Leslie	Midwife
393	Margaret Hutchison	Had a servant
411	Jonet Ewart	"Living under the Laird of Guodtrees"
431	Agnes Williamson	Miller's wife
432	James Welsh	Servant to Minister's wife
576	Major Thomas Weir	Retired Major
577	Jean Weir	Former School Teacher
593	John Scott	A Workman
601	Christian Morison	A poor woman
607	Margaret Clerk	Rich enough to hire an Advocate

No.	Name	Status
623	Gideon Penman	Former Minister
636	Isobell Eliot	Former servant
637	Helen Laying	Had a servant
641	Bessie Gourdie	Midwife
646	Bessie Gibb	Husband a Skipper
661	John Hislop	Weaver
671	Gean Hadron	Poor and sought alms. Baker's widow
672	Elspeth Wood	Miller's widow
673	John Glass	Tenant of Rorie McKenzie of Redcastle
676	Jean Ross	School-Teacher
678	Margaret Duncan	Merchant's widow
680	Jannet Boyd	Servant to Craigton
683	Margaret Alexander	Poor - sought alms
684	Elspeth Tarbat	Spouse a Shoemaker
690	Mary Morisone	Spouse a Skipper
693	Jean Gilmore	Spouse a Beadle in Govan
694	Janet Robertson	Spouse a Smith in Govan
695	Jannet Gentleman	Spouse a Beadle in Glasgow
696	Marion Ure	Spouse a Merchant
699	Agnes Currie	Indweller in Torrieburn
845	Geils Burnet	Had a servant
853	Richard Halywall	Merchant
854	Jannet Hil	Spouse a workman
866	John Hislop	Weaver
872	Nicolas Lawson	Husband a Farmer
895	Katherine Cunynhame	Spouse a Miller
898	Jonnet Listar	Spouse a Gardner
912	Margaret Reoch	Vagabond
924	Jonet Hammyltoun	Spouse a Baker
931	John Stewart	Vagabond
932	Margaret Barclay	Spouse Burgess
953	Jonet Maglene	Spouse a Gardner
1018	Elizabeth Jamesone	Spouse a Skipper
1104	Issobell Miller	Spouse a Cordonner
1114	Helen Gow	Spouse a Cordiner
1129	Alexander Hamiltoun	A vagabond

No.	Name	Status
1136	Katherine Oswald	Spouse a Miller
1147	Isobel Rutherfurde	Vagabond
1149	Jonet Neill	Spouse a Burgess of Dumbarton
1155	Margaret Hunter	Spouse a Sailor
1158	Janet Melros	Midwive
1160	Isobel Gray	Vagabond
1161	Alexander Hunter	Vagabond
1200	Helen Beatie	Midwife
1204	John Graham alias Joke the Graham	Weaver
1214	Agnes Robesoun	Vagabond
1250	Margaret Studgeon	Vagabond
1255	Margaret Hastie	Spouse a Menstrell
1279	Barbara Wod	Spouse a Burgess of Lauder
1283	Janet Allane	Spouse a Burgess of Lauder
1383	Elie Nesbit	Midwife
1388	Marion Hurdie	Vagabond, born in England
1492	Issobell Murray	Husband a Forester
1628	Christian Gray	Husband a Showmaker
1640	Jonnet Burrell	Husband a Maltman
1691	Mary Lawmont	Servant
1767	Beak Nein Ean Duy Vic Finley	Servant
1850	Hendry Wilson	Loadman
1859	Grissell Jaffray	Husband a Maltman
1874	Lizzie Mudie	Servant
1886	Marjorie Anderson	Servant to Agnes Kelly
1900	Catharin MacTargett	Husband a Weaver, became a beggar
1941	The Wives of Magistrates	
2038	Jeane Craig	Husband a Collier
2040	Janet Fairlie	Husband a Maltman
2047	Agnes Tailzeor	Spouse Fudnelle in Bo'ness
2063	Marion Durie	Spouse past Baillie of Innerkeithen
2221	Lyon King of Arms	
2316	Donald Moir	Miller
2385	Jonet Rendall	Poor Vagabond

No.	Name	Status
2441	Helen Hunter	Innswoman
2462	William Scottie	Vagabond
2506	Helen Hill	Husband a Mariner
2598	Margaret Dunham	Innkeeper

The following were merely mentioned in the course of trials, confessions, etc.

No.	Name	Status
50	Wife of the Portaris of Seytoune	
64	Bessie Broune	Husband a Smith
89	Gelie Duncan	Servant
92	Niniane Chirneyside	Servant (to Bothwell)
100	Robert Griersoun	Ship's Captain
115	John Damiet	Italian
116	Michael Clark	Smith
127	Marioun Ersche	Irish
167	Elspethie	"The Spay Wife"
310	Elspeth Colvill	Husband a Baker
312	Elspeth Robertson	Husband a Weaver
321	Marioun Lowrie	Husband a Flesher
323	Margaret Robertson	Husband a Weaver
324	Helen Gibson	Husband a Chapman
493	Margaret Blak	Miller's wife
494	John Homme	Miller
501	Jon Kincaid	Pricker of Witches
534	Wife of George Sandie	Spouse a Cooper
543	Jonet Lowrie	The Baker's wife
547	Jeane Dikson	A Hynd's wife
558		Her son was a Millar
566	George Binnie	Servant to Minister's wife
573	George Lacost	Miller
890	Jonet Drysdaill	Servant to Sir James Newton
926	Jonet Andirsone	Servitor to Johnne Andersone

No.	Name	Status
959	Janet Robertsone	Spouse a Dreger
1192	Janet Hardie	Spouse a Skipper
1297	Lady Manderstone	Spouse Sir George Hume of Manderston
1356	Lady Samuelston	Nobility
1379	Johne Smith	Servant to Lady Bass
1393	Cowie	Brouster
1406	George Semill	Preacher
1421	Gardener's wife	
1447	Cristane Poock	Servant
1459	Margaret Young	Spouse Burgess of Dysart
1471	Margaret Reid	Midwife
1479	The Piper's mother	
1486	Margaret Bartilman	Husband a Maillmaker
1505	Grissell Anderson	Spouse Elder in Painston
1755	John Hay	Messenger
2235	Morven Witches	Employed by Campbell of Ardkinglass
2333	Malcome Toir	Reader at Logie
2336	George Semple	Minister
2447	John Shand	Fugitive
2600	Margaret Henderson, Lady Pittathrow	Nobility
2877	Janet Conochie	Husband a Cooper
2879	Goodaile	Husband a Cooper
2908	Margaret Kirkwood	Had a servant
2937	John MacQueen	Minister
2938	Marion Purdie	Once a Midwife, now a beggar
2940	William Easone	Minister
2979	Molly Redmond	Servant to Lady Tonderghee
2980	Lady Tonderghee	Nobility
2982	Robert Bainzie	An Elder in the Kirk
2995	Mary McNarin	Servetrix
3004	Jean Brown	Servant
3010	Kathrine Taylor	A crippled beggar
3030	John Mill	Minister
3034	Curate of Anstruther	Episcopalian Curate
3035	Archbishop Sharp	

TABLE 11

Distribution of cases by geographical zones broken down by type of court.

COURT TYPE	GEOGRAPHICAL ZONES												TOTAL
	1	2	3	4	5	6	7	8	9	10	11	12	
High Court	13	60	106	21	3	12	44	8	89	26	1	19	402
Circuit Court	14	3	10	5	1	3	16	20	8	23	0	62	165
Privy Council	126	111	94	55	28	93	79	58	101	37	6	3	791
Acts of Parliament	2	53	31	0	0	4	0	0	5	1	0	3	99
Committee of Estates	53	52	41	0	0	9	0	0	4	2	0	9	170
Other	23	18	49	6	18	48	8	3	30	17	40	4	264
TOTAL	231	297	331	87	50	169	147	89	237	106	47	100	1891

KEY TO GEOGRAPHICAL ZONES

		Total
1.	Eastern Borders	231
2.	East Lothian	297
3.	Lothians and Edinburgh	331
4.	North East	87
5.	Banff, Angus and Kincardine	50
6.	Fife	169
7.	Central Scotland (Stirling to Perth)	147
8.	Highlands and Islands including Bute	89
9.	West Scotland including Lanark	237
10.	Western Borders and Galloway	106
11.	Orkney and Shetland	47
12.	Unlocated Cases	100

Note: Most of the cases in Zone 8 were either in Bute or on the eastern seaboard of Ross, Caithness, or Sutherland.

SECTION III

TRANSCRIPTS

This Section consists of a few samples of the material available. Section IV contains information on more extended transcripts in print. Contained below are examples of confessions and indictments and the legislation against witchcraft.

CASE OF Margaret Harvie 1659

The depositioun of Witnesses examined in presence of Colonell Thomas Read Liuetenent Cloberie Major Matlo Williame Stirling of harbertshyre Captaine Carrait and Captain Hunt at Stirling ye 16 march 1659 Against Margrat harvie in Rippon paroch

Agnis Dinven in Rippon depones that hir dochter Margrat milne being seik she cauld Margrat Harvie thairof wha bad hir goe to Isobel Keir hous and carrie of ye charr above ye said Issobell hir doore heid and seik the bairnes health for Gods caus, Which she refuset to obey and ye bairn diet

Jonet miller now in ye prisoun suspect of Witchcraft declaires that about ye 15 of December last by past, she went in to Margrat Gourlay in hir hous efter ye sun set qr she saw Isobell Keir and Margrat harvie and ane blak man with thame, all siting at one tabill covered With ane Whyt cloth and sum boylet beif and bread thairon, And that ye said Margrat gourlay offered to ye deponer ane part of ye meat Which she refuiset to eat And then Margrat Gourlay bad hir goe about hir bussiness And imediatlie yrefter ane bed in ye hous qr they were at meat took fyre Which wes extinguishet be Andrew Wright and Georg Wordie
Also Jonet miller declaires that within aygt dayes or yrby thairefter she saw Isobell keir Margrat harvie and Margrat Gourlay in Androw Wrightis stak yaird and Margrat Gourlay puting in four haulr of Wolen yairn in ane stak And yrefter imediatlie Johne Wright Went out and fand fyre kenilet in syde severall places on ye bak of his hous nearest ye barne yaird And that they took out fyve burning colis out of t places of ye hous qr it was burning and put thame in ye hous fyre qr they craket extraordinerlie And that ane blak reaven came flieing too and again above ye hous And imediatlie yrefter the said stak qr Margrat Gourlay wes standing took fyre Which Wes extinguished by ye cuntrie people

The depositionnes afoirsaid are taken in our hearing and signuret by Us

Thomas Reade
John: Clobriy
W Stirling
Ja: Mutlow

(Case 300)

CASE OF Magdalen Blair 1659

Stirling the 13 Jan'r 1659

Mr Mathias simpsone & Rob Russall baillie haveing mett in duncan buchannan house for visiting of helean ker his spous who for the p(resen)t is heavilie deseased and supposes herself to have gotten by witchcraft And supposeing Madlan blair to be the persone she is conveened And the persones followeing being depones as followes

James andersone baxter declares that about an yeare since or yrby there was a horse belonging to Richart idstone in spitell standing beofre Madlane blairs doore after he was disburdenned of a load of and ther being some scolding words past betwixt the sd Richart & her, schee strake the sd Richards horse saying God ner he shoot to death And the horse died suddenlie the same day after he was taken home

The sd Magdalane here upon examined confest that shee strak the sd horse and uttered the foresd words

The sd Helen ker depones that shee challenges the sd Magdalane about those words and told her the horse was dead and Magdalen ansred it was litle enough althou it had fallin upon the man himself, and shee never gave a malison but what shee saw light

The sd Magadalen hereupon pe'sed , acknowledges that she sayed then That she once prayed a malison upon John steill who had gotten a bairn wt her and would give her nothing to help it and he lay long sick & spent much of his geir

The sd helen farder sayes that the sd Magdalen at that tym sayed to her, what had shee a doe to come speake wt her since her husband & shee were not friends, and yt night The sd Helen goeing in to her bed wch was made found a lump of dead sand betwixt the sheets like a modiwort hillok It being ten ho'rs at ewin, And altho shee was weell in health at yt tym yet yt night shee tooke siknesse wch hath continewed wt her ewer since The extremmetie of it leaying upon her at yt houer of the night till the last saturday when told the minister that shee suspected the sd Magdalen had wronged her, And since her paines come not to her till midnight

The sd Magdalen hereupon p'sed declares That shee onelie sayed to Helen, What have ye a doe to come to me for I have nothing to do wt yow, And being asked about the dead sand how it came in to Helens bed, schee ansred ye should aske yt of the rest leaves For that is also much as ye would make me doer of all

M. Symson
Robert Russall

James Worie clerke of ye sd burgh being like wise auditor to the foresd depos'nes attests the same

William Luckisone maltman declares that about six yeirs since or yrby he contracted a sore siknes, And in the meane tyme haveing occasion to visite katharine Luckisone his sister now spous to james andersone, and finding her and Magdalen blair sitting togither in the foot of andrew cowans yaird The said katharine asked at Magdalen what shee thought aled the deponer And Magaden thereupon asked at the de poner if there was any enmitie or discord betueen Issobell bennet and him, And he ansred that there was none yt he knew of, except that at sometimes when her fowles would be in his fathers victuall, he would throw stones at them to call ym furth of it Whereupon Magdalen desire that he would goe to Issobell bennet and take a grip of hir coat taile and drink a pinte of ale wt her And crave his health from her thrie tymes for the Lords sake and he would be weell But he did it not

The said katharine Luckisone hereupon examined declared the same to be true

I James norie not' & comon clerk of s'ling subves for the sds Wm & katharine at yr comand Becaus they cannot write

The said Magdalen hereupon examined declares that about the foresaid tyme shee was sitting wt the sd katharin Luckison when Wm Luckison came to the, and when katharine asked at her what would doe good to Williame, and shee ansred that a rose cake was good for him, And bad him take it But denyes the rest, And this shee denyed at the first, Till she was confronted before the sds Williame & katharine

James andersone baxter declares that when he was in sute of katharine Luckisone his present spous, There being a dis cord betuixt him & her qr upon he went in sute of an other In the mean tyme he mett wt Magdalen blair as he was goeing to meet wt the woman that he was in sute of, And shee sayed to him, That he would never get an other woman but katharine Luckison his pu't spous; James andersone

The said Magdalen hereupon examined declares that shee onelie sayed to him, sitay at home, For ye neid not seeke an other woman, but katharine sieing shee is as good as another

Stirling the 14 Jan'r 1659

In pr's of Master mathias Simpson min(iste)r & Rot russell baillie and divers others Helen ker being desired to tell if ewer shee made use of any charme for ob e ing her health, schee confest that shee was charmed by on katharine mcgregor in dunblane wt a drink of water and that the same katharine charmed Mr Thomas Lindsay mini(ste)r at dunblane & his wife

And being desired to tell if shee thought that magdalan blair had wronged ~~her by~~ witchcraft Shee held upe her hand in a signe that shee did think so She Being desired soe to doe in regaird shee was speechless throw the extreamitie of her desease And the neernesse she was to her death & being but about tua houres before

M. Symson
Robert Russall

Ja: Wories clerk of Stirling & writ here of attests ye same

Stirling the 18 Jan'ry 1659

The qlk day duncan nairn provest, Andrew buchanan & Robert russell baillies being conveened for farder tryall of the sd Magdalen blair annent the cryme of witchcraft Whereof shee is suspected and haveing conveened before them the persones following for haveing informa'ne yr annent, They deponed as followes viz

Helen fergusone spous to Andrew cowane wright de clares that about the moneth of march 1658 Shee being going upe the way to her husbands workhous, Margaret Hanle spous to Jon allan skinner mett wt her and desired her to goe in to Marjorie wingyets seller next to magdalen blairs house (being in the afternoone) And when they had gone in togither to drink a chappin of ale The sd Magdalen came in to them wt out any desire And sayed to Margaret pawle That shee was kinde when her husband was sik But since shee had not been kinde And imediatlie yrafter shee sayed to the deponer That since shee gave her not meat as shee did formerlie The deponer never threave and the deponer replyed That it was too true

The said Margaret pawle declares the like except annent the last p't yrof, wch to hir memorie was That Magdalen sayed yt helen had no moir in her anirie yn formerlie yt shee got meat fra her

The said Magdalen here upon examined declared that to the best of her knawledge shee went not in to the sd helen ferguson & Margaret paule But nather that she spoke any thing to the sd Margaret as helen depons But about that tyme shee sayed to helen That shee would not be a bow of meat the richer at the years end That the deponer got none of her meat

I James Worie comon clerk S'ling subves as not' for the sd magdalen at her comand Becaus shee cannot write.

(Case 346)

CASES OF The Witches of Libberton 1661

The depositionnes of the Witches in Libberton paroche as follows.

On Monday the 29 of July 1661 Janet Gibsoun confesed that the divel did appear to her as she was going to the Carthall about the tuilight in the evening & asked what she did want & bad her renounce her saviour, & on nyht befair she confesed the divell did ly with her in her bed. She thought his nature was cold & that he had carnall deall(ing) with her & caused her renounce her baptisme by laying her on hand on her head; & the other hand on the sole of her foot, It was at the back of Johne Crichtonnes yaird dyk,

(Case 383)

Margaret Bryssoun confess(eth) about Witsunday by gaine a yeare; she being in a great agonie & grief at her husband (about 10 a clock at nyht) for selling of ane cow, she cried out & bad ather god or the divel come & tak her from them and did run out to the house wall & the nyht to have felld herselfe, & her daughters came foorth & took her in again & she went to her bed, but could get no rest & wase within ane howre efter she had lyon down & cam to the lithe hous door q(uai)r the divel did appear to her & said he sould take her away soul & body, & caused her put her handis on on the head, the uther on her foot & renounce her baptisme to him & she sould want nothing & she did so, & promised to be his servant, the divel niped her on the shoulder (q)(uai)r she thought she was pricked.

(Case 382)

Elsepeth Blackie confessed she met twyse with the divel 1° she mett within Kinghorn yard about 10 a clock at night q(uai)r there was about 40 at the meitting, she kend non of them bot Elspeth Mowat, the rest wer all masked, this was befoir Candlemas, About 2 dayes (th)(ai)rafter, the divel mett with her in that same place, & took her by the hand & bad her lay it on her head, renounce her baptisme & be his servant & she sould want nothing. & confesed to be his servant & renounced her baptisme

(Case 380)

Elsepeth mowat confess(eth) that she sould glorifie god & shame the divel about candlemas there cam a man to her in her own hous, & monie women with him & took her out of her bed; & bad her go with them, and within 14 dayes efter going to Doc land Richesons well in the evening, there came a man to her & said remember now that yow ar myne, and took her by the hand & bad her renounce her baptisme & be his servant & she sould want nothing, & she did so & renounced her her baptisme, And the divel did ly with her

(Case 351)

Margaret porteous, confesed about 4 yearis since, that the divel appeared to her in her owne hous, about 10 a clock at nyht, in the liknes of a man & bad her renounce her baptisme & be his servant, & she sould have al (th) e pleasure of the earth & she did renounce her baptisme & promised to be her servant and since hes delated severall uthers

(Case 400)

Thomas Black confesed in the nyht tyme the doores being fast locked the divel appeared to him, & asked of him if he would be his servant, & he said yes, it is more nor a yeare since, he confeses lykwyse he was 4 tymes in company with the sax that was burnt, the first tyme fall him he lay heavie on He said I sould never want to be his servant, he confeses he was at the dralling doun of Robert Mitchells barne & kill.

(Case 381)

Agnes Pogavie confest as she was lying in her bed, as she thought waking she thought her spirit was carried away, she said the say the divel his a bell that he rings. It is about since he appeared to me first lyke a dog, & he fand on me, a second tyme he appeared to me in my bed & had me renounce my baptisme & I sould not want, the divel had carnall deal with her & he 3 tyme he came to me he gave me a nip on the shoulder. T(he) 4 tyme he came to me q(uhe)n I was gathering stickis lyke a ill kend man & gave me a piece of money & after I had lookit to it, it was but a sclait stone.

(Case 378)

Jonet Hewats confesses about 7 years since a heavy thing cam to her in her bed she being lying with on Helen Spears about halfe a yeare since, the divel appeared to me & bad me renounce my baptisme & I sould nevir want, which she did, she confeses she wes with the divel at the powburne cuming from Edinburgh another tyme betwixt and William Grahams house (illeg)ding home, and that he had carnall dealling with her

(Case 352)

Margaret Greive confeses she was at meitings in the Lady Ligtouns yaird about 6 yearis since & declares Margaret Bruntoun & Jonet Robisone was there She declared she knew all these & that was burnt in Gilmertoun to be at severall meittingis. And cuming from Dalkeith about 22 yearis since or (th)(ai)rby the divel appeared first lyke a dog & then lyk a man & bad her renounce her baptime which she did and delated severall utheris.

(Case 399)

Bessie Flinkar confest the divel cam first to her about 2 years since cuming from Braeds milne, & bad her be his servant & renounce her baptime & she sould want nothing, & at his comand putting her handis on her head gave him all under Againe he came to her in the night tyme lyke her own husband as she thought & lay with her. And she was taken upon the hills by a whirle of wind & masked herselfe, & (th)e(r) danced with the rest, besyds several presump tionnes of malifices laid to her charge, & severall uthers, as Bessie Wil soun & Issobell davis q(uho)m she hes put out for witches, who confesseth & hes the accustomed markis on them.

(Case 396)

Bessie Wilsoun confeseth the divel appeard to her clothed in black lyk a gentleman cuming from Mortoun homeward, alongs Mortounhallpark about 2 yearis since, & asked q(uha)r she was going, she said she was going home The divell said thee art a poor pudled body, Will thee be my servant, & I will give the abundance, & thee sall never want, & she granted to be his servant A second tyme Satan came to her about 6 weekes (th)(ai)rafter in the night tyme she being in her bed, she thought it was her own husband & he lay with her & he bad her put on hand to her head, another to the foot, & give him all betwix with the renouncing of her baptime, which she did, & confest she was at a meeting with Bessie Alovkak & Issobell Dodis amongst the hills.

(Case 379)

CASE OF Margarat Allan 1661

14 Nov.

Curia Justiciarie S.D.N. Regis
Tenta in Pretorio burgi de Edr
decimo quarto die Novembris 1661
per magistrum Alexandrum Colvillis
de Blair justiciarium deputatum —
Int S.D.N. Regis

Witchcraft

Desyrtit

Intram

Margarat Allan. prisoner

Delaititt of severall poyntis of Sorcerie & witchcraft mentioned in her dittay

Persewar

James Bannatyne of New hall

The q(ui)lk day the said Margarat Allan being brought furth of the Tolbuith of ~~Edr~~ To have underlyne the Law for the Crymes of Sorcerie and witchcraft mentioned in her dittay And entrand upon Pannall Offering her selfe willing to abyde ane tryall for the samen And In respect that James Bannatyne of newhall persewar past fra the per suit of the said margarat for the Crymes forsaidis— The justice deputes (th)(ai)rfore be Consent of both parties, Desertis the said dyet pro loco et com pore And Ordaines the said Margarat to be putt to Libertie, she acting her selfe for her good-behaviour in all tyme comeing And that she shall never come nor enter upon the boundis of the Lands of New hall in any tyme comeing under the pain of death.

(Case 405)

THE FRASER MANUSCRIPT

The following is a transcript of pages 307-312 of James Fraser's manuscript notebook in the National Library of Scotland, Edinburgh: "A Collection of Providential Passages Antient and Modern Forreign and Domestick", dated 1670.

Major Weir's birth, Life & death - known to the Author.

One Thomas Weir, whom I saw at Edinburgh, Anno i66o, comonly called Captain Weir, he was born in Clydsdeal, neare to Lanerk anno i607, the sone of one John Weir first a plough maker and afterwards a farmer. about the yeare of the Massacre of the Kingdom, was made seriant, and, about the 45 turned lieutenant. in the 48 he came to Scotland; and Edinburgh being ye Metra politan and Center of the Kingdom. Thomas Weir made acquaintance with many, & not the worst, personating a deale of gravity & mortification; frequented sermons frequently till in end he went under the notice & got the repute of a singular professor. at Length, he got a Charge over the waiters att ye ports of the City, being a check to them, about the year 1650. he got ye place of Major in the town guard and so was ever after called Maior Weir; his garb was still a cleck and somequhat dark, & never went without his staffe. he was a tall black man; & ordinarly looked down to the ground a grim Countenance and a bigg nose. at lenght he became so Notarly regarded among the presbiterian strict sect. that iff 4 mett together. be sure maior Weir was one, and at privat meetings prayed to admiration which made many of that stamp to Court his Converse; he never married But lived in a privat Lodging with his Sister Grisel Weir. many resorted to his house to heare him pray & join with him, but it was observed that he could not officiat in any holy duty without the black staff or rod in his hand leaning upon it, which made those who heard him pray admire his flood in prayer. his ready extemporary expression. his heavenly gesture; so that he was thought more Angell than Man. and was tearmed by some the holy Sisters ordinarily Angelicall Thomas. and yet how amazing is it this vile Counterfit was a Divil and varlot. and was in Compact with the Divil, upwards of 50 year in his service. From whom he had got the gift of utterance, and this inchanted staffe, for by it he was inabled to pray, to Comit filthinesse not to be named, for no woman (when he pleased) with whom he spoke or touched her cloeathes or skin but would yeld to act whordom with. even women of singular reputation & chaste, & have not been mistresses of themselves in Major Weir's Company. by the use of this staff, he was enabled to conciliate the favour of any, to reconcile nighbours, even husband & wife when at variance, which purchased him veneration with all. & brought him vast gain & profit and yet he lived and cohabited in Incest with his own Sister & also in Bestiality, On a Session day he went out of Edinburgh to a place called New mills to a solemn meeting and by the way he lighted of his mare & in to a buish where he committed bestiality with her. a Country maid from an obscure place espied him & came trembling to the Minister & declared it to him in Secret. the Minister told it was Calumny upon a saint, that had such a gospell life as Ma. Tho. Weir did who was a prominent man. he had so charmed the Clergy as well as the laity. But the poor women was whipt for affirming the truth because there were no wittnesses. in short this villan lived all his time in horrid wickednesse, especially the yeares that he abode at Edinburgh. at length like the wild ass was found in his mouth. Coming one day as his custom was to view the waiters he found some of them in a Cellar drinking and neglecting their charge. after a gentle reproach one of them replyed, that some of their number being upon duty, the rest had retired to drink with their old friend and acquaintance Mr. Burn, at which word Maior Weir started back, and casting an eye upon him repeated his the word Burn 4 or 5 times & going home came not abroad for a long time after. it was observed by some that going to Liberton sometimes, he shunned to step over that water brook which is ordinarily called Liberton Burn but went about to Shun it, but this men have coniectured & not a Miss that he had been advised to beware of a Burn or some other thing which the equivocall word might signify - as Burn in a fire, if so he hath forseen his day approach nigh. a year before he discovered his imposture he took a sore sickness during which time he spake to all the visited him like an angel and Came frequently abroad again. A while after this, he tooke some dreadfull tortours of Conscience, &

the terrours of the Almighty being upon his Spirit, Called in several Nighboures to his house to whom he confessed and that most willingly his particular sins, which he was guilty of with sad aggravations which bred amazement to all persons, they Coming from a man of so high repute of Religion and piety. he ended with this remarkable expression, byfore God sayes he I have not told the hundred part of that I can Say more & am guilty of these same very abohminations he confessed before the Judges likewayes, but after this, he would never to his dying hour confesse any more which might have been for the glorifying of God & the edification of others, but remained stupit, having no Confidence to looke any man in the face, or to open his eyes. When two of the Magistrates of Edinburgh Came to his house in the night time, to Carry him to prison, they asked if he had any mony to secure, he said. None. His sister said there was; whereupon there was found in panells here and there, to the value of five dollars in parcels, which they tooke up. His sister advised the Magistrates to secure his staffe especially, which they did. Thereafter he and his Sister both were carried away & secured in the Tolebouth, and The Balioses returning home went into a Tavern at the west bow neare to Weir's house, they mony was put into a bag & the Clouts thrown into the fire, which after an unusual manner made a Circling and dancing in the fire, There was another Clout found with some hard thing in it, which also they threw into the fire, it looked like a root which Circled and sparkled like gunpowder & Passing up the funnell of the chimney it gave a crak like a little Cannon to the amazement of all that were present; The foresaid mony was taken by one of the two Balioses to his own house & laid by in his Closet, during which time his wife & the rest of the family were affighted with a terrible noise within the study, like the falling of a house, three times successively, his wife knocking gave a fearfull Cry, saying my deare are you alive, the Baliose came out unaffraid & said he heard nothing whether he concealed this upon the account that his wife was with Child or otherways is uncertain. The mony was presently sent away to the other baliofs house where was also heare some terrible disturbance, but in broken expressions. During the time of his imprisonment he was never willing to be spoken to & when the Ministers of the City offered to pray for him, he would Cry out in fury. Torment me no more for I am tormented already. one Minister asking him if he should pray for him he replied not at all. The man in a Zealous Anger said I will pray for you in spite of your teeth & the Divil your master too. so he prayed in his heareing & the wittnesses observed that Weir stared weildly & was senseless as a bruit all the while. Another asked him if he thought there was a God, he said I know not. & the other replied. O man the Argument that moves me to think there is a God, is thyselfe for what else moved thee to inform the world of thy wicked life. But Weir answered Let me alone. When he peremptorily forbad one of his own parish Ministers to pray one demanded if he would have one of the Presbiterian persuasion to pray. He answered Sir you are now all alike to me. then said the Minister to him, I will pray with you, do it not said he upon your peril lookeing up to the beams of the house. but prayer was made so much the more heartily because the Company present expected some vision, it is observable that in things Common he was pertinent enugh but when anything about Almight God & his Souls Condition Came about he would shrugg & rub his breast saying torment me not before the time; at last he was sentenced to be burnt; And when the account of this was given him, he stood mute and stupid; when he was at the Stake to be burnt, the City Ministers called to a cunning man there looking on a Presbiterian, which persuasion Weir was formally deemed to be, to speake to him, but no sooner he opened his mouth than the vile wretch made a sign with his hand & his head to be silent. When the roape was about his neck to prepare him for the fire, he was bid say Lord be mercifull to me, but he answered let me alone, I will not I have lived as a beast & I must die as a beast. the Fire was kindled, he dropped a little after into the flames. a sad spectacle to behold. & shortly after his blaik staff was cast into this fire, with him, whatever incantation was in it. the persones present, aver that it gave rare turnings & was long a burning as also himself. it is said that he was much troubled in prison, for causeing the poor woman to be scourged for affirming that he Committed bestiality going to Newmills; the same woman was present spectator to his fatall end & glorified God solemnly. his incest with his own sister was first when she was a young maid, the place where this abommation was Committed remained Cursed for Contrary to nature it Continued alwas bare without grass; the Reverend Minister to whom Maior Weir

Confessed so much declared that the place lay off the rode betwixt Kirkaldy & Kinghorn upon a little hill side which he had the curiosity to go and see & found it so; things neere 40 yeares ago committed Many other horrid things he confessed which Christian eares should not be defiled with One notable remark of him I cannot omit, which I had from two persones of good fame yet liveing, at the foot of the west bow, near Weirs lodging, This gentlewoman a substantial Marchants wife, was very desirous to hear him pray, so much being spoken of his utterance, for the end, spoke to some of her nighboures, that upon he came to their house, shee might be sent for. This was done, but could he never open his mouth before her no not so much as to blisse a cup of ale, he either remaining mute or up with his staff and away. It troubled her then, but her husband and she smiles at it now but doubt Some few daes before he discovered himselfe, this Gentlewoman comeing from the Castle hill where her husbands neice was lying in of a Child about midnight perceaved about the bow head, 3 women in windowes, shouting laughing & claping their hands, the Gentlewoman went forward till just at Ma. Weirs doore, there arose as from the street a woman above the length of two ordinary females, and stepped forward, the Gentlewoman not as yet excessively feared, bid her maid step on if by the lantern they could see what she was, but hast what they could this long legged Spectre was still before them, moving her body with a vehement cachinnation and unmeasurable laughter. at this rate the two strove for plais till the giantess came to a narrow lane in the bow commonly called the Stinking Closs. full of flammy lights and a great multitude of people laughing and gasping with a hissing noise, this sight as so late a time of the night no people being in the windows; respecting the closs mad herself and her maid hasten home wishing that she might have more wittnesses. But she declared all that she saw to her family but more passionatly to her husband and then sick with feare, yet she went the next morning with her maid, to view the notor plais of the former night walk and at the closs enquired who lived there it was answered Maior Weir. The honest couple now reioicing that to Maior Weir's devotion they never said Amen Anent those visions and apparitions, in all probability have been a presage of his approaching death and of the manner of it. links and torches signifying an honourable internment which perhaps has been promised to him. There was one Minister in the City that would never be persuaded to speak with him in prison but no sooner was he dead but he was to the Tulebooth and called for his sister who had some remorse, he told her that her Brother Major Weir was burnt and how he died, she believed nothing of it, but after many attestations, she asked where his staff was. for she knew that his strength and life lay therin. he told her it was burnt with him, where-upon notwithstanding of her age, she nibliy and in a furious rage fell on her knees, uttering words horrible to be remembered, and in reseigning as she was desired, her rageing eufony closed with these words, O Sir I know he is with the Divils for with them he lived, she entreated that minister to assist her and attend her to her death, which at her violent importunity he yeelded unto though it was not his course to wait upon condemned persones. What she said in private to himself he sayes must die with him; she avouched that from her being sixteen years of age to her 56 her brother had the incestuous use of her body and then loathed her for her age she was sexty sex at this time and he when he died was about 70. the Minister asked her if she was ever with child to him? she declared with confidence he hindered that by means abominable, which she beginning to relate the Preacher stopt her. some bystanders were desirious to hear the reste, but says he Gentlemen the speculation of this iniquity is in itselfe to be punished; next she was interogat if she had any hand in her brother's Divilry. She declared but in a passive way and gave this plain instance. a firie chariot of coach as she called it, coming in to his door, at broad day, a stranger invited him and her to goo with a friend at Dalkeith 4 miles from Edinburgh. they bothe entered and went forward in their visit at which time says she one came and whispered in his ears which affected him, they returned after the same manner that they had gone out, and Weir going next day to a visit told them he had strong apprehensions that day the kings Forces were routed at Worcester which within too or three days was confirmed by the post, she affirmed that non saw the Coach but themselves. The Devil, said she hath wrought far greater Farelies in his time than this. She said she knew much of the inchanted staff. which had received from the Divil some yeares agoe, by which he was enable to do what he pleased. She oft hid it from him and because without it he could do nothing, he would threaten and vow to dicover her incest fearing which whe wold deliver it again. Being asked the cause of her much spinning which she was famous for, she denied any assistance from the Divil, but found that she had an extraordinary facility therein. far above ordinary spinsters. for onward that when she came home after being abroad she found there was more yarn on her whell than she left and that her weaver could not make cloath thereof for the yarn braking or falling from the whole look. Once there came a stranger to her while she was at her wheele, and proposed a way to her to make her rich, for they both lived upon alms and got enough of it. The way was this stand up and say, all Crosses and Cares goe out of this house, she answered, God forbid I say that, but let them be welcome when God sends them, after two or three visits more she asked this stranger where shed dwelt she replied in the potter Raw, a street in the suburbs of that city but finding neither such a house nor such a woman I judged, said she, it was the Divil, one of my Brothers acquaintance, for I knew he had familiarity with the Divil. She was asked anent her parents? and said she was perswaided her mother was a witch, for the secretest things that wither I myselfe or any of the family could do when once a mark appeared on her brow, she could tell it to them though done at a distance, being demanded what sort of a mark it was, she answered I have some such mark myselfe when I please on my forehead, whereupon she offered to uncover her forhead, for visible satisfaction, the minister refusing to behold it, and forbidding any discovery, was earnestly requested by some spectators to allow the freedom, he yeelding she put back her headdress, and seeming to frown there was an exact horse-shoe shaped for nailes in her wrinckles, terrible enough I assure you to the stoutest beholder. In the morning before her execution she told the Minister she resolved to die with all the shame she could to expiat under mercy her shamefull life; this he understood to be an ingenuous confession of her sins, in opposition to her brothers despair and desprat silence, to which he did Incourage her at her parting with him. She gave him hearty thanks for his pains, and shakeing and kissing his hands she repeated the same word which he bade her perform; ascending up the ladder she spake somewhat confusedly of her sins, of her brother and his inchanting staffe and with a ghastly countenance beholding a multitude of spectators, all wondering and some weeping, she spoke aloud. There are many here this day wondering and greeting for me but alais few mourns for a broken -------- at which words many seemed angry. others called to her to mind higher concerns and I have heard it said that the preacher declared he had much ado to keep a composed Countenance. The Executioner falling about his duty she prepared to die stark naked, then and not before were her words relating to shame understood, the hangman strugled with her, to keep on her cloaths. and she strugled with him to have them off; at last he was forced to throw her over open faced, which afterward he Covered, after the usuall manner with a cloath.

I set not this on record to reflect upon men of this or that persuasion. the Divil can counterfit what Religion he pleases and ordinarly a good one, true Religion can never suffer any prejudice from a hypocrit his wearing a cloak of it, more than the good angels can suffer stain from Satans transforming himselfe into an Angel of light; it is evident there is a Divil that hurries men on into sin. This maior Weir had that oppression to two Ministers that came to him in prison; There was no temptation which the Divil could propose to him but he was capable to accept of it. it is certain there is either an explicit or implicit Compact between some men and the Divil, horrible sins covered with religion, bring utter dispare at the last and desperation is hell in fiere, some men as well as Divils are tormented before the time: but let us beware that such a man's fall prove not a neck brake to us, let us idolise no man for his profession or that he is of this or that persuasion or of such a party. Let no man rest in a bare profession of Religion men in compact with the Divil may be assisted, both to preach and pray at this, vile Wizard, Weir, a precious person learned (?) of the presbiterian party. all this account I had from an eye and eare witnesse and a man of good credit and repute; Ma. Weir was brought to his dreadfull desperat and yett deserved death April 14 anno 1670 at the gallow Lie bewixt Leith and Edinburgh where he was burnt as aforesaid.

(Case 576)

CASE OF Bessie Paine 1671

Bessie Paine is Indytted for the sin of wichcraft In sua far as she Charmed ane oxe belonging

To John turner Elder In Airdwall by giving him some hay bear & green kaill stoks & gave for signe yt if he should recover he would licke his upper lepp & if not he would die & conforme to what she said the oxe did the samen & recovered;

Item Cuthbert Browne of Craigend his first wyffe being sick He sent for Bessie paine who befoir shoe was spoken to Concerning the nature of the Disease told that Agnes Rowan had witched her And yre-eftir shoe went and cured her

Walter Patersone in Tarranauchtie haveing a chyld sick used all ordinarie meanes for the chyldes recoverie which proveeing uneffectuall he sent to a maiden which being at that tyme incarcerat in the prissone of Dumfries Who told him that Bessie paine wold cure his chyld And haveing sent to the sd Bessie paine she told that upon the nixt sabbath day yreftir at twelff a clock the chyld wold fall dead and yreftir wold recover which accordinglie fell out

Item Agnes Davidsone offeirs to depone that her fathe being sick The sd Bessie paine desyred some of the hair of his head and beard and the pairing of his nailles and his garters Which shoe weassocored thrie tymes from the top of her finger to her elbow and within a week yreftir he died

John Crockett living in Lands haveing ane chyld sick went to the sd Bessie paine and desyred shoe wold use some remidie for his chyld The sd Bessie cam and desyred the mother of the chyld to take the shirt over the chylds head and draw it alongis the den of the bear And to hing the shirt over the north syde of ane thorne bush till it was dry And yreftir to put it on the chyld and putt the chyld in the cra-dell And take the fyer off the hearth staine And the samyne being sweiped clean to put all personnes out of the house except the chyld and herselff And yreftir To take the chyld and the cradell and rocke the Cradell Till yr should a man come in that wold cure the chyld And the sd Jon Crocketts wyffe being affrighted to obey her injunctiones The chyld lay two yeires sick

Item the sd John Crockett haveing had severall tymes kyne which not withstanding being verrie well ffed did never bull He did at Last buy ane Cow And shortlie yreftir the erll of Withsdailles came to gett the Fairdner Mairt Kyne They came to the foirsd John And he haveing delt with them and past his Cow And yreftir went to the sd Bessie paine and took one of her kyne yrupon the sd Bessie Alledging that the sd John had sent them to take her Cow And the nixt Sabbath shoe mett with Jon Crockets wyffe And told her that shoe wold find God to punish and the devill for her cationnar that shoe wold have a Cow when shoe should have none And shortlie yreftir the sd Johns kyne died And for elleven yeir yreftir he had no kyne at all that Lives.

Item Harbert Crockett being at a Laikwak with the sd Bessie paine her husband called Jon Murray some personne did shew the sd Jon Murray and Harbert Crockets breeches togither Which the said Harbert perceaeving Cutting the threds Cutted a peace out the sd Jon Murray his cloak And Bessie paine the nixt day bringing the sd cloak to Harbert Crockets fatheres house shewing the hell of it Shoe said befoir it were Long he should have ane other thing to think upon, And the sd Harbert haveing at that tyme (which was about Candlmes) sevin nolt befoir the first of May yreftir they wes all dead

Item Robert Sturgeone haveing taken a rowme called the Aird wheerine the sd Bessie had former-lie Lived And eftir he was in possession yroff shoe cam to his house And sitteng downe upon her knees upon the hearth staene shoe said all the witchcraft which I have I leave it here And it is well knowne yreftir That within a yeir and a quarter He had above Threttie nolt dead And nothing he tooke in hand did prosper dureing his possession of that rowme

Item the said Bessie paine haveing charmed a Cow belonging to Richard Crocket shoe cured her And told that the first thing that shoe mett with should die And yreftir shoe mett with Threttie two oxen who had bein at work And the first ox belonging to William wright Died immediatlie yreftir

Item Robert huttoune haveing a cow sick His mother in Law sent for the said Bessie paine who caused the Cow to be put thrie tymes throw ane hanck of green yairne speaking some words which the personnes present did not understanding and yreftir the Cow was cured

Item

(Case 599)

CASE OF Mary Sommerveil 1671

3rd July

Curia Jushciciarie S.D.N.Reg
tentam preterio burgi de
Edr tentio die mensis - July
Per Alex ' dominum
de Italcartoim et dominos
Ro ertum Nairn de S trat
hurd re Ivan - em Lockhart
de Castelhill et Joanem B
aird de newbyth
Justicia dicty S.D.N.
Kegis.
Curia legitime aftinmals.

Lord Halcartuim preset

Intram.
Robert Bouar wrightin d uniforuiling
Indytes and accuses for the crymes of
adultirie committed be him in maner
mentionat in his ind peinent.
Persewar
His maties advocat
The Lords comissioners of Justiciarie
ordained him to goe to prison til he
find cantione to ab his apeirance this
day fortnight
Somervaill witchcraft put to libertie
Laidlay witchcraft put to libertie

The which day anent ane petitione present(ed) to his ma(jis)ties justices be Marie Somervail prisoner with in the tolbuith of Jedburgh Make and mentione that wher the petitioner being caleit befor them at Jedburgh for the crym of witchcraft aleadgit comitted. be her, wher upon she was in carcerat and put in prisone and lyen even since in ane sterving conditione. Not with-standing that ther was no informatione given in aganist her nor persone com-peiring to insist aganist her and that she was content to apear before them when ever she should be calet. And thairfore craveing warkanes to th effect understen. The justices haveing considered the foresaid petitione grants the desyre thereof and ordaines the petitioner to be put at libertie.

(Case 591)

CASE OF Grissell Rae, Margaret McCuffock and Janet Howat 1672

15th July

Edr. honorabiles
Viros dominos Jacobum
Lockhart ce lid Justiciancie
Clericum Jacobum foulis de
Colinton Robertum Nairn de
huird I varem Lockhart de
Castelhill Joanem Bain de
Newbyth et Thoman Wallace
de Cringie -

The which day anent ane petition presented to the Lords Comissioners of Justiciance be Grissell Rae Margaret McCuffock and Janet Howat prisoners in Kirkcudbright makonid mentioim that when the petitioners being upon misin for matione apprehendit and incarcerat in a pryle 1671 in on den to have undergone ane tryell before the Southern Circuit hollin at Dumfries in may therefore. For the all eagrit crymes of witchcraft wherof they ware altogeden most innocent being unlie accused thereof by some of them malicious and malevolent neighboures out of splent prejudice, against them. And ther being no Indytement exhibit against the petitioners at the said circuit court they ware by warrand of the Lords Strathuird and Newbyth None of the Comissioners of Justiciarie who held the said Circuit transporred from Dumfries to Kirkcudbright wher they have even since continued in a dark dungeon in a most miserable conditione being alwayes at the point of starving having nothing of ther own nor nothing allowed them for ther sustenance - And on of ther number Issobell pain who was in prisonis with them dyed the last winter through cold hunger other inconveniencies of the prison. And the petitioner ane in such an me pressable miserie that it ware better for them to be dead than alyve. And seing the petitioners are most and maliciously mis-represented as guiltie of the fur said most horid crymes where of ane most innocent and have now coatim lon in such ane intollerable prisone and ane not lyk to be put to ane tryel which they are most willing to undergoe and being no blae longer to subsist in such a miserable conditione thairfore crave in that they ought be put to libertie upon sufficient cautione for ther apeirance befor them the third day of the next Justicreain to be hold in at Dumfries on sooner upon alan citatione of fyftein dayes warneing.

(Grissell Rae Case 603)
(Margaret McCuffock Case 602)
(Janet Howat Case 604)

MARGARET PROVOST, MARGARET BEZOK, and MARY NICINNARICH.

The following transcription is made from a manuscript found among the miscellaneous papers of the Boyds of Trochrigg, in the University Library, Glasgow.

Precognition takin of the persones after named by warrand from the Kings advocat; at ffortross 6th october 1699.

1. The said day The Laird of Suddie adduced as witnes against Margaret Provost declared that he heard her badlie reputed and bruted as a witch, and therfore he went with his servants and pulled down the house about her ears and within a day or two therafter his gardener who was one of the servants in his company swelled as bigg as two men, and in some days more got such a voracious stomach that he would eat as much as six upon all which she being Challenged the gardener became better, and her son came to him and told him that if he would prevail with his master to give her a house again, he should be well.

Mr Thomas ffrazer minister of Suddy declared That Captain McKenzie of Suddy finding ane inconveniencie to have quearns upon his ground, which encouraged the indwellers to abstract their corns from his miln did upon a Certain day case break all the saidis quearns among which he brake that of Margaret Provost within a short time therafter, the said Captain leaping a little brook not above two foot broad fell down and wrested his legg and thigh, which did so enable him that though there was niether breach nor dislocation his thigh and legg became so extraordinarily small that for eighteen moneths time he was confyned to his bed, which being repute a supernatural advent Many did conclude the same was effectuate by the said Margaret Provost her sinistruous means and malefices but for his part he could not be positive.

James Ked in Killern informed against the said Margaret and her daughter That the said Margaret's daughter being Challenged be the said James wife for the skaith done to her by the said Margaret's hens Did tell she would kill them and if she were wronged be the daughters skill she should Challenge her as the instrument therof To which the daughter replyed that if she had skill the said James wife should share therof and that therafter the next morning his best cow failed in his plough and after that the said cow and one of his best horse dyed by ane unknown disease and that himself within a few days fell very unwell and continued so till she was publilie Challenged and therafter she began to amend.

2. Margaret Bezok alias Kyle spouse to David Stewart in Balmaduthy declared she threatened John Sinclair using a phrase that she would quicklie overturn his cart and within a week therafter his wife fell ill, and that she was brought to see the seek wife and touched and handled her and heard that therafter she convalesced.

John Sinclair in Miuren declared that the said Margaret did threaten ut supra and that therafter his wife distracted within less than a week and continued in that distemper till the said Margaret was brought to see her, and that she handled and felt his wife who therafter grew better but continues something weak still and that it is eight weeks since the first threatening.

Katherin Davidson in Balmaduthy declared that upon a day keepin her cows from the said Margaret's hens, she was threatened be the said Margaret That she should have neither sock nor coulter goeing upon that ground, and that therafter she lost ane ox that dyed suddenly and another ox that fell and brake his bones and that therafter she challenged her son and found no more prejudice Agnes Davidson and Jannet Urquhart concurr in this declaration.

3. Alexander Maclay in Kilearnan did upon a certain day in September ninetie four Challenge Murrock Nickinairich her herd, for suffering her beasts to eat his fathers corns, Quairupon the wife appearing threatened him at a high rate and told him that that Challenge should be repented of by him, In a short time upon the morrow therafter The said Alexander haveing fallen in ane extrairdinary and unnatural sickness he continued therin for fyve weeks time, but within a day therafter havving gote a drink of milk from the said Murrock did immediately upon drinking therof recover his perfect

health And further declared that he heard her flyte with two of her neigh-bour-wives, and threatened them that none of them should be upon that hill before that day twelve moneth and both the wives accordingly dyed as he saw. And at another time heard her flyte with Donald Maclady and that she threatened that before eight days she should make him repent his carryage, and accordingly within the eight days his best horse dyed of a strange sickness viz: by his tongue chafts and mouth being cult in twall (?) parts.

John Maclay in Redcastle informed likewise against the said Mary Micinnarich that upon his Challenging her for being the occasion of his brothers sickness he fell himself immediately unwell and continued so still till the minute The Lady Redcastle and Kenneth Mackenzie brother to Muirtown Called for her and Challenged her and therafter he convalesced, besides she is still repute a rank witch.

Hugh: Baillie ilk B.

(Margaret Provost Case 3064)
(Margaret Bezok Case 3065)
(Mary Nicinnarich Case 3066)

CASE OF Mary Morison 1699

petition for Mary Morison alleged guilty of Witchcraft

The said day anent ane petition presented to the sd Lords be Mary Morisone spouse to ffrancis Duncan skiper in Greenock Shewing that where the Supplicant being upon the dilatione of Jannet Shaw Bargarans daughter lately possest to be ane of her tormenters was for her vindication oblidged to inact herself to appear and Undergoe a tryall befor their Lords When called for that effect And for the space of ten eight to come to Edinburgh and apply the Lords of privy Council for a tryall which their Lords were pleased to recomend to my Lord Advocat to prosecute betwixt and the fiftienth of November thereafter During which tyme the petitioner and her husband to their great losse stayed att Edinburgh and all that tyme noe informatione given in alike my Lord Advocat wrote to the severall presbyteries in the west Country where she was borne and Constantly resided for informatione against her But none informing She did again apply to the Lords of his Majesties privy Council for getting up her husbands bond and for liberty to return home Accordingly the twenty second of the said month of November their Lords were pleased to allow her to returne home and to gett up her husbands former bond and to renew the same to her selfe before the Lords of Justiciary to Undergoe a tryall As being Alleadged guilty of the abominable Cryme of Witchcraft how soon she should be informed against which accordingly was obeyed. Thereafter in Apryle sixteen nynty nyne there was ane Indytment raised against the petitioner before the sds Lords of Justiciary founded upon the said Jannet Shaw, Jannet Laird and Margaret Murdock (whom under their fitts of torment) their giving up the petitioner as ane of the tormenters. And a tryall apointed at Glasgow before the Saids Lords in May therafter at which tyme the petitioner Compeired again Continued till october and then adjourned from Glasgow to Edinburgh to the fourth of december last which their Lords adjourned till this dyet All which dyets at Glasgow to the great loss of ther poor family and hazard of her life being very tender and infirme she keeped also her husband came to Edr & keeped the dyets there and at each tyme to his great prejudice always renewed his bond for her Compearance And seing it is very weell proven by all persones of intire fame in the place of her birth and residence that she has bein of undoubted good fame and reputatione during all her life and nowayes tainted with any public guilt or malifice to her neighbours either in their goods or goodname untill the forsaid possest persones in their fitts of torment did alleadge that the devil represented her as one of their tormenters All which they now after their recovery to health again doe utterly dissoun Also it is expected from the precognition taken that nothing will be found against her in the least to the detriment of her untainted reputatione All that the witnesses depone being only upon what they heard from the saids tormented possest persones whill in their fitts which by law are reprobat and that it is beyond measure hard to keep the petitioner under such a process as being alleadged guilty of the forsaid haynous and abominable Crime of Witchcraft soe disgracefull to her selfe and posterity without a tryall now after soe long dependence And Adjournments to her great greife and losse near to the utter ruin of her poor family Therefore Craving the Saids Lords would be pleased Either to appoint my Lord Advocat to insist presently against her or else to give her the benefite of Law and their Lords daylie practise of deserting the dyet that therby she may be restored to her wonted fame and reputatione The Lords Justice Clerk and Commissioners of Justiciary with consent of his Majesties Advocat and sollicitor And for severall good causes moveing them Deserted and be thir presents Deserts the dyet against the said Mary Morisone Simpliciter Wherupon Sir David Shaw advocat as pro locutour for the said Mary Morisone asked and tooke instruments and protested for the Cautioners releise which the said Lords Admitted and hereby admitts.

(Case 690)

CASE OF John Glass 1700

Petition for Rorie Mckenzie of Redcastle

The Said day anent ane petitione given in to the saids Lords be Rorie McKenzie of Redcastle younger Showing that John Glasse histennent in Spittell having Upon certain good reasons and by finding the petitioner Cautioner obtained by their lords delyverance Advocatione of the proofs raised against him before the sh(e)riff of Rosse for the Crymes of Witchcraft and consulting of witches against him But thereafter the Lords of privy Councill having granted Commissiene to certaine gentlemen in the North to trye and Judge the said John Glasse and others accused of Witchcraft at the burgh of ffortrosse and to report befor putting of any sentence to executione The said John Glasse was Accordingly tryed and past under the knouledge of ane assyse there And albeit by their verdict Nothing was found proven against him of all the horrid Crymes lybelled yet the Commissioners were pleased to ffyne and banish him which being reported to the saids Lords of privy Councill by some of the saids Lords of Justiciary and his magesties Advocat who were the Committee appointed to examine the said process Their lords the sd John Glasse from the said sentence and appointed him to be sett at liberty By all which it was evident that as ther wes nae need for the said Johns appearance before their lords upon the dyet of his advocatione so the thet petitioner neither could nor needed present him to his bond of Cautionerie Therefore having their would ordanie ther Clerk to give up the petitioners bond and would dysert the dyet in the Advocatione The Lords Justice Generall Justice Clerk and Commissioners of Justiciary having considered the said petitione They desert the dyet in the advocatione against John Glasse and Ordaine the bond of Cautionery to be delyvered up.

(Case 673)

The admissability of women witnesses

SRO: JC2/14 pp. 259-260

November 1674

A debate anent Receaving
women to be witness' in ane
exculpa(tio)n

My Lord Advocat alleadged that Ailison Ker nor no woman cane be witnes' because by the uncontraverted lawe and pract'qs of Scotland women cannot be witness' no in civillibus and fare lesse in criminibus except in the caice of treason and some fewe excepted caices and occult crymes which are speciallie priviledged And as this is undoubted lawe and pract'q It is also clear by a statut of the Lords of Session and this is urged not so much in relation to this caice as the preparative and in relation to the generall Interst of the kingdome And wheras it is pretendit that the women cannot be witness' for the persewars yet they may be witness' to prove a defence and exculpation It is answered that the distinction is without warrant et ubi lex non distinguit nec nos And if women be testes Inhabiles as to the persewer and in behalf not only of the privat interest of parties And lykwayes of the publict Interest and concernment of the King and the country and his Majesties Advocat persewing upon the account of that interest multo minus cane they be habiles in behalf of the defender and as to the pretence of the civill lawe and practice of any other nation it is of no weight seeing we are to be ruled by the lawe of Scotland And by expresse act of parliament It is pro vydit that we should not be ruled by any other lawes And it cannot be Instanced that upon a debate it wes ever found that women should be receaved witness' in behalf of any defender And it is humblie con ceaved that in a caice which may be of so much consequence that the Lords will judge according to lawe standing and will not make new lawes which is only proper to King and parliament.

Sir Andrew Birnie answers that the habilitie of women to be witness' is acknowledged to be consonant to the common lawe and then being not statut forbidding women and Incapacitating them to be witness' it is warrantable by our lawe to recurre to the common lawe where statut is deficient especiallie when it cane be Instanced that women have bein frequentlie receaved in this court as witness' in capitall crymes and in occultis as in the caice of Suintoun And the poynt wheranent this witnes is to be examined does not concerne the rancounter but that which is altogither forraigne and extrinsicle to witt that it being most dark and dubious and occultissimum who wes the aggressor ther does a stronge presumption aryse from the last words of the defunct wherof thir women were witness' and who are most proper to be about a dyeing person And the pannall being in defence is more favourable then the persewer himself who having cited women as witness' is in pessima fide to object ag't them in the exculpation

The interloquiter

The Lords in regard they find there wes no penuria testium tempore mortis they therfor refuse to admitt the women witness'

WITCHCRAFT LEGISLATION

1. 16 Mary, c. 73 from Acta Parliamentorum Mariae, A.D. 1563
   from A.P.S. Vol. II, p.539

ITEM Forsamekeill as the Quenis Maeistie and thre Estatis in this present Parliament being informit that the hauy and abominabill superstition vsit be divers of the liegis of this Realme be vsing of Witchcraftis Sorsarie and Necromancie and credence geuin thairto in tymes bygane aganis the Law of God And for avoyding and away putting of all sic vane superstitioun in tymes tocum it is statute and ordanit be the Quenis Maiestie and the thre Estatis foirsaidis that na maner of persoun nor persounis of quhatsumeuer estate degre or conditioun they be of tak vpone hand in ony tymes heir efter to vse ony maner of Witchcraftis Sorsarie or Necromancie nor gif thame selfis furth to have ony sic craft or knawlege thairof thairthrow abusand the pepill Nor that na persoun seik ony help response or consultatioun at ony sic vsaris or abusaris foirsaidis of Witchcraftis Sorsareis or Necromancie vnder the pane of deid alsweill to be execute aganis the vsar abusar as the seikar of the response or consultatioun. And this to be put to executioun be the Justice Schereffis Stewartis Baillies Lordis of Regaliteis and Rialteis thair Deputis and vthers Ordinar Jugeis competent within this Realme with all rigour hauing power to execute the samin.

2. 1 Jac. I c. 12, 1604
   from Statutes of the Realm, London 1818, Vol.IV, pp.1028-9

Be it enacted by the King our Soveraigne Lorde the Lordes Spirituall and Temporall and the Comons in the present Parliament assembled, and by the authoritie of the same, That the Statue made in the fifte yeere of the Raigne of our late Soveraigne Ladie of most famous and happie memorie Queene Elizabeth, intituled An Acte againste Conjurations Inchantments and Witchcrafts, be from the Feaste of St. Michaell the Archangell nexte cominge, for and concerninge all offences to be committed after the Same Feaste, utterlie repealed. II. And for the better restrayninge the saide Offenses, and more severe punishinge the same, be it further enacted by the authoritie aforesaide, That if any person or persons after the saide Feaste of Sainte Michaell the Archangell next cominge, shall use, practise, or exercise any Invocation or Conjuration of any evill and wicked Spirit, or shall consult covenant with entertaine employ feede or rewards any evill or wicked Spirit to or for any intent or purpose; or take up any dead man woman or child out of his her or theire grave, or any other place where the dead bodie resteth, or the skin bone or any other parte of any dead person, to be imployed or used in any manner of Witchcrafte Sorcerie Charme or Inchantment; or shall use practise or exercise any Witchcrafte Inchantment Charme or Sorcerie wherebie any person shalbe killed destroyed wasted consumed pined or lamed in his or her bodie or any part thereof; that then everie such Offendor or Offendors, theire Aydes, Abettors and Counsellors, being of any the saide Offences duelie and lawfullie convicted and attainted, shall suffer pains of deathe as a Felon or Felons, and shall loose the priviledge and benefit of Cleargie and Sanctuarie.

III. And further, to the intent that all manner of practise use or exercise of Witchrafte Inchantment Charme or Sorcerie should be from henceforth utterllie avoyded abolished and taken away, Be it enacted by the authoritie of this present Parliament, That if any person or persons shall from and after the saide Feaste of Saint Michaell the Archangell next cominge, take upon him or them by Witchcrafte Inchantment Charme or Sorcerie to tell or declare in what place any treasure of Golde or Silver should or might be foune or had in the Earth, or other secret places, Or where Goods or other things lost, or stolen, are become: Or wherebie any Cattell or Goods of any person in his, or her bodie although the same be not effected and done; that then all and everie such person and persons so offendinge, and beinge thereof lawfullie convicted shall for the said Offence suffer imprisonment by the space of one whole yeere, without baile or maineprise, and once everie quarter of the saide yere shall in some Markett Towne, upon the Markett Day, or at such Tyme as any Faire shalbe kepte there, stande openlie upon the Pillorie by the space of sixe houres, and there shall openlie confesse his or her error and offence; And if any person or persons beinge once convicted of the same offences as is aforesaide, doe eftsoones perpetrate and comit the like offence, that then everie such offender, beinge of any the saide offences the second tyme lawfullie and duelie convicted and attainted as is aforesaide, shall suffer pained of death as a Felon or Felons, and shall loose the benefitt and priviledge of Clergie and Sanctuarie: Savinge to the wife of such person as shall offend in any thinge contrarie to this Acte, her title of dower; and also to the heire and successour of everie such person his or theire titles of Inheritance Succession and other Rights, as though no such Attaindor of the Ancestor or Predecessor had bene made: Provided alwaies, That if the offender in any the Cases aforesaide shall happen to be a Peere of this Realme, then his Trial therein to be had by his Peeres, as it is used in cases of Felonie or Treason, and not otherwise.

3. 9 Geo. II c. 5

from The Statutes at Large, London 1764, Vol.VI, pp.206-7

An act to repeal the statute made in the first year of the reign of King James the First, intituled, An act against conjuration, witchcraft, and dealing with evil and wicked spirits, except so much thereof as repeals an act of the fifth year of the reign of Queen Elizabeth, Aginst conjurations, inchantments, and witchcrafts, and to repeal an act passed in the Parliament of Scotland in the ninth parliament of Queen Mary, intituled, Anentis witchcraftis, and for punishing such persons as pretend to exercise or use any kind of witchcraft, sorcery, inchantment, or conjuration.

Be it enacted by the king's most excellent majesty, by and with the advice and consent of the lords spiritual and temporal, and commons, in this present parliament assembled, and by the authority of the same, That the statue made in the first year of the reign of King James the First, intituled, An Act against conjuration, witchcraft, and dealing with evil and wicked spirits, shall, from the twenty fourth day of June next, be repealed and utterly void and of none effect (except so much thereof as repeals the statute made in the fifth year of the reign of Queen Elizabeth, intituled, An act aginst conjurations, inchantments, and witchcrafts.

II. And be it further enacted by the authority aforesaid, That from and after the said twenty fourth day of June, the act passed in the parliament of Scotland in the ninth parliament of Queen Mary, intituled, Anentis witchcrafts, shall be and is hereby repealed.

III. And be it further enacted, That from and after the said twenty fourth day of June, no prosecution, suit, or proceeding, shall be commenced or carried on against any person or persons for witchcraft, sorcery, inchantment, or conjuration, or for charging another with any such offence, in any court whatsoever in Great Britain.

IV. And for the more effectual preventing and punishing any pretences to such arts or powers as are beforementioned, whereby ignorant persons are frequently deluded and defrauded; be it further enacted by the authority aforesaid, That if any person shall, from and after the twenty fourth day of June, pretend to exercise or use any kind of witchcraft, sorcery, inchantment, or conjuration, or undertake to tell fortunes, or pretend from his or her skill or knowledge in any occult or crafty science, to discover where or in what manner any goods or chattles, supposed to have been stolen or lost, may be found; every person so offending, being therof lawfully convicted on indictment or information in that part of Great Britain called England, or on indictment or libel in that part of Great Britain called Scotland, shall for every such offence suffer imprisonment by the space of one whole year without bail or mainprize, and once in every quarter of the said year in some market town of the proper county upon the market day there stand openly on the pillory by the space of one hour, and also shall (if the court by which such judgement shall be given shall think fit) be obliged to give sureties for his or her good behaviour, in such sum, and for such time, as the said court shall judge proper according to the circumstances of the offence, and in such case shall be further imprisoned until such sureties be given.

9 Geo. II c. 5. was repealed in 1951, by the Fraudulent Mediums Act.

SECTION IV.

SOURCE MATERIAL

This section contains

1. The abbreviations for all source material mentioned in the case lists. Many of these are local histories which have only one or two cases of witchcraft. The main sources are listed separately on page 2 in addition to appearing below.
2. References for those marked Gilmore or Truckell.
3. A list of manuscript sources in the Scottish Record Office for centrally administered trials.
4. Printed sources for centrally administered trials.
5. Short list of books on Scottish witchcraft. This list excludes recent popular literature on Scottish witchcraft which is not based on any new research. It also excludes all general works on witchcraft unless they have a considerable section on Scotland, or unless, like Sir Walter Scott's Letters on Demonology, are written from a Scottish perspective.

No attempt has been made to list the local source material. Researchers should start with J.M. Thomson's The Public Records of Scotland (Glasgow 1922) and supplement this with enquiries at the Scottish Record Office in Edinburgh where a new guide is being prepared. As noted (p.x), a survey of all legal and ecclesiastical sources for crime in the early modern period is currently being made by Bruce Lenman and Geoffrey Parker of the Department of Modern History, University of St. Andrews.

1. ABBREVIATIONS.

Works which have been abbreviated in more than one way have been entered under each form.

Abdn Krk Sess R	<u>Aberdeen Kirk Session Register</u>, Spalding Club, Aber. 1946
Abdn Sh C.R.	<u>Aberdeen Sheriff Court Records</u>
Anal. Scot.	R. Wodrow, <u>Analecta Scotica</u>, Edin. 1842-3
Anderson	Patrick Anderson (1575-1624) 'History of Scotland'. MS in the National Library of Scotland
Andrson	Maureen Anderson, St. Andrews undergraduate dissertation, 1976. (References are not given.)
Ann. Banff	<u>The Annals of Banff</u>, New Spalding Club, Aber. 1891-3
APS	<u>Acts of the Parliament of Scotland</u>, London 1814
Archae Scot.	<u>Archaelogia Scotica</u>, Transactions of the Society of Scotland, Edin.
Arnot	H. Arnot, <u>Celebrated Criminal Trials in Scotland</u>, Edin. 1785
Balfr	J. Balfour, <u>Historical Works</u>, Edin. 1824-5
Bann	R. Bannatyne, <u>Journal of the transactions in Scotland</u>, Edin. 1806
Berwickshire Nat. Cl.	<u>History of the Berwickshire Naturalists' Club</u>, Edin. 1834
Bev	D. Beveridge, <u>Culross and Tulliallan</u>, Edin. 1885
Birrell	R. Birrell, <u>Diary</u>, Edin. 1795
Bk Kirk Sc.	<u>Booke of the Universall Kirk of Scotland</u>, Edin. 1839
Bk Old Edin. Cl.	<u>The Book of the Old Edinburgh Club</u>, Edin. 1908-45
Bk Perth	J.P. Lawson, <u>The Book of Perth</u>, Edin.1847

Boul	R. Boulton, Compleat History of Magick Sorcery and Witchcraft, London 1716
Br'ness & Dist.	T. Salmon, Borrowstouness and District, Edin. 1913
Brodie	D. Laing, editor, The Diary of Alexander Brodie of Brodie and of his son, James Brodie of Brodie, Spalding Club, Aberdeen, 1863
Brown	P. Hume Brown, Scotland before 1700, Edin. 1893
Bucha Fld Cl.	Buchan Field Club Transactions 1807-1890
Buchan	J. Buchan, History of Peeblesshire, Glasgow, 1925-27
Buckner	Buckner, Rambles in and around Aberdour, 1881
Cal.	Calendar of State Papers Relating to Scotland, Edin. 1936
Calndr State Papers	Calendar of State Papers Relating to Scotland, Edin. 1936
Cam	J. Campbell, Balmerino and its Abbey, Edin. 1867
Canisay Kr Sess. R	Parish Registers of Canisbay, 1652-1666, Scottish Record Society, 67, Edin. 1914
Ch.	R. Chambers, Domestic Annals of Scotland, Edin. 1861
Cham.	R. Chambers, Domestic Annals of Scotland, Edin. 1861
Chron. Perth	The Chronicles of Perth, Mairland Club, Edin. 1831
Cldr	Calder, Sketches, 1724
Clelnd	J. Cleland, Rise and Progress of the City of Glasgow, Glasgow, 1820
Cook	Annals of Pittenweem
Cowan, S.	Cowan, S. The Ancient Capital of Scotland, London, 1904
Craig-Brown	T. Craig-Brown, History of Selkirkshire, Edin. 1886

D	Circuit Court Minute Books, Scottish Record Office
Dal.	J.G. Dalyell, The Darker Superstitions of Scotland, Edin. 1834
Dalyell	J.G. Dalyell, The Darker Superstitions of Scotland, Edin. 1834
Diur Rem Occ	Diurnal of Remarkable Occurents, Maitland Club, Edin. 1833
Doc. Pbles	Charters and documents relating to the Burgh of Peebles, Scottish Burgh Records Society, Edin. 1872
Dvdson	J. Davidson, Inverurie and the Earldom of Garioch, Edin. 1878
Dunbar	E. Dunbar, Documents relating to Moray, Edin. 1895; and E. Dunbar, Social life in Former Days, Edin. 1865
Edin Mag & Lit Misc	Edinburgh Magazine and Literary Miscellany, Dumfries 1909
E. Fife R.	Records of East Fife
Firth	C.H. Firth, Scotland and the Protectorate, Edin. 1899
Foun	Lord Fountainhall, Historical Notices, Edin. 1848
Frgson.	J. Ferguson, "Bibliographical notes on the witchcraft literature of Scotland", Proceedings of the Edinburgh Bibliographical Society, Edin. 1899
Fyfe	W.W. Fyfe, Summer life on land and water, Edin. 1851
G	J. Gilmore, "Witchcraft and the Church in Scotland subsequent to the Reformation", Unpublished Ph.D. thesis in Glasgow University Library, 1948. See (2) below for details
Gl. Brgh. R.	Records of the Burgh of Glasgow, Maitland Club, Glasgow 1832
Gunn	C.B. Gunn, The Book of Stobo Church, Peebles 1907
Hay	G. Hay, Arbroath, Arbroath, 1876

Hewison — J.K. Hewison, *Isle of Bute in the olden tyme*, Edin. 1893-5

Hghd. Pps — Ed. J.P.N. Macphail, *Highland Papers*, Scottish History Society, Edin. 1914

Hibbert — S. Hibbert, *Description of the Shetland Islands*, Edin. 1822

His. Brechin — D. Black, *History of Brechin*, Edin. 1867

His. Ch. Sc. — *Records of the Scottish Church History Society*, Glasgow 1924-44

His. Dumfrs — *Transactions and Journal of the Dumfriesshire and Galloway Natural History and Antiquarian Society*, Edin. and Dumfries, 1884-

His. Pbles. — W. Chambers, *History of Peeblesshire*, Edin. 1864

His. Renfrew — W.M. Metcalfe, *History of Renfrew*, Paisley 1905

Histrcl Notices — Lord Fountainhall, *Historical Notices*, Edin. 1848

Hndrson — E. Henderson, *Annals of Dunfermline*, Glasgow 1879

Hnarson — Henderson, *History of Banchory-Devenick*

Hntr — W. Hunter, *Biggar and the House of Fleming*, Biggar 1862

Irv. — J. Irving, *The Book of Dumbartonshire*, Edin. 1879

J.C. — Justiciary Court MS: Scottish Record Office

Krk Sess. R. Dunfermline — *Parish Registers of Dunfermline* 1561-1700, Edin. 1911

Laing — A. Laing, *Lindoes Abbey and its burgh of Newburgh*, Edin. 1876

Lamont — J. Lamont, *Diary*, Maitland Club, Edin. 1830

Low — G. Low, *Tour through Orkney and Shetland*, Kirkwall 1879

Ltrs & Pps — *Letters and papers illustrating the relations between Charles the Second and Scotland in 1650*

Lyon	C.J. Lyon, *History of St. Andrews*, Edin. 1843
Mack	Mackintosh, *Elgin Past and Present*
Mait. Cl. Misc.	*Miscellany of the Maitland Club*, Edin. 1833-47
McCall	H.B. McCall, *History of Mid Calder*, Edin. 1894
McDwll	McDowall, W., *History of the Burgh of Dumfries*, Edin. 1867
McKnlay	Mackinlay, J.M., *Folklore of Scottish Lochs and Springs*, Glasgow 1893
McKnzie	G. Mackenzie, *Laws and Customs of Scotland in Matters Criminal*, Edin. 1678
Min. Krk-Sess. Kinghn	*Minutes of the Kirk-Session of Kinghorn*
Min Syn Fife	*Selections from minutes of Synod of Fife, 1611-1687*, Edin. 1837
Murray	J. Murray, *Kilmacolm*, Paisley 1907
New Stat Acc	*The New Statistical Account of Scotland*, Edin. 1845
Nicoll	Nicoll, J., *A Diary of Public transactions and other occurrences chiefly in Scotland, from January 1650 to June 1667*, Bannatyne Club, Edin. 1836
Old Stat. Acc. Scot	*The Statistical Account of Scotland*, Edin. 1791-99
Ork & Shet Flklre	Black, *Orkney and Shetland Folklore*
Orkney Ct. Bk.	*The Court Books of Orkney and Shetland*, Edin. 1967
Pit.	R. Pitcairn, *Criminal Trials in Scotland*, Edin. 1833
Pres. Bk. Kirk	*The Presbytery Book of Kirkcaldy*, Kirkcaldy 1900
Pres. Bk. Strathbogie	*Extracts from the Presbytery Book of Strathbogie*, Aberdeen 1843
Pride	Pride, D., *A History of the Parish of Neilston*, Paisley 1910
Proc. Antiq.	*Proceedings of the Society of Antiquaries*

Proc. SRO List	Scottish Record Office hand list of processes
Ptson	J. Paterson, History of Ayr and Wigton, Edin. 1863-66
Ramsay	Elninthologia, London 1668
Regal Kirriemuir	Reid, Regality of Kirriemuir
Reid	Reid, Regality of Kirriemuir
R. Old Abd.	Records of Old Aberdeen
R. Brg. Kirk	Records of the Burgh of Kirkcaldy, Kirkcaldy 1908
R. Brgh Lnrk	Extracts from the records of the royal burgh of Lanark, Glasgow 1893
R. Brgh Stir	Extracts from the records of the Royal Burgh of Stirling, Glasgow 1887
RCE PA 11	Records of the Committee of Estates, Scottish Record Office
Reg. Pres. Lnrk	Selections from the registers of the Presbytery of Lanark 1623-1709, Edin. 1839
Reg. Krk. Sess. St And.	Register of St. Andrews, Edin. 1889-90
Reg. St. And.Pres.	Selections from the minutes of the Presbyteries of St Andrews and Cupar 1641-1698, Edin. 1837
R. Elgin	W. Cramond, The Records of Elgin, Aberdeen 1903-8
Reliq. Antiq. Scot	Reliquiae Antiquae Scoticae
R. Inv	Records of Inverness, Aberdeen 1911-24
R. Mlrse	Selections from records of the regality of Melrose
Rog	C. Rogers, Social Life in Scotland, Edin. 1846
Ross	W. Ross, Aberdour and Inchcolme, Edin. 1885
R.P.C.	Register of the Privy Council of Scotland, 3 series, Edin. 1877-1970
R. Pres Brechin	Register of the Presbytery of Brechin

R. Pres. Kelso — *Register of the Presbytery of Kelso*

Ronald — Ronald, *Landmarks of Old Stirling*

R. Regal. Mlrse — *Selections from records of the regality of Melrose*

Salmon — T. Salmon, *Borrowstouness and district*, Edin. 1913

Sc. Antiq — Cornelius Hallon, A.W. & J.H. Stevenson, editors, *The Scottish Antiquary* or Northern Notes and Queries, Edin. 1888-1903

Sc. Nts and Quer — Cornelius Hallon, A.W. & J.H. Stevenson, editors, *The Scottish Antiquary* or Northern Notes and Queries, Edin. 1888-1903

Sc. Rem. — *Scottish Reminiscences*

Sess. Bk P'hame — Paton, H., editor, *The Session Book of Penninghame*, Edin. 1933

Sharpe — C.K. Sharpe, *A historical account of the belief in witchcraft in Scotland*, London 1884

Simpkins — J. Simpkins, *Folklore of Fife*, London 1914

Sinclair — G. Sinclair, *Satan's Invisible World Discovered*, Edin. 1685

Sinclar — G. Sinclair, *Satan's Invisible World Discovered*, Edin. 1685

S.J.C. — *Selected Justiciary Cases*, Stair Society, Edin. 1953

Sp. Cl. Misc. — *Spalding Club Miscellany*, Aberdeen 1841-52

Spott Misc. — Maidment, J., editor, *Spottiswoode Miscellany*, Edin. 1844-1845

Soc. Antiq — *Proceedings of the Society of Antiquaries of Scotland*

S.P. Misc. — *Spalding Club Miscellany*, Aberdeen 1841-52

SRO adj List — Index to the Books of Adjournal, Scottish Record Office

Stat. Acc. Ayrshire — *New Statistical Account of Ayrshire*

Stir	Stirling, R.M., Inveresk Parish lore, from Pagan Times, Musselburgh 1891
Thom.	A. Thomson, Lauder and Lauderdale, Galashiels 1902
Truckell	A.E. Truckell, Unpublished list of witchcraft cases in Galloway and Dumfriesshire and transcripts. See (2) below for details
Waddell	P.H. Waddell, An Old Kirk Chronicle, Edin. 1893
Webster	D. Webster, Tracts on Witchcraft, Edin. 1820
Webstr	D. Webster, Tracts on Witchcraft, Edin. 1820
Whit	Bulstrode Whitelock, Memorialls of the English Affairs, London 1682
W'locke	Bulstrode Whitelock, Memorialls of the English Affairs, London 1682
Wood	J.M. Wood, Witchcraft and superstitions recorded in the south-western district of Scotland, Dumfries 1911
Wodrow	R. Wodrow, Analecta Scotica, Edin.1842-3

2. References to John Gilmore "Witchcraft and the Church in Scotland, Ph.D thesis Glasgow University Library 1948.

Case	
2228	Spottiswoode Miscellany, Vol. 2, pp.266-267
2234	Macphail, J.R.N., editor, Highland Papers, Edinburgh, 1914, pp.165-167
2235	Macphail, J.R.N., editor, Highland Papers, Edinburgh, 1914, pp.165-167
2300	Spalding Club Miscellany, Vol. 1, Aberdeen, 1841, p.166
2311	Booke of the Universal Kirk of Scotland, Edinburgh, 1839, pp.28-31
2333	Fergusson, R.M., Alexander Hume, Paisley, 1899, p.108
2335	Cramond, W., The Records of Elgin, Aberdeen, 1903, p.135
2336	Maitland Club Miscellany, Edinburgh, 1833, pp. 420, 421, 424
2361	Pagan, J., Annals of Ayr in the Olden Times 1560-1692, Ayr, 1897, p.108
2362	Stuart, J., Selections from the Records of the Kirk Session, Presbytery and Synod of Aberdeen, Aberdeen, 1846, p.87
2367	Spottiswoode Miscellany, Vol. 2, p.304
2368	Spottiswoode Miscellany, Vol. 2, p.304
2370	Maidment, J., The Chronicle of Perth, Edinburgh, 1831, pp.92-93
2371	Maidment, J., The Chronicle of Perth, Edinburgh, 1831, p.89
2381	Maitland Club Miscellany, Vol. 1, p.467
2382	Irving, J., The Book of Dumbartonshire, Edinburgh, 1879, p.37
2436	Lorimer, G., The Early Days of St. Cuthbert's Edinburgh, Edinburgh, 1915, pp.144, 145
2476	Kinghorn, Extracts from the Ancient Minutes of the Kirk Session of Kirkcaldy, Kirkcaldy, 1863, p.50

Case

2484 Robertson, D., South Leith Records, Edinburgh, 1911, p.49

2485 Robertson, D., South Leith Records, Edinburgh, 1911, p.49

2526 Robertson, J., Selections from the Registers of the Presbytery of Lanark, Edinburgh, 1839, p.54

2527 Lorimer, G., The Early Days of St. Cuthbert's Edinburgh, Edinburgh, 1915, pp.135-136

2528 Kinloch, G.R., Selections from the Minutes of the Presbyteries of St. Andrews and Cupar, Edinburgh, 1837, p.106

2529 Kinloch, G.R., Selections from the Minutes of the Presbyteries of St. Andrews and Cupar, Edinburgh, 1837, p.106

2530 Kinloch, G.R., Selections from the Minutes of the Presbyteries of St. Andrews and Cupar, Edinburgh, 1837, p.106

2536 Salmon, T., Barrowstounness and District, Edinburgh, 1913, p.183

2539 Henderson, E., Extracts from the Kirk Session Records of Dunfermline, Edinburgh, 1865, p.31

2540 Henderson, E., Extracts from the Kirk Session Records of Dunfermline, Edinburgh, 1865, p.31

2541 Henderson, E., Extracts from the Kirk Session Records of Dunfermline, Edinburgh, 1865, p.31

2542 Henderson, E., Extracts from the Kirk Session Records of Dunfermline, Edinburgh, 1865, p.31

2552 Arnot, H., A Collection and abridgement of celebrated criminal trials in Scotland, Edinburgh, 1775, p.393

2573 Cramond, W., Extracts from the Records of the Kirk Session of Elgin, Elgin, 1897, pp.31-35

2582 Extracts of the Records of the Presbytery of Brechin, Dundee, 1876, p.39

2586 R.P.C., 2nd Series, Vol. 8, p.198

2587 Paton, H., Kingarth Parish Records, Edinburgh, 1932, pp. 12, 13, 15

2588 Paton, H., Kingarth Parish Records, Edinburgh, 1932, pp. 12, 13, 15

<u>Case</u>

2592 Robertson, D., <u>South Leith Records</u>, Edinburgh, 1911, p.90

2593 Ferguson, R.M., <u>Alexander Hume</u>, Paisley, 1899, p.259

2594 Paton, H., <u>Kingarth Parish Records</u>, Edinburgh, 1932, pp. 12, 13, 15

2595 Paton, H., <u>Kingarth Parish Records</u>, Edinburgh, 1932, pp. 12, 13, 15

2656 Wood, J.M., <u>Witchcraft and Superstitious Record in the South Western District of Scotland</u>, Dumfries, 1911, p.97

2657 Beveridge, D., <u>Culross and Tulliallan</u>, Edinburgh, 1893, p.237

2671 H.M. Commission; 14th Report, App. 3, Marchmont MSS, pp.109-110

2672 Craig-Brown, T., <u>The History of Selkirkshire</u>, Edinburgh, 1886, Vol. 1, p.201

2683 Paterson, J., <u>History of the County of Ayr</u>, Ayr, 1847, Vol. 11, p.92

2684 <u>Proceedings of the Society of Antiquaries</u>, Vol. 4, p.474

2685 <u>Proceedings of the Society of Antiquaries</u>, Vol. 4, p.474

2686 H.M. Commission, 14th Report, App. 3, Marchmont MSS, pp.109-110

2687 Craig-Brown, T., <u>The History of Selkirkshire</u>, Edin. 1886, Vol. 1, p.201

2733 Craven, J.B., <u>A History of the Episcopal Church in the Diocese of Caithness</u>, Kirkwall, 1908, p.101

2737 Simpkins, J., <u>Country Folklore</u>, Vol. 7, London, 1914, pp.98-99

2751 Hunter, J., <u>The Diocese and Presbytery of Dunkeld</u>, London, N.D., p.370

2752 Hunter, J., <u>The Diocese and Presbytery of Dunkeld</u>, London, N.D., p.370

2753 Hunter, J., <u>The Diocese and Presbytery of Dunkeld</u>, London, N.D., p.370

Case

2754 Hunter, J., The Diocese and Presbytery of Dunkeld, London, N.D., p.370

2807 Paton, Rothesay Parish Records, 1931, pp.24-26

2812 Scots Law Times, 20th July, 1935, p.169

2820 Cramond, W., The Records of Elgin, Aberdeen, 1903, Vol. 1, pp.369-370

2822 Cramond, W., Extracts from the Records of the Kirk Session of Elgin, Elgin, 1897, p.289

2834 Cramond, W., The Records of Elgin, Aberdeen, 1903, Vol. 1, pp.369-370

2835 Cramond, W., The Records of Elgin, Aberdeen, 1903, Vol. 1, pp.369-370

2836 Cramond, W., The Records of Elgin, Aberdeen, 1903, Vol. 1, pp.369-370

2848 Macphail, J.R.N., Editor, Highland Papers, Edinburgh, 1914, Vol. 3, pp. 7, 8

2868 Macgill, W., Old Ross-shire, Inverness, 1909, (Supplementary Volume) p.76

2872 Cramond, W., Extracts from the Records of the Kirk Session of Elgin, Elgin, 1897, p.300

2876 Paton, H., Kingarth Parish Records, Edinburgh, 1932, pp.57-58

2895 Wood, J.M., Witchcraft and Superstitions Recorded in the South Western District of Scotland, Dumfries, 1911, p.131

2903 Kinloch, G.R., Selections from the Minutes of the Presbyteries of St. Andrews and Cupar, Edinburgh, 1837, pp.90, 91

2905 Metcalfe, W.M., A History of the County of Renfrew, Paisley, 1905, p.327

2906 Henderson, E., Extracts from the Kirk Session Records of Dunfermline, Edinburgh, 1865, p.70

2907 Henderson, E., Extracts from the Kirk Session Records of Dunfermline, Edinburgh, 1865, p.70

2934 Mackay, W., Records of the Presbyteries of Inverness and Dingwall, Edinburgh, 1896, p.344

Case	
2937	Mackay, J., History of the Barony of Broughton, Edinburgh, 1869, pp.69, 70
2940	R.P.C., 3rd Series, Vol. 14, p.385
2942	Buchan, J., A History of Peebleshire, Glasgow, 1925, pp.333-334
2957	Metcalfe, W.M., A History of the County of Renfrew, Paisley, 1905, pp.328, 333
2960	Wood, J.M., Witchcraft and Superstitions Recorded in the South Western District of Scotland, p.97
2961	A History of the Witches of Renfrewshire, Paisley, 1877, p.132
2971	Hunter, J., The Diocese and Presbytery of Dunkeld, London, N.D., pp.59, 60
2979	McKerlie, P.H., History of the Lands of Galloway and their Owners, Edinburgh, 1870, pp.487, 488
2980	McKerlie, P.H., History of the Lands of Galloway and their Owners, Edinburgh, 1870, pp.487, 488
2990	Sinclair, G., Satan's Invisible World Discovered, Edinburgh, 1871, p. lxxv
2992	Webster, D., Collection of Rare and Curious Tracts on Witchcraft and Second Sight, Edinburgh, 1820
2995	Paton, H., The Session Book of Penninghame, 1933, pp. 161-163
2996	Paton, H., The Session Book of Penninghame, 1933, pp. 161-163
2997	Mackenzie, W.M., The Book of Arran, Glasgow, 1914, p.298
3006	Paton, H., The Session Book of Penninghame, 1933, pp. 161-163
3007	Pitcairn, R., Ancient Criminal Trials in Scotland, Edinburgh, 1833, Vol. 3, pp. 520, 521
3011	Mackenzie, W.M., The Book of Arran, Glasgow, 1914, p.298
3012	Johnstone, A. and A., Old Lore Miscellany of Orkney, Shetland, Caithness and Sutherland, London, 1907, Vol. 4, p.47
3022	Wodrow, R., Analecta, Edinburgh, 1842, Vol. 2, p.339

Case

3023 Gunn, C.B., The Book of Linton Church, Peebles, 1912, p.109

3024 Gunn, C.B., The Book of Linton Church, Peebles, 1912, p.109

3029 Macnaughton, C., Church Life in Ross and Sutherland, Inverness, 1915, p.199

3030 Goudie, G., The Diary of the Rev. John Mill, Edinburgh, 1889, p.23

3031 Stuart, J., Extracts from the Council Register of the Burgh of Aberdeen, Edinburgh, 1871, Vol. 2, pp. 144, 145

3032 Calendar of State Papers Relating to Scotland, London, 1858, Vol. 1, p.461

3033 R.P.C., 2nd Series, Vol. 8, p.125

3034 Kirkton, J., History of the Church of Scotland, Edinburgh, 1817, p.189

3035 Kirkton, J., History of the Church of Scotland, Edinburgh, 1817, p.84

3036 Robertson, D., South Leith Records, Edinburgh, 1911, pp. 51, 52

3037 Kinloch, G.R., Selections from the Minutes of the Presbyteries of St. Andrews and Cupar, Edinburgh, 1837, p.16

3038 Cramond, W., The Records of Elgin, Aberdeen, 1903, pp. 183, 184, 300

3039 Cramond, W., The Records of Elgin, Aberdeen, 1903, pp. 183, 184, 300

3040 Kinloch, G.R., Selections from the Minutes of the Presbyteries of St. Andrews and Cupar, Edinburgh, 1837, p.19

3043 Robertson, J., Selections from the Register of the Presbytery of Lanark, Edinburgh, 1839, p.79

3044 Kinloch, G.R., Selections from the Minutes of the Synod of Fife, Edinburgh, 1837, p.61

3045 A History of the Witches of Renfrewshire, Paisley, 1877, p.28

3046 Robertson, J., Selections from the Register of the Presbytery of Lanark, Edinburgh, 1839, p.20

Case

3047 Maxwell, A History of Dumfries and Galloway, p.259

3048 Extracts from the Presbytery Book of Strathbogie, Aberdeen, 1843, p.14

3049 Paton, H., Kingarth Parish Records, Edinburgh, 1932, pp. 12, 13, 15

3051 Jervise, A., Memorials of Angus and Mearns, Edinburgh, 1885, pp. 69, 70

3052 Stevenson, W., The Presbytery Booke of Kirkaldy, Kirkcaldy, 1900, p.136

3053 Stevenson, W., The Presbytery Booke of Kirkaldy, Kirkcaldy, 1900, p.125

3054 Jervise, A., Memorials of Angus and Mearns, Edinburgh, 1885, pp.69, 70

3055 Robertson, J., Selections from the Registers of the Presbytery of Lanark, Edinburgh, 1911, p. 79

3056 Robertson, J., Selections from the Registers of the Presbytery of Lanark, Edinburgh, 1911, p. 79

3057 Robertson, J., Selections from the Registers of the Presbytery of Lanark, Edinburgh, 1911, p. 79.

References to A.E. Truckell Unpublished List of Witchcraft Cases in Galloway and Dumfriesshire.

Case	
2499	Kirkcudbright Burgh Court Book
2500	Kirkcudbright Burgh Court Book
2501	Kirkcudbright Burgh Court Book
2502	Kirkcudbright Burgh Court Book
2503	Kirkcudbright Burgh Court Book
2760	Dumfries Kirk Session Records
2773	Dumfries Kirk Session Records
2774	Dumfries Kirk Session Records
2804	Dumfries Town Council Records
2805	Dumfries Town Council Records
2889	Letter from Glendonying, Stewart Depute of Kirkcudbright
2890	Letter from Glendonying, Stewart Depute of Kirkcudbright
2977	J.M. Wood, *Witchcraft and Superstitions Recorded in the South-Western District of Scotland*, pp. 82-87
3984	Session Book of Twynholm
3002	Session Book of Penninghame
3003	Session Book of Penninghame
3004	Session Book of Penninghame
3005	Session Book of Penninghame
3009	Dumfries Kirk Session Records

3. Manuscript sources for centrally administered trials in the Scottish Record Office and National Library of Scotland.

<u>Scottish Record Office</u>

1. Books of Adjournals - Court of Justiciary J.C.2.

1.	16 Oct. 1576	-	28 Nov. 1584
2.	1 Dec. 1584	-	20 Oct. 1591
3.	15 May 1596	-	26 Jun. 1604
4.	25 Jul. 1604	-	19 Jul. 1611
5.	24 Jul. 1611	-	7 Oct. 1619
6.	7 Oct. 1419	-	24 Mar. 1631
7.	26 Mar. 1631	-	15 Nov. 1637
8.	17 Nov. 1637	-	17 Jul. 1650
9.	15 Oct. 1652	-	5 Jul. 1655
10.	29 Jun. 1661	-	23 Jan. 1666
11.	29 Jun. 1661	-	14 Jun. 1667
12.	24 Jan. 1666	-	14 Dec. 1669
13.	24 Dec. 1669	-	1 Aug. 1673
14.	4 Aug. 1673	-	13 Mar. 1678
15.	3 Jun. 1678	-	4 Jul. 1682
16.	5 Jul. 1682	-	21 Aug. 1685
17.	25 Aug. 1685	-	22 Mar. 1690
18.	24 Mar. 1690	-	17 Apr. 1693
19.	3 Jul. 1693	-	13 Nov. 1699

2. Boxes of Processes J.C. 26
J.C. 27

3. Circuit Court Records J.C. 10

1. 1622–1628. Now reclassified to be PC8/5 and printed in RPC Vol. 14, pp. 667–714 (no witches)

2. 1655–1658
1658–1659
1666

3. 1671–

4. 1678–1684

5. & 6. (bound now as one) 1677, 1607–1699. Contains the Paisley witches only

7. 1682–1686 now reclassifies to be PC8/7

8. 1701–1702

4. Records of the Committee of Estates RCE. PA. 11

National Library of Scotland

Extracts from Books of Adjournal.

ADV. MSS	24	6	6
	24	6	17
	25	2	9
	25	4	8
	6	1	20
	23	1	23
	25	2	8

4. Printed sources for centrally administered trials.

Acts of the Parliament of Scotland, London 1814

Arnot, H., Celebrated Criminal Trials in Scotland, Edin. 1785

Black, G.F., Some Unpublished Scottish Witchcraft Trials, N. York 1941

Pitcairn, R., Criminal Trials in Scotland, Edin. 1833

Register of the Privy Council of Scotland, Edinburgh

Scott-Moncreiff, R., Records of Proceedings of the Justiciary Court, Edinburgh 1661-1678, Scottish Historical Society Vol. 48

A.E. Truckell, 'Unpublished Witchcraft Trials' in Transactions of the Dumfriesshire and Galloway Natural History and Antiquarian Society, L1 1975.

5. Short List of Books on Scottish Witchcraft.

Anon. De Excerabili ... conjuratione, Edin. 1601

Anon. News from Scotland, London 1591

Anon. Relation of the Diabolical Practice of above Twenty Wizards and Witches of the Sherriffdom of Renfrew, London 1697

Anon. Trial Confession and Execution of Isobel Inch et al for Witchcraft at Irvine anno 1618, Ardrossan, N.D.

Anon. True and Full Relation of the Witches of Pittenweem, Edin. 1704

Anon. True Narrative of the Sufferings and Relief of a Young Girl, Edin. 1698

Black, G.F., Calendar of cases of witchcraft in Scotland 1510-1727, New York 1938

Campbell, J.G., Witchcraft and Second Sight in the Highlands and Islands, Glasgow 1902

Dalyell, J.G., The Darker Superstitions of Scotland, Edin. 1834

Ferguson, John, "Bibliographical Notes on the Witchcraft Literature of Scotland" in Proceedings of the Edinburgh Bibliographical Society, Edin. 1899

Gilmore, John, Witchcraft and the Church in Scotland subsequent to the Reformation, Unpublished Ph.D. thesis, Glasgow University Library 1948

Hutchisone, James, Sermon, Paisley April 1697, Scottish Historical Review, Vol. VII 1910

James VI of Scotland, Daemonologie, Edin. 1597

Keiller, Alex, The Personnel of the Aberdeenshire Witchcraft Covens, London 1922

Larner, Christina, "Anne of Denmark, Queen of Scotland: A Demonological Dowry?", Glasgow University Gazette, June 1975

Larner, Christina, "James VI and I and Witchcraft" in The Reign of James VI and I, ed. A.G.R. Smith, London 1973

Larner, Christina, Scottish Demonology in the Sixteenth and Seventeenth Centuries, Unpublished Ph.D. thesis, Edin. U. Library 1962

Larner, Christina, 'Two late Scottish Witchcraft tracts' in The Damned Art, ed. S. Anglo, London 1977

Law, Robert, Memorialls, Edin. 1818

Legge, F., 'Witchcraft in Scotland' in The Scottish Review, Vol. 18, October 1891

Linton, Lynn, Witch Stories, London 1861

Mackenzie, Sir George, Laws and Customs of Scotland in Matters Criminal, Edin. 1678

Mackenzie, Sir George, Pleadings in some remarkable cases, Edin.1672

Millar, John, ed., History of the Witches of Renfrewshire burnt on the Gallow-green of Paisley, Paisley 1809

Mitchell, J and Dickie, J., The Philosophy of Witchcraft, Paisley 1839

Neill, W.N., "The Professional Pricker and his test for witchcraft", Scottish Historical Review, 19 (1922)

Paterson, Rev. John, The Belief in Witchcraft Unsupported by Scripture, Aberdeen 1815

Scott, Sir Walter, Letters on Demonology and Witchcraft, London 1830

Sharpe, C. Kirkpatrick, Historical Account of the belief in Witchcraft in Scotland, London and Glasgow 1884

Sinclair, George, Satan's Invisible World Discovered, Edin. 1685

Stafford, Helen, 'Notes on Scottish Witchcraft Cases 1590-1591' in Essays in Honor of Conyers Read, ed. Norton Downes, Chicago 1953

Summers, Montague, The Geography of Witchcraft, London 1927

Telfair, Rev. Alexander, True relation of an apparition, Edin. 1696

Wood, J.M., Witchcraft and Superstitions recorded in the south west district of Scotland, N.P. 1911

Webster, David, Collection of Rare and Curious Tracts on Witchcraft, Edin. 1820

INDEX OF NAMED INDIVIDUALS

The arrangement of cases under types of court and source in Section I means that some individuals appear more than once. Where these are matched with certainty the references are collated. Where it is clear that different individuals are concerned, or where there is any doubt about the matching, the name is replicated as appropriate. Further research will certainly produce more matching cases.

Lightning Source UK Ltd.
Milton Keynes UK
UKOW07f2340100416

271942UK00004B/9/P